Hard Bodies

D1215828

Hollywood Masculinity in the Reagan Era

SUSAN JEFFORDS

Rutgers University Press • New Brunswick, New Jersey

Library of Congress Cataloging-in-Publication Data
Jeffords, Susan, 1953–
    Hard bodies : Hollywood masculinity in the Reagan era / Susan
Jeffords.
        p. cm.
    Includes bibliographical references and index.
    ISBN 0-8135-2002-9 (cloth) — ISBN 0-8135-2003-7 (pbk.)
    1. Men in motion pictures.   2. Machismo in motion pictures.
3. Reagan, Ronald.   I. Title.
PN1995.9.M46J44   1993
791.43'652041'09048—dc20   93-18282
                                                                  CIP

British Cataloging-in-Publication information available

Third paperback printing, 2004

DESIGN BY JOHN ROMER

To Montana, a rose blooming in my life

CONTENTS

ACKNOWLEDGMENTS

There are many people who deserve my thanks for their part in the production of this book. If there is an academic heaven populated by saintly and indefatigable colleagues, then Evan Watkins is its earthly representative. His consistent and good-natured support have been invaluable to my work. I also deeply appreciate H. Bruce Franklin's incisive comments on a draft of this book. Tom Byers and Steve Cohan deserve thanks for prompting me to rewrite two chapters and offering me the opportunity to try them out before including them in this book. Audiences at the Twentieth-Century Literature Conference and at Portland University contributed helpful questions that encouraged me to develop ideas further. Portions of Chapter 3 appeared in *Genre*, and I thank the editors for allowing me to reprint those sections. Great thanks go as well to my editor at Rutgers, Leslie Mitchner, for supporting this project from its instigation and making many useful suggestions along the way. Dev Stahlkopf was a research magician, always producing references at the drop of a hat. Andrew B. Lewis deserves great thanks for his thoughtful and thorough copyediting and my appreciation for being a just plain good reader.

Daily thanks go to Greg, Andrew, and Matthew, for offering me a happiness that enables all my work to be a pleasure.

Hard Bodies

"In their impact on social, economic, political/governmental life, and on the attitudes and personal values of Americans, the eighties were the most important years since World War II."

HAYNES JOHNSON

"In any revolution, two battles must be fought, one over ideology and one over control of the state."

RICHARD NIXON

Life as a Man in the Reagan Revolution

I n November of 1981, after suffering numerous legislative defeats at the hands of the new coalition of Republicans and Reagan Democrats, Speaker of the House "Tip" O'Neill suggested that one of the reasons that Ronald Reagan was such an effective president was that people simply "like him as an individual." He went on to say, "They're rooting for him because we haven't had any presidential successes for years—Kennedy killed, Johnson with Vietnam, Nixon with Watergate, Ford, Carter, and all the rest."[1] As journalist Roger Rosenblatt phrased it at the beginning of 1981, "the U.S. is famished for cheer."[2] Coming after the agonizing national standoff with Iran over the hostages, Ronald Reagan's election to the White House was to change this sense of presidential failure. Chosen as *Time* magazine's "Man of the Year" in 1980, Reagan went on to become, according to the Gallup poll, the most admired man in America throughout the eight years of his presidency.[3] His approval rating when he left office in 1989 was higher than any outgoing president's during the previous forty years.[4]

Reagan came to the White House during a troubled period in U.S. history. In summing up why Ronald Reagan was the "man of the year" in 1981, *Time* magazine declared: "The events of any isolated year can be made to seem exceptionally grim, but one has to peer hard to find elevating moments in 1980."[5] As Rupert Wilkinson characterized the period,

Ronald Reagan as Time's *"Man of the Year." (*Time *magazine, 1981)*

The 1980 election came at a postimperial moment, when Americans were not at all sure what role they wanted or could obtain either for their presidents or for their country in world affairs. In crises affecting sensitive national honor, many Americans wanted their president to get tough yet realized the past costs and current limits of such toughness. Economically, too, the idea was growing that America had entered a period of fundamental decline, reversing its history. This prompted new worries about the people's vigor and ambition, industriousness and will.[6]

According to Richard Nixon, Reagan's chief accomplishment while in office was that he was able to counter this "postimperial" malaise and "restore America's spiritual strength. He renewed America's faith in its ideals and recommitted America to a responsible world role."[7] Reagan himself was to draw the same conclusion in his farewell address in January of 1989: "The way I see it, there were two great triumphs, two things that I'm proudest of. One is the economic recovery. . . . The other is the recovery of our morale. America is respected again in the world and looked to for leadership."[8] Reagan's own personal confidence, biographer Lou Cannon explains, "had not been ruined by the introspection of the post-Vietnam era or by the national humiliation inflicted on the United States when Americans were held hostage in the U.S. embassy in Tehran during the last painful year of Jimmy Carter's presidency."[9] As president he tried to "restore national self-confidence by transferring his own self-confidence to his countrymen."[10] Martin Anderson, who worked as Reagan's economic policy adviser, concludes that "he led the United States back to greatness—in the power of its military defenses, the strength of its economy, the freedom of its people—and by so doing established our country as a towering model of a good society."[11] It was, in fact, this success that partly contributed to the widespread public determination that the years from 1980 to 1988 were a "Reagan Revolution."

One of the reasons that Reagan was able to carry out these social, economic, and cultural changes was his link to one of the most pervasive and influential features of American culture, the Hollywood film industry. Certainly, Reagan's path to the White House was paved at least in part by his experiences as a popular film star. He was usually cast as a trustworthy, likeable, and good-hearted leading man, and that eventually landed him the General Electric Theatre job that launched him on a national speaking tour of G.E. factories which formed the base for his later gubernatorial and presidential campaigns. His position as president of the Screen Actors Guild during the turbulent years of the House Un-American Activities Committee (HUAC) hearings solidified the anticommunism that would become such an elemental part of his presidential years. Indeed, the Hollywood film industry itself shaped the Reagan presidency and the 1980s through the many images, characters, and narratives that Reagan borrowed from film and used in his work as president. Journalists Bob Schieffer and Gary Paul Gates conclude that "once he left the Midwest, Reagan's movie career became the beacon that led him to everything else that followed, and when he ventured into a political career, a part of him remained firmly anchored to his Hollywood past. It provided him with a secure frame of reference in the insecure world he now found himself in, and it was the prime source of the anecdotes that he was so prone to relate."[12] From the moving World War II anecdote about the captain of a damaged B-17 bomber who told a trapped and frightened ball-turret gunner, "We'll ride it down together," when all the other crew had bailed out, a story that Reagan told as true but in fact lifted from the film *A Wing and a Prayer* (1944, Henry Hathaway); to his narration of the plot of *War Games* (1983, John Badham) as part of a discussion with congressional representatives concerning the MX missile; to his failure to review a briefing book for an upcoming economic summit in 1983 because *The Sound of Music* (1965, Robert Wise) was on television; to his veto challenge to a congressional tax increase inspired by Clint Eastwood's *Sudden Impact* (1983), "Go ahead. Make my day"; to his borrowing the concept of a nuclear-free world from the science fiction film *The Day the Earth Stood Still* (1951, Robert Wise); to his reference to the United States as "the A-team among nations,"[13] Ronald Reagan's speeches, negotiations, and policies were often shaped by Hollywood. As Lou Cannon puts it,

> Hollywood had been the center of Reagan's life from the time he was twenty-six years old until after he turned fifty. Even when he was gone from Hollywood, Hollywood was never gone from him. He watched movies whenever he could, and the movies were the raw material from which he drew scenes and sustenance. He converted movie material into his own needs.[14]

But more than specific images, lines, or characters, Hollywood shaped Reagan's "plots" as well, inclining him to create narratives in which he could be featured, as he had been during his acting days, as the hero of the story. For example, he retold his testimony before HUAC in terms that glorified his own role. Though, according to Cannon, Reagan was "not outwardly obsessive about his anticommunism, . . . as the events receded into the past, their importance increased to Reagan, who made of his experience a morality tale in which he was a hero as well as wholesome innocent."[15] One of Reagan's favorite stories to tell about himself, the stories that Roger Rosenblatt describes as the ones he "seemed genuinely happy to hear," was of how he got the job as a radio sports announcer for station WOC in Davenport, Ohio, in 1932. When asked by the program director to describe a game, Reagan recounted one of his own games at Eureka College: "As a blocking guard, I was supposed to get the first man in the secondary to spring our back loose, and I didn't get him. I missed him. And I've never known to this day how Bud Cole got by and scored that touchdown. But in the rebroadcast I nailed the guy on defense. I took him down with a magnificent block." From this account of his earlier football game, a narration in which he changes himself from victim to hero, Reagan learned a vital political lesson: that the success of the story, especially a story in which he could figure as a hero, was more important than any facts involving the events themselves.[16] This was the role he wrote for himself by "rescuing" U.S. medical students in Grenada, confronting Mu'ammar Qaddafi over Libyan-sponsored terrorism, and sending military aid to the Nicaraguan contras. It was also the role he played in the story that came to be known as the Reagan Revolution. For, as Martin Anderson assesses the Reagan years, Ronald Reagan did not "cause" the revolution; rather the circumstances made it possible for him to stand at the head of a changing social and political situation: "Neither Goldwater nor Nixon nor Reagan caused or created the revolutionary movement that often carries their name, especially Reagan's. It was the other way around. They were part of the movement, they contributed mightily to the movement, but the movement gave them political life, not the reverse."[17]

Reagan cast himself as hero, but many in the country seemed to be reading from the same script. As linguist Robin Lakoff suggests, "[Americans] act modern, cool and sophisticated. But underneath, we want a daddy, a king, a god, a hero, . . . a champion who will carry that lance and that sword into the field and fight for us."[18] Folklorist Alan Dundes puts it more succinctly: "There is an unconscious aspect in politics, where we are looking for a hero who will turn out to be a father figure for the country."[19] It was in the search for such a hero in the 1980s that Hollywood plot lines and presidential politics became intimately confused.

A close look at historian George Mosse's study of nationalism and sexuality can suggest that *visibility*—that which links nationalism and racism with stereotyping—is the key mode of national identity formation. In other words, it is how citizens *see* themselves and how they *see* those against whom they define themselves that determines national self-perception. Because of the close ties between the production of nations and the development of the middle classes in Europe and the United States—a class that was itself grounded in a sense of display and self-recognition through visible markers of success and achievement—it is possible to conclude that the very idea of a nation is itself dependent on this visual realm. A nation exists, in other words, as something to be *seen*. In such a case, examining one of the chief distributors of images in this country—Hollywood films—offers clues about the construction of American national indentity. And examining Ronald Reagan, both one of the best manipulators of those images *and* one of the best images himself, can show how that identity worked in the 1980s.

Ronald Reagan stands then as an image of popular culture and as an emblem of American national identity. He is an icon of the New Right and a Hollywood star, the leader who confronted the Soviets and the entertainer who said to the surgeons about to operate on him after the 1981 assassination attempt, "Please tell me you're all Republicans."[20] He links in one image popular and national narratives, making them somehow the same story. As a result, it is impossible to discuss some of Hollywood's most successful films of the 1980s without also discussing "Ronald Reagan,"[21] the image that was conveyed through and as the presidency during the years of 1980–1988.

In 1990, Robert Bly, in his influential book *Iron John: A Book About Men*, argues for a history of masculine models in the United States. "The Fifties male . . . got to work early, labored responsibly, supported his wife and children, and admired discipline. . . . His view of culture and America's part in it was boyish and optimistic." In addition, "the Fifties man was supposed to like football, be aggressive, stick up for the United States, never cry, and always provide. . . . The Fifties male had a clear vision of what a man was, and what male responsibilities were, but the isolation and one-sidedness of his vision were dangerous."[22]

The "Sixties male," Bly goes on to say, was influenced by the Vietnam War and the women's movement. He sought to learn about the "feminine side" within him and to treat women differently. Bly finds "something wonderful about this development," but is concerned nonetheless. As he puts it, "There is something wrong. The male in the past twenty years has become more thoughtful, more gentle. But by this process he has not become more free. He's a nice boy who pleases not only his mother but also the young woman he is living with."[23]

Bly calls "seventies males" soft, possessed of "a gentle attitude toward life in their whole being and style of living," but "not happy," principally because they lacked the "energy" or the ability to be "life-giving." Such men held within them deep wells of "grief" and "anguish"; and although they could be "nurturing," they could not "say what [they] wanted, and stick by it. *Resolve* of that kind was a different matter."[24]

In speaking of the same period, Richard Nixon, in his 1992 treatise on America's future, *Seize the Moment: America's Challenge in a One-Superpower World*, offers a similar assessment: "In the mid-1970s the United States began to lose its sense of purpose. . . . In the late 1970s a malaise enveloped the nation's dominant elites. America's confidence was broken. We lost our geopolitical bearings. . . . Instead of shaping history, the nation let itself be buffetted by events."[25] Echoing Bly's terminology, Nixon comments elsewhere that the "hard-headed detente" he had practiced as president had become, by the mid to late seventies, the "soft-headed detente" of President Jimmy Carter.[26]

Nixon attacks Carter, directly or indirectly, throughout his 1980 book *The Real War,* in which he lays out the foreign and domestic policies that Reagan followed for the next eight years. From arguing for increased expenditures on nuclear armaments to move the United States back to a position of parity with the Soviet Union, to attacking the "cultural elite" who had led the nation astray, Nixon articulated the agenda that would dominate U.S. politics during the 1980s as the "Reagan" philosophy. Key to the force of Nixon's proposals for the 1980s was his assessment of the 1970s, a period that, like Bly, he characterizes as one of a failure of resolve, or what Nixon prefers to call a failure of will.

Nixon centers his attack on Jimmy Carter, the man he holds responsible for the loss of 100 million people to communism: "Angola, Ethiopia, Afghanistan, South Yemen, Mozambique, Laos, Cambodia, and

South Vietnam, all have been brought under communist domination since 1974; nearly 100 million people in the last five years." Ronald Reagan responded directly to this attack on Carter when in 1988 he declared: "In the 2,765 days of our Administration, not one inch of ground has fallen to the communists."[27] Accusing Carter of "piecemeal temporizing," Nixon condemns him for canceling the B-1 bomber, "one of the greatest strategic blunders this nation has ever made," and for caving in on SALT II: "The Carter administration gave in to the Soviets on almost every important point." He even criticizes Carter for what would seem to be an accomplishment—not having any U.S. soldiers killed in combat while he was president: "When a President repeatedly makes a political issue out of the claim that no American has been killed in combat during his administration, he wins points at home but loses clout abroad; other leaders must wonder how far he would let himself be pushed before he would risk that record."[28]

Nixon portrays the Carter years as the nadir of U.S. strength and "resolve." Under Carter, the nation was "drifting," "lost in uncertainty or paralyzed by propriety," "waffling," "wavering," "floundering," "uncertain," and "irresolute," which for Nixon raises the question of whether the United States is a nation of "steel or mush." And although Nixon's main target, as in the 1980 Republican Party platform, was the Carter administration, he does not spare the nation as a whole, which to him seemed to be following the same troubled path:

> Only in very recent years has the notion taken hold that life is meant to be easy. Coddled, pampered, truckled to, a generation of Americans has been bred to believe that they should coast through life. . . . Where abundance comes easily, it becomes too easy to assume that security comes with comparable ease. "Street smarts," jungle savvy, that edgy wariness that comes naturally to those whose precarious existence keeps them ever on the alert—these atrophy in the cushioned luxury of a life in which ease and deference are taken for granted.

As Nixon looks at the last years of the 1970s then, he sees a weakened nation, led by a president whose own softness has culminated not only in the loss of national "will" and strength but in the triumph of communism around the globe and the possible reduction of the United States to a minor power. As he puts it, "Thus reduced we will not survive—nor will freedom or Western values survive." In what

Nixon believes to be the battle of World War III, fought with or without weapons, the Soviet Union wants to end the war, "not with a bang, but with a whimper,"[29] a sound he seems to have heard Carter making.

Nixon's adjectives are clearly loaded within a gendered context. He favors strong and willful presidents, who are decisive, "steely," resolute, and certain, and disparages a weakened president, whom he calls "paralyzed" (castrated), uncertain, "mushy," and wavering. Yet, he does not draw any direct references to masculine or feminine qualities. Robert Bly, leader of one of the most popular gender cults of the eighties, the "men's movement," however, leaves no such doubts about the sources of his judgments of men, nations, and their behaviors. For Bly, "the United States has undergone an unmistakable decline since 1950," one that he attributes to the increasing power of women and the parallel "diminishment and belittlement of the father." This decline of the position of the father is linked for Bly, both historically and symbolically, to the killing of kings. After centuries of king-worship and the presence of kingly bodies, to which common citizens anchored their notions of spiritual kings, the dethroning of the earthly king created a vacuum, leaving nowhere for people to attach their understandings of "The Sacred King," he who "acts as a magnet and rearranges human molecules," he who "send[s] energy down" and "affect[s] our feelings and actions the way a magnet arranges tiny flakes of iron." Because, according to Bly, "our visual imagination becomes confused when we can no longer see the physical king," the image of the physical father has suffered as well: "In our time, when the father shows up as an object of ridicule (as he does, as we've noted, on television), or a fit field for suspicion (as he does in *Star Wars*), or a bad-tempered fool (when he comes home from the office with no teaching), or *a weak puddle of indecision* (as he stops inheriting kingly radiance), the son has a problem."[30]

Bly's criticism of the situation of men since the 1970s is that because sons cannot locate a father as model or source of guidance, they turn to women for help: "Some sons fall into a secret despair. They have probably adopted, by the time they are six, their mother's view of their father, and by twenty will have adopted society's critical view of fathers, which amounts to a dismissal. What can they do but ask women for help?" Bly acknowledges that "that request is not all bad," but he cautions that "even the best-intentioned women cannot give what is needed," because for Bly, although "women can change the embryo to a boy, . . . only men can change the boy to a man."[31]

Raising what would become the key domestic policy theme of the Reagan administration, Bly targets the family as the source of this gendered scenario and of the sons' "problems." Because, Bly argues, "between twenty and thirty percent of American boys now live in a house with no father present, . . . the demons there have full permission to rage." Not only is there no father around to provide a "kingly" model for the son but, he adds, "If the son learns feeling primarily from the mother, then he will probably see his own masculinity from the feminine point of view."[32] Bly condemns the consequences for the son of the loss within the family of a physical king, but the Carter administration, for many, writ large Bly's conclusions and deliberately weakened itself by enhancing Rosalynn Carter's powers as First Lady. As John Orman, in his comparative study of the Carter and Reagan presidencies, concludes: "Carter did not project the image of being a 'real man.' . . . Carter considered the advice of his wife, Rosalynn Carter, when making many important decisions. Some observers criticized the new liberated role that Rosalynn Carter was establishing for First Ladies, that is, of policy advisor to the president."[33] In defining the construct of "toughness" as it has affected personal and national identity in American history, Wilkinson even includes Rosalynn Carter in a group of women he sees as having fulfilled the "tough guy" characterization in spite of their gender.[34] As Orman's study calculates, Rosalynn Carter had one hundred scheduled policy advisory meetings with President Carter during his tenure of office, ranking her in the top ten advisors during his presidency.[35] Perhaps having fallen into a "secret despair," Jimmy Carter had no recourse but to "ask women for help."

Combining Jimmy Carter's attention to Rosalynn Carter's advice on policy matters with his apparent "indecisiveness" on foreign-policy issues led some to openly characterize Carter as a feminine president. In a 1984 article for the *Wall Street Journal,* John Mihalic talks about the Carter presidency in these terms:

> Jimmy Carter first presented himself to the nation as a masculine personality. Naval academy. Submariner. Nuclear Engineer. Farmer. Loner. Tough governor. But once in office, he lost no time revealing his true feminine spirit. He wouldn't twist arms. He didn't like to threaten or rebuke. . . . And we watched how far this approach got him in the jungles of Washington and the world. So in a sense, we've already had a "woman" president: Jimmy Carter.[36]

It is exactly this kind of characterization that underlies Nixon's and later Reagan's consistent diatribes against the "soft-headed" policies of "the late 1970s." Because that period was dominated by a president who seemed to have turned "feminine" in midstream, not only was the nation in peril but the world as a whole was at risk of becoming "slaves" to the Soviet Union. Though Nixon does not say as much, Bly and Mihalic do: because Carter was not "man enough" to run a superpower nation, the world was in a crisis, a crisis that only a return of the "physical king" and father could resolve.

Robert Bly "discovered" this anguish, pain, and lack of resolve in men in 1980, the same year that Richard Nixon published *The Real War*, the same year that Ronald Reagan was elected to the White House. Bly promoted a revival of personal and domestic manliness during the 1980s; Nixon outlined foreign-policy positions that would contribute to a revival of U.S. "manliness" through a hard-edged anti-Soviet philosophy backed by increased weapons production. Ronald Reagan was able to capture both of these roles, to portray himself as both a "real man" and a "real president," as both a father and a king. For this reason he was able to foster what many have come to recognize as a revolution in U.S. social organization and to implement clear-cut policies—both foreign and domestic—that would define the nation's identity and agenda for the next eight years. It was a revolution defined by what it was not. It was not Jimmy Carter or the Carter policies, which it rewrote as weak, defeatist, inactive, and feminine. Consequently, it was a revolution whose success pivoted on the ability of Ronald Reagan and his administration to portray themselves successfully as distinctively masculine, not merely as men but as decisive, tough, aggressive, strong, and domineering men. Fulfilling here both Nixon's and Bly's desires for the United States and for men by restoring economic and military as well as spiritual strength, Ronald Reagan became the premiere masculine archetype for the 1980s, embodying both national and individual images of manliness that came to underlie the nation's identity during his eight years in office.

When Bly notes that the son faces "problems" when all father images have been diminished, he asks what became a key question for U.S. culture in the 1980s: "How does [the son] imagine his own life as a man?"[37] One answer to that question can be found in Hollywood films. The masculine characters that populated some of the decades' most popular Hollywood films offered narratives against which American men and women could test, revise, affirm, or negate images of their own conceptions of masculinity, which, because of a changing economy, altering gender relations, increasingly tense race relations, refigurings of U.S. geographic distributions, a technologized militarism, and a reconfigured work force, were themselves in flux throughout this period. Certainly countless films came out of Hollywood production studios during the 1980s that conveyed often contradictory and ambivalent masculine characters. Nonetheless, the films that U.S. moviegoing audiences chose to see in large numbers during this period were largely and consistently concerned with portrayals of white male action heroes. Such films provided a narrative structure and a visual pleasure through which consumers actively responded to and constructed a U.S. popular culture. Indeed, it can be argued that the question of masculine identity—"How does [the son] imagine his life as a man?"—circumscribes the relationship between Hollywood films and U.S. popular culture during the 1980s.

Nixon's and Bly's scenarios link the crisis of a nation with the crisis of manhood. It cannot be an accident that one of Ronald Reagan's most powerful and effective activities in the White House was to convey certain distinctive images of himself as a president *and* as a man—chopping wood, breaking horses, toughing out an assassination attempt, bullying Congress, and staging showdowns with the Soviet Union—making himself into what John Orman called "the quintessential macho president."[38] The question then of how the son is to "imagine his life as a man" must be answered not only in terms of the relationship between Hollywood films and U.S. popular culture but also in terms of the relationship between the Reagan presidency and the popular construction of national identity: to the extent that the president stands for the nation, and to the extent that a particular president constructs that standing in distinctly masculine terms, then national identity must itself be figured in relation to popular masculine models and narratives of masculine generation and power. Lauren Berlant calls this relationship "national fantasy," to designate "how national culture becomes local—through the images, narratives, monuments, and sites that circulate through personal/collective consciousness."[39] "Ronald Reagan" became one of these sites of "national fantasy" in his ability to combine for many Americans the national and the individual, the public and the personal, the global and the local. "Ronald Reagan" became one of the ways through which many Americans felt a personal connection to their national identity.

In their analysis of the formation of national identities, Jochen and

Linda Schulte-Sasse suggest that "the pleasurable collective experience of a unified national body, in which the individual experiences a reconciliation of agonistic and decentering desires, has become a major ingredient ensuring the cultural reproduction of modern societies."[40] The search for a "unified national body" may remain constant over a certain period, but the ambivalent and often contradictory experiences that motivate this search cannot remain stable (logically, if they did, the desire for such a unified body would dissipate). Thus, although definitions of the masculine body were key to the formation of national and popular cultures throuhgout the 1980s, those bodies and definitions were neither stable nor consistent. My project in this book is, on the one hand, to argue for the centrality of the masculine body to popular culture and national identity while, on the other hand, to articulate how the popularizations of that body altered during the years of the Reagan and Bush presidencies. In the broadest terms, whereas the Reagan years offered the image of a "hard body" to contrast directly to the "soft bodies" of the Carter years, the late 1980s and early 1990s saw a reevaluation of that hard body, not for a return to the Carter soft body but for a rearticulation of masculine strength and power through internal, personal, and family-oriented values. Both of these predominant models—the hard body and the "sensitive family man"—are overlapping components of the Reagan Revolution, comprising on the one hand a strong militaristic foreign-policy position and on the other hand a domestic regime of an economy and a set of social values dependent on the centrality of fatherhood.

Throughout the Reagan era, there was what Lawrence Grossberg insightfully recognizes as an effort by the New Right, which supported Reagan's presidency, not simply to redefine the nation but rather to establish "a new relationship between people and the nation."[41] The arena for this new relationship was, according to Grossberg, "in the conjuncture of economics and popular culture rather than that of economics and the State."[42] In other words, during the Reagan era popular culture became the mechanism not simply for identifying but for establishing the relationship between the people and the State, through the articulation of that State as the unified national body of masculine character. Consequently, the reformulation of the relationship between the people and the nation, as configured in the popular discourses of militarism, patriotism, individualism, family values, and religious beliefs, was accomplished largely through the rearticulation of both the individual and the nation in terms of masculine identities in such a way that actions by either side—individual or nation—were to be seen as impinging on and in many ways determining the other.

Such a systemic interdependence between individual and nation as linked through the masculine body would go a long way toward explaining what many perceive to be contradictory impulses of the Reagan philosophy—a hands-off policy toward corporations and states combined with an interventionist and prescriptive policy toward individual citizens.[43] In order to revise the relationship between people and nation, the Reagan presidency, in conjunction with the New Right, nationalized *bodies* by equating individual actions with national actions in such a way that individual failings were to be seen as causes for national downfall (precisely its critique of Jimmy Carter and the "cultural elite," but equally its justification for attacking single mothers, substance users, homosexuals, and welfare recipients). What better way to repair such a "failing" than to prescribe the kind of popular body through which individuals could position themselves in relation to "their" nation? And what better body to use than that of a president/Hollywood actor/father figure whose very character came to define the parameters of a national popular identity?

There is much debate among pundits and historians about how much Ronald Reagan knew about what he was doing in the White House and about how much control he had over the policy changes, social upheavals, and economic alterations—both nationally and internationally—that came to be recognized as part of the Reagan Revolution. Tale-bearing insiders such as David Stockman, Donald Regan, and Larry Speakes generally characterize Reagan as an uninformed and bumbling fool who didn't understand the economic policies he put forward and who was swayed in his decisions by colorful diagrams and entertaining charts.[44] Journalists who had followed the Reagan presidency generally agree.[45] In stark contrast, Martin Anderson, Reagan's economic adviser who worked with him throughout two presidential campaigns, cites Reagan's two-term election to the governorship of California, his two-term presidency, his high public-approval ratings, his success at achieving his goals of nuclear disarmament, his deliberate and open challenges to communism that many believe contributed to the rapid downfall of the Soviet Union, and his turnaround of the U.S. economy and concludes: "If Ronald Reagan did all this and was only half as dumb or as removed from the decision-making process as his critics claimed, then he had to be the luckiest man ever to walk on this good earth. No one is that lucky."[46]

This is not a debate I want to join. Whether Reagan deliberately or ignorantly stood as the head of the "revolution" that bears his name is, for my purposes, irrelevant. For me, the roles Reagan played—as president, as national spokesperson, as military commander-in-chief, as father-figure, as hero, as emblem of a "national fantasy"—and the narratives in which they figure are what is important. For it is how those roles were understood by the millions of people who elected him president and "most admired man of the year" that matters, particularly to the extent that many of those people were the same who contributed their dollars to making the *Rambo* and *Lethal Weapon* sequences, *Batman* (1989, Timothy Burton), and *Top Gun* (1986, Tony Scott) among the top-grossing films of the decade.[47]

This book then is not about Ronald Reagan himself, or even Ronald Reagan's presidency, so much as it is about the correspondences between the public and popular images of "Ronald Reagan" and the action-adventure Hollywood films that portrayed many of the same narratives of heroism, success, achievement, toughness, strength, and "good old Americanness" that made the Reagan Revolution possible. I am not suggesting that Reagan in any way "caused" these stories to be told, or that he even consciously exploited the imagery of the films he viewed weekly in the White House. It is more that both Reagan and Hollywood participated in a radical shift away from the attitudes, public policies, and national concerns that characterized the late 1970s and the Carter administration. And whereas both Reagan and Hollywood aided and abetted that shift through the promulgation of their own interests, both as well clearly capitalized on it to reap their own political and economic benefits—with consequences that we are still struggling to come to terms with in the 1990s.

Robin Wood has stated that "since the early 60s, the central theme of the American cinema has been, increasingly, disintegration and breakdown,"[48] citing as examples *The Chase* (1966, Elia Kazan), *Nashville* (1975, Robert Altman), *California Split* (1974, Robert Altman), *The Poseidon Adventure* (1972, Ronald Neame), *Towering Inferno* (1974, John Guillermin), and *Earthquake* (1974, Mark Robson). But, he goes on to argue, this plot was replaced in the late 1970s by a run of " 'moral' reactionary movies" such as *Star Wars* (1977, George Lucas), *Rocky* (1976, John G. Avildsen), *Urban Cowboy* (1980, James Bridges), and *Star Trek*. These films, he concludes, indicate that the 1970s was "the period when the dominant ideology *almost* disintegrated."[49] In his analysis of the history of the American "tough guy" image, Rupert Wilkinson also views the

1970s as a time of contradictory characterizations of masculinity that challenged traditional notions of power and domination:

> In popular literature and the media, the early-to-mid-1970s pro-
> duced a cafeteria of choices from thoroughgoing, countercultural
> assaults on the tough guy to celebrations of virility that paid the
> merest lip service to the new critiques. In the middle range, films
> like *Marathon Man* . . . enabled viewers to have it both ways, to
> distance themselves from the most obvious tough guys, but to iden-
> tify with a sensitive, reluctant hero when he stumbled into a tough
> and exciting role.[50]

Seth Cagin and Philip Dray call this period Political Hollywood, the time when Hollywood made movies for a growing youth counterculture that wanted to see challenges to the political system that had come under attack during the civil rights, antiwar, and women's movements of the 1960s.[51] But, according to Cagin and Dray, that "golden age" of the 1970s gave way to a time of disillusionment and disorientation that left Hollywood at sea about its place in popular culture. Though economically assailed by the new cable and video industries, Hollywood's "distress," they argue, was more a result of no longer having a secure audience than the pressure of a specific technological challenge:

> Whatever the precise chemistry involved, when the movies are reas-
> signed a new position in the hierarchy of popular culture they must
> reestablish a rapport with their audience, to justify their existence;
> for when they no longer have something to offer a *popular* audience,
> the movies as we know them will cease to exist. . . . Hollywood
> movies, which by 1982 cost an average of $10.6 million to produce
> and another $10 million to market and distribute, can only be manu-
> factured in a spirit of confidence that the filmmakers know what
> audiences want to see.[52]

Certainly the election of Ronald Reagan in 1980 and his reelection in 1984 by the largest electoral college margin in U.S. history offered Hollywood some insight into "what audiences want to see": spectacu-lar narratives about characters who stand for individualism, liberty, militarism, and a mythic heroism. Through the blockbuster successes of films such as *First Blood* (1982, Ted Kotcheff), *Superman* (1978, Richard Donner), *Die Hard* (1988, John McTiernan), *Lethal Weapon*

(1987, Richard Donner), *Terminator* (1984, James Cameron), *Robocop* (1987, Paul Verhoeven), *Raiders of the Lost Ark* (1981, Steven Spielberg), *Top Gun,* and *Batman,*[53] Hollywood indicated that it had overcome the "fragmentation" and "distress" of the late 1970s and come successfully into a multimillion dollar era of action films that seemed to be "what audiences want to see." Like his own popular presidency, coming on the tail of a "fragmented" and "distressed" Carter administration struggling with the Iranian hostage crisis, Ronald Reagan and the conservative movement that heralded him as its leader also seemed to have found "what audiences want to see."

Most of the popular films of the 1970s fit Wood's framework, but one series of box office hits seems to speak more to the hard-body films of the 1980s—*Dirty Harry* (1971, Don Siegel), *Magnum Force* (1973, Ted Post), *The Enforcer* (1976, James Fargo), and *Sudden* 1983 *Impact*—than to the "disintegration" films of the 1970s. In these films, Clint Eastwood plays a hard-edged, unemotional, individualistic, and violent San Francisco police officer whose method of choice for dealing with criminals is to shoot them with his .357 Magnum pistol, a method these films show to be far more effective than the law. If the kinds of shifts between the 1970s and the 1980s that have been described here in fact occurred, how could such apparently anomalous films as the Dirty Harry series have been produced in the "countercultural" 1970s? And how, if at all, are they any different from the hard-body films of the 1980s? Cagin and Dray situate the Dirty Harry films within a broader sequence of what they call vigilante films, in which a larger-than-life superhuman hero battles alone against an increasingly deteriorating society in which the only recourse from crime, violence, and corruption is the determined individual who acts on his own principles and commitments. "Misunderstood by their superiors and unappreciated by the public they serve, they achieve satisfaction only from their skill and its ultimate vindication."[54] Vigilante films such as *Dirty Harry, Billy Jack* (1971, Tom Laughlin), *Walking Tall* (1974, Phil Karlson), and *Death Wish* (1974, Michael Winner) are, they conclude, "marvel[s] of cross-purposes and a testament to the confusion and loss of social cohesion that arose out of bitter resistance to the counterculture, as well as resistance to the resistance."[55]

The Dirty Harry films confirm this sense of bitterness and nihilism that Cagin and Dray identify. Though Harry Callahan may kill the serial murderer Scorpio in *Dirty Harry*, he throws away his badge at the

*The 1970s' "hard body" hero, Dirty Harry. (*Magnum Force, *Warner Brothers)*

end of the film in disgust at the inability of the police department to jail a known murderer (Callahan failed to read Scorpio his Miranda rights, and he was released to kill yet again). Callahan successfully eliminates a vigilante police group that had formed within the police force in *Magnum Force,* but, as the lieutenant who organized the young officers declared, there are many more where they came from; Harry is again alone in his sense of how a police officer should operate and what causes he should serve. And in spite of the fact that Callahan kills the members of the "Revolutionary Strike Force" who kidnapped the mayor and terrorized the city in *The Enforcer,* his partner is killed, and the mayor—who has been shown to be an egoistic buffoon—is still in power. In each of these 1970s films, though Callahan "solves" the crimes by killing the culprits, the institutions that enabled these criminals to operate in the first place retain power, and the incompetent individuals who run them remain in charge. There is no "happy ending" for Callahan, only a brief respite between crimes.

As one of the series's opening motifs suggests, Harry Callahan barely has time to finish a meal before he is caught up in another crime. Harry's heroism has a nihilistic edge to it that cannot reassure audiences that any of his actions have mattered or have changed the social order in any way.

In contrast, the heroes of hard-body films suggest a different kind of social order, one in which the men who are thrust forward into heroism are not heroic in defiance of their society but in defiance of their governments and institutional bureaucracies. In each case, these heroes are shown to be representing the will and desires of the "average" citizen against the self-serving empowerment of government bureaucrats who are standing in the way of social improvement. This is one reason why many popular films of the 1980s are POW rescue films in which an obdurate government is trying to hide its own incompetence at the expense of the lives of individual citizens: four of the most popular were *Rambo: First Blood, Part 2* (1985, George P. Cosmatos), *Missing in Action* (1984, Joseph Zito), *Missing in Action 2* (1985, Lance Hool), and *Uncommon Valor* (1983, Ted Kotcheff). The heroes of these films are those who defy government policies (when Rambo is ordered to just take pictures, he instead saves a "live American") and rescue citizens from their leaders. Unlike the Dirty Harry films, in which a lone hero is pitted against a widely corrupt society, the hard-body films of the 1980s pose as heroes men who are pitted against bureaucracies that have lost touch with the people they are to serve, largely through the failure of bureaucrats themselves to attend to individual needs. This was, of course, one of the primary themes of Reaganism. Ronald Reagan promised that when he entered the White House he would decrease the size of government itself and cut unwieldly bureaucracies that had come, according to Reaganites, more to serve the interests of the lawmakers and bureaucrats who depend on their budgets than to address real needs of citizens. It is this edge—that institutions had been misdirected by self-serving government officials—that enables the films of the 1980s to retain a sense of social cohesion despite the hero's need to defy many of society's chief institutions. Because individuals have come to misuse government institutions, the institutions themselves cannot be blamed for the failure and can be resuscitated, often by the hard-body heroes themselves.

Robocop, a half-human and half-computerized police robot, for example, is designed to circumvent the "live Americans" who work in the police force and who have come to complain about their wages, working conditions, and lack of support from their boss, Omni Consumer Products corporation. His triumph is to eliminate the egoistic and power-hungry boss of OCP who is interested only in profits, and to restore control of the police force and the city of Detroit to the "Old Man," the founder of OCP (though he is by no means an entirely admirable character either). The police officers themselves are consistently depicted as overworked, committed, and good-hearted people who are trying to rein in a rapidly deteriorating social order. What *Robocop* reveals is that this deterioration is largely a product of OCP's own management structure, in which profit is the sole criterion for administrative decisions, and in which the the boss is himself profiting from the sales of drugs and illegal weapons that are the chief causes of crime in Detroit. Consequently, the "average" citizens—the police officers—are not only being badly served by their governing officials but are in fact being deliberately abused by them for personal profit. What makes Robocop a hero is that he supports the work of those average citizens and succeeds both in toppling the drug ring and unseating the corrupt officials of OCP. *Dirty Harry* also depicted government officials who were not fulfilling their civic obligations, not because they were individually bad or corrupt but simply because the system favored the advancement of incompetents who were too rule-bound and indecisive to make any significant changes. Such sentiments were logical outcomes of a post-Watergate era, in which it seemed that institutions of government corrupted individuals who in turn corrupted society (sentiments that led to the passage of the War Powers Act, for example). In contrast, *Robocop* never suggests that the police force is useless or a failed institution, but simply that it needs to be returned to the hands of the hardworking officers who populate it. In similar ways, the *Rambo* films never argue for the elimination of the military, *Top Gun* for the elimination of the Navy, *Die Hard* for the elimination of the police force, or *Superman* for the elimination of the justice system. In each of these films, the removal of a few bad individuals—whether incompetent police captains or hardened criminals such as Lex Luthor—will presumably return the system to its operating purpose: serving average Americans.

Ronald Reagan, like Robocop, touted himself as the defender of the average citizen who needed a break from too much government. In his 1981 inaugural address, he told the American people, "Our government has no power except that granted by its people. It is time to check and reverse the growth of government which shows signs of having grown beyond the consent of the governed."[56] But, like the heroes of hard-body films, he went on to say: "It is not my intention to do away with government. It is rather to make it work—work with us, not over us; to stand by our side, not ride on our backs."[57] The "us" that Reagan celebrated in this speech was exactly those "average Americans" he purported to speak for against big government:

> Those who say that we're in a time when there are no heroes, they just don't know where to look. You can see heroes going in and out of factory gates. Others . . . produce enough food to feed all of us and then the world beyond. You meet heroes across the counter. . . . Now, I have used the words "they" and "their" in speaking of these heroes. I could say "you" and "your," because I'm addressing the heroes of whom I speak—you, the citizens of this blessed land. Your dreams, your hopes, your goals are going to be the dreams, the hopes, and the goals of this administration, so help me God.[58]

It is these kinds of remarks that have led many to label Reagan a "populist" president, having a "powerful appeal to the average man in America."[59]

The heroes of the hard-body films of the 1980s can more appropriately be identified as "populist" heroes than the vigilantes that typified action heroes of the 1970s. And though they may possess hard bodies like Rambo's or Martin Riggs's, seventies heroes seem more isolated from the social order than a part of it. Martin Riggs (Mel Gibson) can be invited into Roger Murtaugh's (Danny Glover's) home at the end of *Lethal Weapon*, but Dirty Harry ends all of his films outdoors, with long-range crane shots emphasizing his isolation not only from other people but from any center of social life at all. Consequently, in a narrative format that focuses on the vigilante's separation from society, it is difficult to establish that character as a national body, as the source of the kind of popular identification that made Reagan and Rambo both national icons. The separation from the "average man" means a separation from the national identity as well.

It is important thus to note how the same story elements—muscular physiques, violent actions, and individual determination—can serve such different social and political ends. For this reason in this book I focus not on the hard-body character, who can certainly be traced back to Teddy Roosevelt and Jim Corbett, but on what the hard-body came to figure in a particular era, an era that saw a resurgence of both national and masculine power, both of which were embodied in the person of Ronald Reagan as president.

I trace how hard-bodied heroes developed during the 1980s, how the vigilante cops of *Dirty Harry* turned into the child-loving police officers of *Kindergarten Cop*. I do so by placing these films in the context of the social and political thematics of the Reagan Revolution. Beginning with an examination of the hard-body iconography, I go on to look at the aspect of that heroic masculinity which attracted Robert Bly and seems to structure so many popular narratives of the 1980s—the father/son relationship. Although the express focus of this book is on the Reagan years, it is also important to understand how the Reagan legacy has shaped subsequent political and cultural debates. Consequently, I look at how the Bush presidency and the later years of the 1980s indicated changes in the hard-body mythology, particularly in the apparent negation of that body in favor of a more internalized and emotional kind of heroic icon. Finally, I conclude with a look at how the themes of the Reagan Revolution have been carried over into Hollywood films of the early 1990s, culminating in an examination of where the hard body appears today and what its possible future might be.

I cannot speak about all 1980s Hollywood films, nor do I mean to suggest that the cultural narratives I am trying to identify here would fit *all* films that were made during the Reagan era. Clearly, there are many Hollywood films that attempted to counter some of the prevailing social and political messages of the Reagan presidency, films such as *Salvador* (1986, Oliver Stone), *Hamburger Hill* (1987, John Irvin), *E.T.* (1982, Steven Spielberg), *Out of Africa* (1990, Sidney Pollack), *Blade Runner* (1982, Ridley Scott), *Do the Right Thing* (1989, Spike Lee), and more, as well as numerous independent films that challenged the mainstream narratives of American culture. I chose to examine some of the most popular films—by box office figures[60]—of the period precisely because their popularity must, I believe, indicate something about what kinds of stories mainstream audiences were interested in seeing, what characters they found compelling, and what images they found worth repeating—what, in other words, they found *pleasurable*. As polls, voting tallies, t-shirts, and public iconography indicate, many found, during this same period, images of "Ronald Reagan" and the nation he seemed to revive pleasurable as well. What I hope to suggest here are some of the ways in which these pleasures overlapped, intermixed, and mutually informed each other, producing a body of films that can show us some of the key narratives, images, and icons that came to be part of the "Reagan Revolution."

This book ends its analysis with the election of Bill Clinton to the White House, an event that indicates a shift in the American voting public's sense of its national identity. By turning away from foreign-policy issues that George Bush offered as justification for his reelection and toward domestic concerns about jobs and social services, voters indicated that the hard-bodied warriors who fought imaginary, external enemies of the 1980s seemed no longer to provide the same kinds of "national pleasure" they had in earlier years. As of 1992 the Reagan Revolution was certainly far from over, as can be seen in the altered conservative strategy of localized legislative change rather than instituted national mandates: in the state rather than federal efforts to write more restrictive abortion laws; in the several state referenda against "homosexual rights" (one such succeeded in Colorado, and another was barely defeated in Oregon); in the commitment of the Christian Coalition to elect more members to local school boards; or in the efforts, in many cases quite successful ones, explicitly to turn the Republican party toward the New Right agenda (as can be seen in the conservative Republican party platform at the 1992 convention, or in the Washington state Republican party platform banning homosexuality, witchcraft, and yoga). Whatever more "liberal" effects the election of Bill Clinton promises to bring about—such as the end on the ban against homosexuals in the military, the reorientation of tax dollars to support education, or the provision of national health care—that administration will continue to struggle with the legacies of Reaganism, both in local referenda and in the Supreme Court. But the very conflicts and divisions that these different and vocal strains of U.S. political culture exhibit will undoubtedly yield "new" definitions of national identity and "new" conceptions of masculinity in relation to it. Already, Bill Clinton's relative youth, his partnership with Al Gore, his forthright discussions of marital infidelity, his acknowledgment of his opposition to the Vietnam War, and his open reliance on Hillary Clinton's advice and insight define a different kind of masculine image in the White House. Whether Clinton will prove another brief aberration in the Republican domination of the presidency since 1968 or whether he will begin a "Clinton Revolution" remains to be seen. But it is highly likely that his administration, like those before him, will contribute to yet another redefinition of the masculine, which will be seen in Hollywood films of the next few years, and that his administration and those films will propose yet another phase in the extended narrative of "American identity."

Hard Bodies: The Reagan Heroes

The Reagan era was an era of bodies. From the anxieties about Reagan's age and the appearance of cancerous spots on his nose; to the profitable craze in aerobics and exercise; to the molding of a former Mr. Universe into the biggest box-office draw of the decade; to the conservative agenda to outlaw abortion; to the identification of "values" through an emphasis on drug use, sexuality, and child-bearing; to the thematized aggression against persons with AIDS— these articulations of bodies constituted the imaginary of the Reagan agenda and the site of its materialization. And whereas heated debates over "ideas" and "values" took place throughout this period, they generally took as their justification and target of success the bodies each "value" declared as its own. But as Amnesty International and other civil and human rights organizations can attest, Reagan's policies were geared not so much to the individual human body as it might be the material location of suffering, pain, or deprivation, as they were to the control of the *idea* of the body, as the Reagan ideology vied for and captured the power to define how bodies were to be perceived, touched, fed, regulated, and counted.

In the dialectic of reasoning that constituted the Reagan movement, bodies were deployed in two fundamental categories: the errant body containing sexually transmitted disease, immorality, illegal chemicals, "laziness," and endangered fetuses, which we can call the "soft body"; and the normative body that enveloped strength, labor, determination, loyalty, and courage—the "hard body"—the body that was to come to stand as the emblem of the Reagan philosophies, politics, and economies. In this system of thought marked by race and gender, the soft body invariably belonged to a female and/or a person of color, whereas the hard body was, like Reagan's own, male and white. In Reagan's self-promoted image—chopping wood at his ranch, riding horses, standing tall at the presidential podium—his was one of these hard bodies, a body not subject to disease, fatigue, or aging. "Ronald Reagan lifted the double-edged ax above his head and slammed it into the tree branch lying on the ground. He swung again, his right hand sliding the length of the long wooden handle, and kept swinging for two full minutes. His face glistened with sweat. . . . In his faded denim shirt, leather gloves, scuffed boots and cowboy hat, he looked fit and even young."[1] This hard body became for Reaganism what Jurgen Link has called a "collective symbol," what he defines as "collective pictures that are culturally 'anchored' in the most literal sense and that act as carriers of symbolic meaning."[2] The depiction of the indefatigable, muscular, and invincible masculine body became the linchpin of the Reagan imaginary; this hardened male form became the emblem not only for the Reagan presidency but for its ideologies and economies as well.

To understand the broad functions of these bodies as collective symbols, it is important to see them not simply as images for Reagan's own self-projections or idealizations of an outdated Hollywood heroism but to recognize their successful linkage in Reaganism to the national body as well. As such, these hard bodies came to stand not only for a type of national character—heroic, aggressive, and determined—but for the nation itself. In contrast to what Reagan's public relations workers characterized as the weakened—some even said "feminine"[3]—years of the Carter administration, in which the United States government was brought to a standstill by a Third World nation, the Reagan America was to be a strong one, capable of confronting enemies rather than submitting to them, of battling "evil empires" rather than allowing them to flourish, of using its hardened body—its renewed techno-military network—to impose its will on others rather than allow itself to be dictated to. As Roger Rosenblatt's assessment of Reagan's popularity suggests, part of the reason why so many Americans were disillusioned with Carter was that he made them feel "small" as a nation and, we can only conclude, as individual bodies as well:

> There was Carter himself . . . who was perhaps most bitterly resented for shrinking those hopes down to the size of a presidency

characterized by small people, small talk and small matters. He
made Americans feel two things they are not used to feeling, and
will not abide. He made them feel puny and he made them feel
insecure.[4]

In this sense, those hard bodies heralded by Ronald Reagan were not
just self-images; they were national identities.

Jochen and Linda Schulte-Sasse, like Link, describe how such identifications work by referring to collective images:

The experience of an imaginary unity such as the nation cannot take
place without the construction of signs or images of that unity; the
self seeks to overcome its separation and the extreme differentiation
of modern societies by mirroring itself in signs that facilitate the
illusion that the very difference that establishes the sign as sign is
overcome in the experience of the sign. It takes pleasure in experi-
encing itself not so much as unity, but as unified in the image of
unity.[5]

The Schulte-Sasses are speaking in this passage primarily of objects
for national identification, such as flags or caricatures of enemies, but
it is clear that the image of a body could serve equally well as a sign of
unity, to the degree that the image of that body is widely accepted as
the projection of the national body itself. In this sense, there is a dual
identification taking place: first, with the individual body, as citizens
might choose to see themselves *as* that body, desiring its strengths,
expressions, and stances; and second, with that body as a national
emblem, as a collective symbol for a nation that individual citizens
receive pleasure from feeling themselves a part of. The Schulte-
Sasses insist that this second form of identification must be understood as a form of pleasure, what they call "national pleasure,"[6] deriving from the sense of "substitute mastery" the image provides: "The
average subject's illusion of being a historical agent . . . demands the
aesthetic representation of substitutes with which we can identify and
depends on images that contain nothing messy or confusing. . . .
Such substitute mastery reconciles us with the nonreadability of everyday events."[7] In these terms, the hardened bodies that emblematized
Reaganism assisted citizens/viewers in perceiving not simply those
bodies but themselves as masterful, as in control of their environments (immediate or geopolitical), as dominating those around them
(whether they be the soft bodies of other citizens or of enemies), and

as able to resolve crises successfully (whether domestic or international in scope). Such bodies assist in the confirmation of this mastery by themselves refusing to be "messy" or "confusing," by having hard edges, determinate lines of action, and clear boundaries for their own decision-making. "The purpose of the masculine ego," Antony Easthope explains, "is to *master* every threat. . . . The castle of the ego is defined by its perimeter and the line drawn between what is inside and what outside. To maintain its identity it must not only repel external attack but also suppress treason within."[8] It is in keeping with this focus on hard edges that Reagan established so many policies concerning the integrity of international boundaries.

One of the functions of the hard edges of such individual bodies is, of course, not simply to invoke similarly defined national boundaries but in fact to reinstate them. According to Reaganites, the Carter presidency not only squandered the national strength and will but failed to maintain the distinctive boundaries of the national identity as well. In a simple but symbolically powerful act of boundary definition, Ronald Reagan, on taking office, restored many of the trappings of the office of the president that Carter (or his predecessor, Gerald Ford) had discarded, including the playing of "Hail to the Chief" (Carter had chosen Sir Arthur Bliss's "Jubilation"), wearing a suit coat while in the Oval Office (Carter had worn a sweater), and reviewing troops at arrival ceremonies.[9] Just as Reagan reestablished the boundaries of the presidency, hard bodies reestablished the boundaries not only of the individual masculine figure but of the nation as a whole.

To understand the diverse functioning of these hard bodies in the Reagan era, it is imperative to keep in mind the collective pleasure that can be derived from imaging and narrating them.[10] One of the key mechanisms for that collective imaging and narration during the 1980s and one of the most visible locations for the "collective symbol" of hard bodies was the Hollywood film, in the viewing of which the pleasure of feeling a part of a national unity could be achieved, not through a speech, a flag, or even a war, but through the narration and movement of hard bodies themselves—their confrontations, actions, decisions, and victories. Film theorists have established that the pleasures of cinema are deeply rooted in psychological, emotional, and personal pleasures, that audience members are able to establish diverse forms of identification with characters and scenarios on the screen.[11] What Jochen and Linda Schulte-Sasse's comments suggest is that this relationship with the characters and events on the screen can function to promote mass unity as well. In such terms, the cinematic narrative offers two ways to a feeling of "mastery": at the level of plot, in which the hard-body hero masters his surroundings, most often by defeating enemies through violent physical action; and at the level of *national plot*, in which the same hero defeats national enemies, again through violent physical action. Viewers can experience personal power by identifying with an individual hero's victory over fictional antagonists and national power through the "pleasurable collective experience" of identifying with one of the key images that came to embody the political, economic, and social philosophy of the 1980s— the hard body. The substitute mastery offered by Reaganism is never simply personal or national but a combination of both. It is for this reason that the hard body was able to function more effectively even than the American flag or individual wars to support Reaganism— because it served both forms of identification simultaneously.

One of the most popular icons of the Reagan era was the film character of Rambo, played by Sylvester Stallone, a man whom audiences watched develop his hard body throughout the *Rocky* films. While those on the left caricatured Reagan's militarism by referring to him in political cartoons as "Ronbo," Reagan himself quipped at a press conference after the release of the hostages in Lebanon, "Boy, I saw *Rambo* last night. Now I know what to do the next time this happens."[12] The films themselves were among the most popular of the decade, suggesting that they had, for whatever reasons, successfully tapped into a strain of American thinking. In three films that span the years of the Reagan presidency, John Rambo, a Vietnam veteran, takes on and defeats a series of enemies—a small-town sheriff and the National Guard in *First Blood* (1982), Vietnamese and Russian soldiers in *Rambo: First Blood, Part 2* (1985), and Soviet military commandos in Afghanistan in *Rambo III* (1988, Peter MacDonald). Because the films focus on Rambo's physical prowess, and because Stallone himself did extensive body-building for the part, the films can be used to illustrate how the hard-body imagery evolved during the eight years that Ronald Reagan was in office. Taken in order, the *Rambo* films narrate the production of the hard body during the Reagan years.

A CBS News–New York Times Poll taken shortly after the 1980 election showed that although 11 percent of the people voted for Ronald Reagan because he was conservative, 38 percent voted for him because he was *not* Jimmy Carter. John Orman explains in his study of the Reagan and Carter presidencies that "Reagan, by most accounts, won the [1980] election essentially because he was not Jimmy Carter."

*The 1980s' "hard body" hero, John Rambo. (*Rambo III, *Tri-Star Pictures)*

By 1984, however, "Reagan won precisely because he was Ronald Reagan."[13] In the intervening years, Reagan's personal and national body image was enhanced by two significant events—the assassination attempt on his life in 1981, and the invasion of Grenada in October of 1983. In both cases, Reagan was able to show that incidents that could have defeated a lesser man—or, more to the point, a lesser body— were unable to overcome him. Indeed, in all of American history, five presidents have been shot at and hit by assassins' bullets, and of those five—Lincoln, Garfield, McKinley, Kennedy, and Reagan—only Reagan survived. And he not only survived, he stayed in character throughout. As Haynes Johnson concluded, Reagan's optimistic and upbeat actions after the shooting "conveyed a sense to the public that Reagan possessed larger-than-life qualities."[14] And as Lou Cannon put it, "The president rattled off one-liners in the face of death and emerged from the ordeal as a hero."[15] Perhaps more important, the assassination was taken not only as a personal triumph for Reagan but as a national one as well: "His survival from a bullet wound lodged an inch from his heart was taken as an augury of a national turn for the better; it signaled the breaking of the skein of bad luck that had plagued the nation and its leaders for nearly twenty years."[16] And when the deaths of more than two hundred U.S. Marines in Beirut threatened to bring back the national trauma and sense of helplessness that had surrounded the Iran hostage crisis during the Carter years, Reagan distracted the public away from Beirut by invading the small island nation of Grenada only two days later, ostensibly to protect U.S. bodies—students at the medical school in St. George's.

In 1982, however, the year in which *First Blood* appeared, the image of the personal and national hard body was not yet culturally solidified. The nation was still reeling under the traumas of the Vietnam War and the Iranian hostage takeover. Stepping out of both scenarios was John Rambo, veteran of the Vietnam War and an escaped POW who had been tortured in captivity. But although the Reagan hard body was not yet fully configured, there is no doubt from this movie that the focus on the body had already begun.

As the film begins, John Rambo is shown from a long shot, walking down a tree-lined road. Only after viewers have assessed his full body does the camera turn, as it does with dramatic effect in the trademark opening of each film, to a close-up of Rambo's calm, emotionless, almost peaceful face. Rambo has arrived at the home of the last surviving member of his Special Forces unit from the war, Delmar Berry, only to be told by Berry's mother that he had died the previous summer from cancer, a cancer brought on, she believes, by Agent Orange contamination. When Rambo shows the photograph of Berry, remarking on how he was so much bigger than all of the other men in his unit, the mother graphically describes how the cancer had so deteriorated his body that she was able to carry him in her own arms. The film opens then with an invocation of an absent strong body—the big man who had been taken down to a less than feminine size by a disease brought on by the war itself—and Rambo's isolation as now the only surviving body from that war. The question the film has posed is one that the Reagan presidency soon would answer: Would that body go the way of its companions and deteriorate as well, or would it find a way to survive the onslaughts of captivity, contamination, and public betrayal?

In the opening scenes of the film, it seems that the answer to this question will be in the negative, as Rambo is arrested and beaten by a small-town sheriff's department, essentially because they did not like the *way he looked*, in other words, not for any particular behavior, belief, or expressed attitude but because his body did not conform to the town's expectations of what a citizen's body should look like. As the sheriff (Brian Dennehey) advises him when he first escorts Rambo out of town, "Get a haircut and take a bath. You won't get hassled so much." The sheriff's animosity is focused solely on how Rambo's body looks and smells. And when he arrests Rambo for vagrancy, he immediately instructs his deputies to "clean him up" so that he'll be able to face the judge the next morning.

It is the act of "cleaning him up" that propels the plot forward into the explosive and violent spectacle for which the Rambo films have become famous. For it is only when the deputies physically strip, hose down, and then attempt to shave Rambo that he exhibits his first overtly physical and aggressive acts of the film, as he uses his expert combat techniques to maim the deputies who have trapped him. To insure that viewers condemn the deputies, the director, Ted Kotcheff, mixes flashbacks to Rambo's torture by the Vietnamese with his treatment by the deputies. When one of the deputies waves a straight razor in Rambo's face in an attempt to shave him, Rambo balks. Deputy Galt then places his nightstick around Rambo's neck in a choke hold. Rambo flashes to a scene in the POW camp where a Vietnamese soldier is slicing at his chest with a long-bladed knife, yielding the multiple scars that viewers saw on Rambo's torso earlier in the scene. His body is presented not as unclean or unshaven but as victimized, as wrongly, harshly mistreated by enemies foreign and domestic who would like to redefine and reshape that body and its presentations.

The opening scenes of *First Blood* then show that, within the United States in 1982, there were reasons for concern about the future status of the masculine body. The town's guardian, Sheriff Teasle, has, for example, a body that contrasts markedly with Rambo's. Brian Dennehey was an excellent choice to play the part of Teasle, making Rambo's judge and opponent the possessor of a corpulent male body, which in its weakness and lack of stamina and self-assured fullness represents all that Rambo sets out to defeat. If, this film argues, the masculine body is to be reclaimed, it will have to be done, not simply by reclaiming some value or usefulness for that body (for example, its serviceability in time of war), but by rejecting the corpulent body altogether, showing *its* uselessness and destructiveness even in time of peace. Another highly popular 1982 film, *An Officer and a Gentleman* (Taylor Hackford), works out the same tension between the weakened and the strong masculine body, again explicitly in terms of a national military and identity. The very plot of the film—how a no-good, flip, useless, and soft male body is changed into a triumphant, resilient, and determined heterosexual hard body—narrates the transformations promised by the Reagan presidency. The softened, pampered, and ill-trained male body will become, for the Reagan imaginary, the body of the Carter presidency, the body that was unable to defend its country/its town/its values against outsiders. This is the body, the Reagan logic will declare, that cost American citizens a unified national strength, in the same way that Teasle's unwillingness to accept Rambo's presence in his town eventually cost the town many of the bodies of its male citizens and a large portion of the town's property.

First Blood clarifies the consequences of the "weakened" years of the Carter presidency, when strength and preparedness were, according to the Reagan historians, abandoned in favor of negotiation and capitulation. The "waffling" and "wavering" that Nixon believed characterized the Carter years[17] typified the inability of the national body to defend its principles and national values. Consequently, *First Blood* shows audiences that inadequate, unprepared, and weakened masculine bodies simply cannot compete with the forces of a strengthened and prepared body.

After Rambo escapes from the prison and flees to the mountains, his survival skills already activated, the sheriff and his deputies pursue him, joking about the "hunt" they are on and having no clear idea of who Rambo is. Skillfully and methodically, Rambo maims each of the deputies, each time with a different type of assault. Later, Colonel Trautman (Richard Crenna), the man who trained Rambo, comments that he must be slipping up, since he had been trained to kill, not injure. But the film requires that Rambo not kill these deputies:[18] first, because it would be difficult to maintain his characterization as a victim if he became a successful killer; and second, because helpless, screaming men far more effectively portray the consequences of a weakened masculinity than silent corpses do. Each deputy in turn appeals for help to Sheriff Teasle, who cannot help him, and the soundtrack begins to echo with the pitiful and plaintive voices of disabled men, all at the mercy of their own weakness.

But *First Blood* is not satisfied to show the weakened individual masculine body of the small towns of America. It must show the weakened national body as well. When Teasle calls in the National Guard to help him capture Rambo, the focus shifts away from what might be simply a poorly trained sheriff's department to the national military itself. Led by Lieutenant Clinton Morgan (Patrick Stack), the National Guard unit walks right by Rambo, who has concealed himself in the river. Later, when Rambo holes up in an abandoned mine, Morgan orders each of his men in turn to go in after him. Each refuses. When Rambo fires at them, they throw themselves down in fear. As a last resort, and against Teasle's orders not to kill Rambo, Morgan orders one of his troops to fire a rocket launcher into the mine shaft. When the mine explodes, Morgan is certain that Rambo is dead. Later, when Teasle orders him to clean up the mess made by the explosion, Morgan whines, "Aw, Will! I have to be back at the drugstore tomorrow!"

Here is the film's harshest criticism of the country's military preparedness: a veteran who has been out of combat for at least five years easily defeats the backbone of U.S. national security. Admittedly, as Trautman reminds Teasle, "Rambo was the best." But these soldiers and deputies are clearly the worst. As Trautman figures it, the odds of two hundred such men against one Rambo are "about right." When the body that had been trained for warfare in the sixties (Rambo joined the Army in 1964) confronts the body trained for warfare in the late seventies, the outcome is clear: the soft body, even when massed in numbers and equipped with up-to-date technology, will lose. And it is this soft masculine body, *First Blood* declares, that represents the national body as a whole.

The film thus presents a short history of this national deterioration. Rambo's body was not foreign born or trained, but one that the country's military was more than capable of producing through the early seventies. The absence of more bodies like his is attributed in the film to two sources: the Vietnam War, which brought on the deaths of all of the other members of Baker team; and the United States itself, which has failed to produce more bodies like these to replace the lost ones. In the intervening years, the country has produced men who view battles as weekend jaunts or hunting sprees, rather than, as

Rambo does, struggles for individual and national survival. Indeed, the country is so unaccustomed to seeing bodies like Rambo's that Rambo's soft-bodied adversaries repeatedly fail throughout the film to recognize it. When Teasle first sees Rambo on the road, he takes him for a hippie, even though Rambo is wearing an Army jacket decorated with an American flag. When the deputies see the scars on his body, they cannot imagine what caused them. And when Rambo disarms all of the deputies and escapes from the prison, they cannot explain his skill. Later, when they're tracking him in the woods, the deputies send attack dogs after a piece of plastic draped over some branches or shoot one another by mistake. They simply cannot recognize his body when they see it because, the film implies, they are not used to seeing men like him anymore.

The film's dynamics work on this assumption, that the audience, like these deputies, is not used to seeing bodies like Rambo's anymore and that the more they see them, the more they will desire them, not only at an individual but at a national level. The true success of *First Blood*, both symbolically and as a marketing tool, is to have created the desire in citizens/audiences to see more bodies like Rambo's, an achievement to which the blockbuster films of the 1980s can attest.

In *First Blood* Rambo's body was continually contrasted to the soft bodies of the deputies and National Guard soldiers to show audiences its sufficiency; the later films have found such comparisons unnecessary. If, as Orman put it, in 1980 Reagan was elected "because he was not Jimmy Carter" and in 1984 "because he was Ronald Reagan," by 1985, the release date of *Rambo: First Blood, Part 2*, Rambo was now popular because he was Rambo. There are no recognition problems in this film. When Rambo enters a room, heads turn. Nor is there any ambivalence about the status of his body. In the first film it was unclear whether his body was clean or dirty, lawful or unlawful, strong or weak; by 1985 Rambo's body-strength is indisputable. In the opening shots the camera pans across the bodies of men hammering rocks in a prison yard and stops at Rambo's bulging physique. No longer the contemplative figure walking through the woods at the opening of *First Blood*, Rambo's is now an even more active, muscular, and hardened body. The camera is not ambivalent about and needs no narrative justification to display his physical prowess.

One of the reasons for the success of Rambo's body and the ease of its recognition in 1985 lies in Ronald Reagan's own achievement of the hard-body imaginary that would typify his presidency. Through his first term as president, Reagan was able to establish himself in the mold of what Orman has called the "macho presidential style," which he defines by the following seven qualities:

1. Competitive in politics and life
2. Sports-minded and athletic
3. Decisive, never wavering or uncertain
4. Unemotional, never revealing true emotions or feelings
5. Strong and aggressive, not weak or passive
6. Powerful
7. A "real man," never "feminine."

As Orman goes on to say, "The macho presidential style places the ability to portray strength, aggressiveness, and power at the top of its demands." And though Orman will claim that to some degree "each president more or less embodied the seven components of the macho presidential style," he also concludes that "Ronald Reagan is the quintessential macho president."[19]

Reagan established these qualities as significant in his presentation of the presidency and his embodiment of the national character. Just as the Rambo films provided narrative models of these characteristics in action, the invasion of Grenada and the bombing of Libya provided concrete, historical instances of the same thing. In particular, the plots of the three films enabled the Reagan hard body to lay to rest the anxieties displayed in the opening scenes of *First Blood* about the future of the masculine body. *First Blood*, for example, establishes Rambo's determined competitiveness. When Trautman tries to encourage Rambo to give himself up so that no one else will get hurt, Rambo reminds him that "they drew first blood" and so the fight must go on. Rambo's strength, speed, and endurance underscore his physical agility, and, when combined with his physique, mark his athleticism. His decisiveness is shown at each stage of his narrative, whether in jumping hundreds of feet into a pine tree to escape a pursuing helicopter in *First Blood* or rescuing an American POW in *Rambo*. And though Rambo broke down at the end of *First Blood* and cried on Trautman's shoulder for his lost friends and uncertain status at home, by *Rambo*, he is emotionless. Even when Co Bao (Julia Nickson) asks him to take her to America with him and then kisses him, he shows no response. The most emotion he shows is in his anger toward Marshall Murdock (Charles Napier) when he learns that Murdock aborted the

Rambo rescuing POWs. (Rambo: First Blood, Part 2, *Tri-Star Pictures)*

mission that was to pick up Rambo and a rescued POW, leaving them to the Vietnamese and Soviet torturers. Even here, Rambo shows only a curled upper lip, as he tells Murdock, "I'm coming to get you." And because Rambo is consistently depicted as strong, aggressive, and powerful, these films conclude, he can be nothing other than a "real man." The promised presidential pardon offered to Rambo at the beginning of *Rambo* if he completes his mission successfully solidifies early in the movie the connection between Rambo and Reagan. It is as if Ronald Reagan has personally promised to free the hard-bodied man from his confinement in return for bringing back more men like him, the survivors from before the decade when masculine bodies were methodically weakened by a "soft" presidential style.

The shift toward the hard body as a *national* emblem takes place in this second film as well. Whereas in *First Blood* Rambo's own body was assaulted by the sheriff and his deputies, which implies that Rambo alone is the victim of Teasle's form of American domestic torture, in *Rambo* the initial focus has shifted away from Rambo's individual body to that of the anonymous and collective body of the men Rambo is sent to rescue. In a similar fashion, Reagan, by this point in his presidency, had managed to redefine the focus on hostages/captives that had so mesmerized the Carter presidency away from the individual captives to the general status of American bodies. Jimmy Carter knew the names of each Iranian hostage, became friends with their families, and prayed for their rescue individually. As he recorded in his memoirs, "The hostages sometimes seemed like part of my own family."[20] Reagan, however, chose to characterize American hostages as collective and representative groups. From the early days of his first term, when he proclaimed a National POW-MIA Day, to the 1983 Grenada invasion staged to "rescue" American medical students, whom Reagan argued could then be taken as hostages, to the crisis over the TWA hostages in 1985, Ronald Reagan treated hostage situations as if America itself was held captive rather than individual diplomats, students, or soldiers. As he told the returning TWA passengers during a White House reception for them, "None of you were held prisoner because of any personal wrong you had done anyone; you were held simply because you are Americans. In the minds of your captors, you represented us."[21]

In the filmic logic of *Rambo*, the forgotten POWs were not individual soldiers who might have committed atrocities or participated in the devastation of an entire nation. Audiences never hear any of their individual stories or learn any of their names. They are referred to in the film as simply "American POWs," Americans who have been left behind to suffer and starve because Congress is unwilling to appropriate money for their rescue (and there is no doubt in this film that it is Congress and not the president who is to blame for this failure). In this sense, these hostages come to represent a crisis in the national body, an effort to suppress a part of the national body that had been, presumably, "forgotten" but has in fact, as this film makes clear, actually been actively suppressed by a weakened government. As Colonel Podovsky (Steven Berkoff), a Soviet adviser, observes as he is torturing Rambo, "It seems you were abandoned on direct command." As *Rambo* goes on to say, it is exactly the deliberate suppression of this part of the national body that has led to the production of the kinds of masculine bodies shown as now in charge of U.S. affairs. Marshall Murdock, the key figure here, is weakbodied and weak-willed, and he surrenders both body and will to Rambo on his return from the mission. He wears a long-sleeved shirt and tie, which contrasts with Rambo's military gear and then exposed muscular torso. Murdock sweats uncomfortably throughout the film, drinking imported Cokes and positioning himself in front of fans as protection against the climate of Vietnam. In this crucible that crystallized the hardened body of a John Rambo, Marshall Murdock's body is shown to be out of place, ineffective, and weak, in other words, soft.

Ronald Reagan's shift from individual to national bodies had, obviously, a number of consequences. He excluded many from the national body by characterizing them as part of the "soft body" that posed an internal threat to the well-being of the United States. From welfare recipients to homosexuals, from Cuban refugees to university professors, Reagan succeeded in establishing a domestic equivalent to the "foreign terrorist." But, as Richard Nixon argues in *The Real War*, the linchpin for the entire Reagan philosophy was the Soviet Union. If Reagan had not been able to "demonize," to use Michael Rogin's term,[22] the Soviet Union, he would have found it impossible to make his parallel accusations of internal weakness. Only a "hard" external opponent justified the call to strengthen U.S. bodies to meet that threat.

Rambo shows American audiences that threat in the bodies of Soviet "advisers" to the Vietnamese prison camp. For the Reagan logic to work, those Soviet bodies are presented as much harder than those of the sheriff or his deputies in *First Blood*. As both Reagan and *Rambo* declare, during all those years when American bodies were getting fat and comfortable, Soviet bodies were hardening themselves for the coming battle. Sergeant Yushin (Vojo Goric), assistant to the colonel interrogating Rambo, is the only man in any of these films whose muscles are actually larger than Rambo's. His firm-jawed indifference to inflicting pain is only the most obvious indication of his preparedness. As the film goes on, it becomes clear that the only body who could stand up to Yushin's is Rambo's, a body that the U.S. government had rejected and sentenced to hard labor. And whereas the Soviet Union has rewarded Yushin for his hard body, the U.S. government has punished Rambo. Where then, this film invites audiences to worry, would they find the bodies needed to defend the United States against Soviet attack? Like *First Blood*, *Rambo* is geared toward manufacturing a national desire to produce more hard bodies like Rambo's and reject the soft bodies that have come to inhabit the government.

At one point *Rambo* seems to contradict Reagan's enthusiasm for technology, especially military technology. Although Reagan's increased funding of the military was geared largely toward improved weaponry and sophisticated technologies, Rambo not only does not need such weapons, he is hindered by them: he has to cut himself free of all of Murdock's sophisticated equipment in order to parachute into Vietnam. Though Trautman has referred to him as "a pure fight-

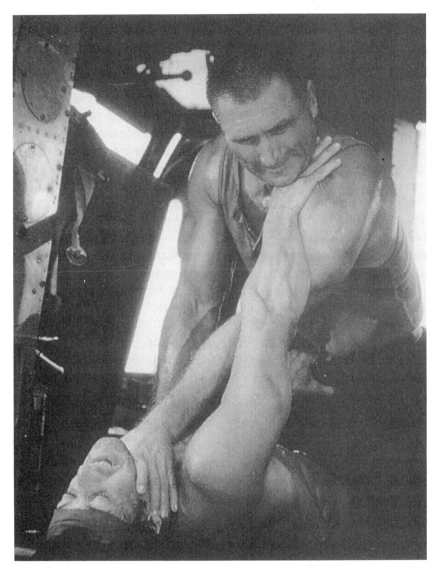

Sergeant Yushin, the only man with muscles bigger than Rambo's. (Rambo: First Blood, Part 2, *Tri-Star Pictures*)

ing machine," Rambo prefers to think of his brains and not his body as his most important asset (he may be the only one in Hollywood who believes this). As he tells Murdock, who has just proudly displayed the banks of computers at Rambo's disposal, "I've always believed the mind was the best weapon."

It is not my goal here to show that the *Rambo* films adhere entirely to the Reagan ideology,[23] but I think it important to work through this apparent contradiction between technology and the individual (one that plagued the entire decade, as can be seen in such films as *Alien* and *Terminator*), largely because it was a contradiction inherent in the Reagan philosophy itself, which continued, despite its insistence on technological innovation, to rely on individuality and not technology as the true basis for American superiority over Soviet thinking. Lou Cannon summarized Reagan's feelings on the matter in these words: "Reagan was always easily convinced that American ingenuity could overcome technological obstacles of great magnitude."[24] With SDI, conceived in the year of *First Blood*'s release, Reagan tried, unsuccessfully, to combine these two visions of American progress, since it would be the individual ingenuity of American scientists and the individual support of a visionary American president that would launch the technology that would, in Reagan's mind, ensure world peace. But the uneasiness of the marriage between technology and individualism is reflected in the rocky rhetoric of Reagan's 1988 Moscow summit speech:

> Like a chrysalis, we are emerging from the economy of the Industrial Revolution, an economy confined and limited by the earth's physical resources, into [one] in which there are no bounds on human imagination and the freedom to create is the most precious natural resource.
>
> Think of the little computer chip. Its value isn't in the sand from which it is made, but in the microscopic architecture designed into it by ingenious human minds. In the new economy, human invention increasingly makes physical resources obsolete. We are breaking through the material conditions of existence to a world where man creates his own destiny.[25]

As these remarks make clear, one of the key features of the Reagan hard body was mental as well as physical superiority over its enemies. In the contrast between Yushin and Rambo, for instance, Yushin, though strong, does not seem to be very bright. He never speaks, and acts only when commanded by Podovsky. He seems to be *only* a "fighting machine." Rambo, on the other hand, decides when to work with Murdock and when to disobey his orders (in bringing the POWs back, for example). He uses his body not only to defeat the Soviet soldiers but to outsmart them as well. Given that so much of Reagan's characterization of the Soviet Union as an "evil empire" is grounded on communism's ostensible disregard for human individuality, it is imperative that Rambo be more than a fighting machine. In order to be the embodiment of Reagan democratic ideals, he must be both muscular *and* independent of mind. As Reagan went on to conclude at the Moscow summit, "Progress is not foreordained. The key is freedom of thought, freedom of information, freedom of communication." For Ronald Reagan, the best "weapon" to use against the Soviet Union is not then a tank or a nuclear bomb but the "free" American mind inside a hard body. This would be, as Rambo tells Colonel Zaysen in *Rambo III*, the Soviets' "worst nightmare."

> *Rambo:* Do you really think you're going to make a difference?
> *Trautman:* If I didn't, I wouldn't be going.
> *Rambo:* It didn't before.
> *Trautman:* That was another time.

These early lines in *Rambo III*, as Trautman tries to explain to Rambo why he is going in to deliver weapons to Afghani fighters rebelling against Soviet occupation, declare the changes that have taken place in Hollywood's representation of the hard body between 1982 and 1988. In *First Blood* Rambo won his battle only at the expense of a prison sentence; in *Rambo* he was told that winning this time was up to him; but in *Rambo III* his only friend tells him that times have changed, that battles such as those they fought in Vietnam are now winnable, not just by individuals like Rambo, but by the country as a whole. And though Rambo is again fighting the evil Soviet empire, he does it this time not on behalf of a handful of POWs but for an entire nation.

Whereas the first Rambo films ground their plots in the loss in Vietnam, a war that spanned the administrations of five presidents and has influenced the policies of an additional four, *Rambo III* takes as its narrative target a specific "loss" of the Carter administration, the Soviet takeover in Afghanistan in 1979, an act that Richard Nixon, setting the tone for the Reagan administration, described in these terms:

> What made the fall of Afghanistan so significant a loss to the West was not just the fate of its 18 million people. . . . Not even its strategic location would make its loss so significant, if that loss had occurred in isolation. But it did not occur in isolation. It was part of a

pattern . . . of ceaseless building by the Soviets toward a position of overwhelming military force, while using subversion and proxy troops, and now even its own, to take over one country after another, until they are in a position to conquer or Finlandize the world.[26]

Afghanistan, in Nixon's and then Reagan's logic, was more than simply another country that the Soviet Union had come to control. For these men, Afghanistan was one more stepping stone to eventual Soviet domination of the world. In such terms, Rambo's defeat of the Soviet garrison in Afghanistan is not simply a victory for himself, Trautman, or even the Afghani mujahideen, but for the entire free world. This is what the Reagan hard body has, by 1988, been advertised to achieve.

Here, as in *Rambo*, the national body is in peril of capture and death at the hands of the Soviet Union, as Trautman, on his mission to deliver weapons to the mujahideen, is captured by soldiers commanded by Colonel Zaysen (Marc de Jonge). And though Rambo enters Afghanistan only to rescue Trautman, his eventual support of the Afghanis escalates the battle from one for the national body to one for the Western body, or, more precisely, is staged as a battle in which the U.S. national body is now valued as *the* Western body itself. The numerous shots of Soviet aircraft firing on defenseless women and children, the tales of Soviets hiding bombs in childrens' toys, the scenes of Afghanis being tortured in the Soviet prison—all arouse not only images of the "evil empire," but imply that the Soviets would commit such atrocities in any country that stood in the way of its intended goals of domination. Because these practices are, according to the film, typical of Soviets and not specific to their fight in Afghanistan, the people of Afghanistan come to stand in here for any people in the world who are struggling to maintain their freedom against the Soviet Union. It is here that Trautman's body is not simply the body of a captured American officer, but the imprisonment of the warrior for freedom, the one who is willing to confront the Soviets before it is too late. The battle that had been domestic in *First Blood* and against Vietnam's Communist government in *Rambo* is now a battle for democracy around the world. And the only body who can wage this battle for the beleagured West, according to *Rambo III* and those who endorse its policies, is the hardened American body.

As a mark of how thoroughly this is a "different time," the problem of recognition that plagued Rambo in *First Blood* has not only disappeared, as it did in *Rambo*, but become commonplace enough to

Rambo leading Afghani rebels to rescue an entire nation. (Rambo III, *Tri-Star Pictures*)

become a joke within the narrative. The deputies of Hope could never be sure who Rambo was and whether they were seeing him or not; the government officials of *Rambo* knew Rambo on sight because of his reputation; but *Rambo III* moves into the world outside U.S. territories and bases to test Rambo's identity. And as the chanting Bangkok crowds attest at the opening of the film, even the people of Thailand know who Rambo is. As he battles another man in a brutal stick fight in order to gain money for the Buddhist monks who have allowed him to live with them, the crowds of gamblers surrounding the two fighters cheer "Ram-bo! Ram-bo!" It is in many ways more important that they know him, not for his credentials as a soldier—as Ericson says in *Rambo*, "You made a helluva rep for yourself in Nam"—but for the status of his body. They know Rambo as a tough and winning stick fighter in the gambling dens of Bangkok. To them, his popularity is not based on past accomplishments and medals won decades before but on his current abilities. This is, of course, the claim that Ronald Reagan would make about the U.S. hard body, that its reputation for toughness, strength, and superiority should not be

Bangkok betting on Rambo's hard body. (Rambo III, *Tri-Star Pictures)*

determined by acts undertaken decades before but by the acts of that body in the present—Grenada, Nicaragua, El Salvador, the Soviet Union. And when those acts are widely known, as they are here, they are approved by the masses of people who see them and the bodies that achieve them. Their approval and confidence is so great, in fact, that they are willing to bet on those bodies to win.

When Rambo meets Hamid (Doudi Shouka), the Afghani guide who is to take him to the village near the prison where Trautman is being held, Hamid does not recognize him at all. He even says to Rambo, to the great delight of Rambo fans, "You look like you have not been in war." But by the end of the film, after Hamid has seen Rambo fight Soviet commandos and risk his life to save Afghani women and children, he asks Rambo to stay and continue to fight with the mujahideen. But this is, after all, how Reagan has set up the U.S. national hard body, that it would not be known by its appearance or words but by its deeds, its willingness to risk itself for the welfare of women and children and to fight Soviet commandos anywhere in the world. The hard body must act, not profess, its strengths and to do so must continue to have stages upon which to perform its spectacular feats of muscular politics.

But although Hamid must be shown Rambo's abilities in order to believe them, film audiences demand no such tests of credibility. As director Peter MacDonald knew, audiences had, by 1988, become familiar not only with Rambo but with the hard-bodied president he emblematizes. So the source of skepticism in Afghanistan is a source of humor at home, as audiences gain an insider status, defining "us" against "them," on the basis of being able to recognize Rambo. After Hamid asks Rambo if he is a soldier or a mercenary and receives a negative answer to both inquiries, he is perplexed about Rambo's identity. "Are you a tourist?" he asks, incredulously. Rambo's simple reply—"I'm no tourist"—allows U.S. audiences to have a joke on the simple-minded Afghanis who have not yet been introduced to this U.S. product.

But the joke extends to the Soviets as well, marking their naïveté in not believing in this new U.S. body, assuming that all Americans are like those they met in the 1970s. An Afghani informer who overheard Hamid's conversation with Rambo tells Colonel Zaysen that Rambo has arrived and that he is a "tourist." After Rambo makes his first failed attempt to rescue Trautman, exploding half the compound and killing many soldiers, Zaysen screams to Trautman, "Who is this tourist?!" Zaysen is placed in the position of Sheriff Teasle, who was equally perplexed about how Rambo could possibly do the things he did. But as an important indication of the increasingly positive attitudes toward the military and foreign interventions in the intervening years, the ignorant are now no longer U.S. citizens, or even the citizens of our allies (it was, after all, the security of Thailand that was the real concern after Vietnam), but the Soviets and those who have come under their influence. It is the Soviets, thanks to Rambo and Reagan, who will be most surprised when they have to confront the new American body, a body that is no longer that of a vulnerable tourist (think of Klinghoffer and the *Achille Lauro* incident or the TWA hijacking, all of which involved U.S. tourists), but instead that of a primed soldier.

This warrior identity is one of the key subthemes of *Rambo III* and a new twist to Rambo's character. Whereas in *First Blood* and *Rambo*, Rambo seemed the reluctant warrior, only fighting where others had drawn "first blood," and though he professes to not want to fight in *Rambo III*, Trautman, Rambo's trainer and mentor, confronts him about this ambivalence. When Trautman first asks Rambo to accompany him to Afghanistan, Rambo refuses, saying that it's not his fight and that his battles are over. Trautman replies: "You may try, but you cannot get away from what you really are . . . a full-blooded combat soldier." When Rambo objects, "Not any more. I don't want it," Trautman concludes, "That's too bad. 'Cause you're stuck with it." He then goes on to tell Rambo a parable about a sculptor who produced a great work of art out of a rough rock. When praised, the sculptor declared that his was not the achievement of having produced this sculpture where there had been only rock, but simply of having revealed what had always been hidden within the rock, the figure that was now called art. Similarly, Trautman explains to Rambo, "We didn't make you this fighting machine. We just chipped away the rough edges. You're going to be tearing away at yourself until you come to terms with what you are. Until you come full circle." True to the Reagan narrative about the country, Trautman's parable suggests that bodies (and nations) like Rambo's are not manufactured out of nothing, but are simply fulfilling their inner destinies. Any ambivalence or confusion the "owner" of this body may feel can be attributed not to questions about that identity but to repression and denial, deliberate efforts to forget who and what those bodies are and the purposes they serve. Within this narrative, Rambo's stay at the Buddhist monastery or Carter's celebration of peace and negotiation are the products of active repressions of the true identity of Rambo and the nation he came to stand for. While in a different context, the nonviolence of Buddhism or of Carter's human-rights agenda could be viewed as alternatives to the aggressiveness of Reaganism, the plots of *Rambo III* and "Reagan 2" depict them not as alternatives but as weaknesses and denials. And while those denials are being made, the Reagan story tells, both Trautman and Afghanistan were taken prisoner by a country whose narrative has never wavered from its goal of world domination. For Reaganism, the warrior hard body *is* the American identity, and the scenario of the Reagan presidency is one in which Ronald Reagan must simply play the part of the modest sculptor who has been able to see behind the "rough edges" to the true inner nature of the American people and thereby produce a work of art to be appreciated by all the world.

Through the *only* focused shot of a woman in the entire film, audiences are invited to imagine how that appreciation will look. As Rambo first enters the Afghani village, the camera cuts from shots of men to boys and back again. But as Hamid's voiceover explains, "They never see man look like you," the camera cuts to a close-up of a woman's eyes, seen above the veil that covers the remainder of her face, as she watches Rambo walk through the village. Though it is difficult to draw exact conclusions from one shot, these eyes clearly do not show distaste, fear, or repulsion, but instead interest, possibly admiration, at the least fascination. As Hamid narrates, the world is not used to seeing men like Rambo—hard bodies like those of Reagan Americans—but when they do see them, they are intrigued and fascinated, ready to learn what those bodies can do, not reject them out of hand. Through this woman's gaze, the camera discovers a boy following Rambo and Hamid, full of curiosity about Rambo's weapons and body. Though Hamid sends the boy away, he appears again in the film, following Rambo into the Soviet prison, where he is wounded in the leg. When Rambo sends him away to recover, he gives him the necklace he took from Co Bao's body after she had been shot in *Rambo*, indicating the place the boy has in Rambo's affections. This boy, and the woman who prefigured him, stand in the film and in the Reagan imaginary for the relationship non-Western, nonwhite peoples and women will have to this new American body, one not of equality but of child-like appreciation. Harking back to earlier representations of nonwhite peoples Americans are sent to rescue (think of John Wayne's smiling pat on the head to Hamchung, the Vietnamese orphan in *The Green Berets* (1968, John Wayne and Ray Kellog), as he tells him, "You're what this is all about"), *Rambo III* reaffirms that the hard body Reaganism celebrates can be only white and male, while the grateful peoples of the world follow curiously behind, infatuated by the image of the men who "look like you."

In what became one of the most memorable and quoted scenes of the film, Trautman confirms for viewers the status of this hard body as superior to all others. When Colonel Zaysen asserts that he will hunt Rambo down, Trautman calmly replies, "You don't have to hunt him. He'll find you." Astounded, Zaysen exclaims, "Are you insane?! One man against trained commandos?! Who do you think this man is? God?!" To the cheers of U.S. audiences, Trautman cooly answers, "No. God would have mercy. He won't." In the hierarchy of the Reagan imaginary, the hard-bodied U.S. male is tougher even than God, for God might exhibit some of the weaknesses characteristic of the Carter presidency, particularly those of forgiveness and love (two days after his inauguration, Carter declared amnesty for Vietnam War draft evaders; during his campaign, he was criticized for speaking too often of love and compassion[27]). Thus Rambo is declared superior to non-Western and nonwhite peoples, white Soviets, and, finally, God in his commitment to carrying out his missions and punishing his enemies. This is the image that Reagan wanted to put forward about the military and government—that it would show no mercy toward its Soviet enemies and would fight them relentlessly and indefatigably until the battle was won. There would be no hesitant incursions or half-prepared rescue missions—only victory.

Rambo III is so secure in its portrayal of the U.S. hard body that it can even close the film with a joke about the possibility of Rambo becoming "soft." Where joking about such things would have been too risky in 1982 or 1985, by 1988, Trautman can confide to Rambo, after defeating an entire Soviet garrison, "We're getting soft." When Rambo replies, "Just a little," this hypermodesty evinces, not the worries of the audience that such might actually be the case, but their snickers, as the audience is invited to join in the private joke that only two such hard-bodied men can afford to make, thereby sharing those bodies as national identities and national securities. As Rambo and Trautman drive off to the desert, the audience can rest assured that no one is worried about the status of Rambo's and Trautman's bodies except the Soviets.

But for all of the frolicking insider humor and camaraderie that the *Rambo* films invite U.S. audiences to share, like the Reagan social philosophy, there is a line drawn to separate the true hard bodies, who will rescue not only the country but the world, from the bodies of the remaining U.S. citizens. Although the demonization of the Soviet Union and the infantilization of the Third World serve to create a sense of national identity as a form of "national pleasure" and suggest that this nation is superior to all others, there is a division created within that national identity that insures that although Rambo's body may serve as an emblem for audience identification with national strength, the members of the audience understand as well that they cannot all *be* Rambo. Because Reaganism as both a political and an economic philosophy was grounded on hierarchies and divisions between those who would benefit from government policies and those who would not, there had to be some way to distinguish *between* groups of Americans, especially among those people who might imagine that they had most to gain from Reagan's assertive masculinities—men. In order for Reaganism to succeed, it had to have some way to lure men into a sense of shared mission with the Reagan state *at the same time* that it had to insist that there was some way to differentiate

from and explain the discrepencies between those were able to benefit from the profits of that state and those who, for reasons the Reagan
logic made clear, *chose* not to. As one mechanism for drawing that line,
the *Rambo* films offer the hard body itself.

In each of the *Rambo* films, there is a moment when his body is
wounded. In *First Blood*, when Rambo first confronts Teasle's deputies in the wooded mountains to which he has escaped, one rabid
deputy intent on killing Rambo begins firing at him from a helicopter
as he is perched precariously on the wall of a sheer cliff. As they both
hover above the rocky ravine below, Rambo realizes that Galt will kill
him if he remains where he is, so he leaps out from the wall to the
pine trees below. As he crashes through the pine branches, one
catches his right arm and rips it open. After causing Galt to fall from
the helicopter to his death below, Rambo takes a needle and thread
from his knife handle and proceeds to stitch together the bleeding
skin of his wound. In *Rambo*, he is tortured by Sergeant Yushin. Tied
to an electrified bed spring, Rambo's body is continually jolted with
higher and higher levels of electricity, enough to make the lights in
the camp dim and flicker. Finally, after Podovsky has been forced to
admit that Rambo is "the strongest so far," Yushin takes Rambo's
knife from a brazier where it has been heating. Placing it against
Rambo's face, he slowly cuts a line down Rambo's cheek with the
glowing knife. Rambo only grimaces. But the best scene is reserved
for *Rambo III*, where a piece of flying shrapnel from an explosion
during the prison escape is lodged in Rambo's right side. After rescuing Hamid and the boy and sending them away to safety, Rambo
works on his wound by firelight. Using his thumb, Rambo forces the
piece of wood out through his body. Then, after pouring gunpowder
from a bullet into the back of the wound, Rambo lights it with a stick
from his fire. The gunpowder explodes out both sides of his body,
cauterizing the wound.[28]

In each of the many times that I watched these films in public, these
scenes never failed to arouse discomfort, especially among the male
members of the audience. From subtle fidgeting to outright disgust,
viewers who had been in synch with Rambo's triumphs a minute before
seemed suddenly distanced from him. Those who could fantasize easily about replicating Rambo's assaults on tanks, rescues of prisoners, or
uses of weapons seemed now to have difficulty imagining suturing or
cauterizing gaping wounds in their own bodies. In each film, the
wounds of Rambo's body worked against audience identification with

him. Although the overall plot continued to invite identifications with his mission, methods, and muscles, these single moments suggested that such identifications could not be complete.

Such scenes are full of ambivalence and potential contradictions for the ideologies of the films. On the one hand, the ability to endure severe pain underscores how truly hard these bodies are. But on the other hand, the wounds indicate that the hard body *can* be wounded, that it isn't invulnerable or invincible, that it is not a machine but human flesh. On the one hand, these scenes suggest that viewers would all want to have bodies like these, bodies that can overcome pain in order to achieve a goal, bodies that recover from damages to go on and fulfill their mission. On the other hand, they can indicate that viewers would not want a body like this if having such a body means having to undergo such hardships, pain, and isolation. Why risk these contradictions? What can be gained from them?

On the most straightforward filmic level, such moments rationalize sustained attention to the exposed male body, scenes that, as Steve Neale pointed out some time ago, are sources of anxiety in a Hollywood film tradition in which the female body is usually the exclusive object of erotic desire.[29] Although all three films are devoted almost exclusively to the portrayal of Rambo's body, these scenes are among the few in which that body is still, in which Rambo is not pursuing enemies, firing weapons, or blending in with trees and mud. Consequently, audiences can examine Rambo here at some leisure and explain any anxieties aroused by that examination as anxieties of plot and not pleasure. But the eroticization of the male body can be achieved in other kinds of portrayals than suturing and cauterizing bleeding body parts. Why the wound?

There are several ways in which these scenes reinforce rather than contradict Reaganism. By arguing, for example, that the national body *can* be wounded—a case that one would think Reagan's image of national strength could not tolerate—Reaganism can insist on providing adequate protection for that body. If the national body were in fact invincible, there would be no need for arms buildups, weapons development, or billion-dollar military budgets. But by voicing concerns about vulnerabilities, Reaganism can argue that more needs to be done to insure that those vulnerabilities not be exposed. This cautionary logic can work on two levels—the individual and the national. Taking, as it so often did, the Iranian hostage situation as an indication of a vulnerability, the Reagan administration could argue that individual American lives are at risk and made vulnerable because of inadequate protection against terrorists. Reagan was to say exactly this about Grenada, that "American lives are at stake."[30] Reagan's response to this projected fear was to train Special Forces units as hostage rescue teams, to target Mu'ammar Qaddafi and the PLO as leaders of international terrorist organizations, to subsequently bomb Libya and ban the PLO from any U.S. dealings, and to invade Grenada to insure that more U.S. hostages would not be taken. Reagan's "Star Wars" proposal promised to protect the national body from any vulnerabilities it might have in relation to a Soviet nuclear attack, since the country no longer possessed the numerical superiority in nuclear weapons that it had in earlier decades. The need for such a space-based weapons system is contingent on the insistence that the national body *can* be wounded. So although the Reagan military and foreign policy philosophies worked to construct a successful image of the national hard body, they could do so only within the context of acknowledging that that body was vulnerable.

Reagan's own vulnerability becomes an important correlative here, as his hard body was the object of an assassin's bullet. On the one hand, John Hinkley's shot proved the president vulnerable; on the other hand, Reagan's recovery proved him strong and resilient. This is a second reason for the portrayal of vulnerability—that the national body can be shown capable of recovering from a past wound. This is one of the necessary premises of Reagan's attacks on the Carter administration. If the "wounds" suffered by the national body during the Carter years—Iran, hostages, inflation, Afghanistan, Nicaragua, and so on—were irreparable, Reagan would lose the force of one of his most frequent claims, that his leadership would make a difference to the nation ("Are you better off now than you were four years ago?"). Like Rambo, the nation can repair itself. Without the need of outside assistance—from NATO, Japan, China, or other allies—the United States will be able to suture and cauterize its own gaping wounds. Relying only on its own ability to repair itself, the nation can return, like Rambo, to the fight against the Soviet Union.

But by far the most important function of these scenes is to simultaneously offer and deny the promise of Reagan prosperity to the viewers of Rambo's films. Rambo's painful self-surgery insists that the national body can both heal itself and remain strong and combat-ready despite its wounds, offering a reassuring form of "national pleasure" as audience members can identify with the hard national body that survives and defeats its enemies. But these scenes also declare that, at the level of the individual body, there are differences between Rambo and most of the viewers of his films, ensuring that the feelings of sameness and unification that inspire such national pleasures do not "trickle down" to the level of the individual, where sameness and unification would be antithetical to the very mechanisms of prosperity Reaganism holds out. Most viewers, especially male viewers, are invited to recognize through these scenes that their bodies and Rambo's are not the same. Specifically, although viewers' bodies could be as vulnerable as his, suffering wounds and pain, their bodies, many men sense, could not survive those wounds as Rambo has done, because they could not perform the self-repair that enables Rambo to go on. This can only be perceived as a failing, a weakness brought out by the comparison to Rambo's hard body, which places such viewers in a position of inferiority to Rambo and the bodies like his that emblematize the Reagan social and economic system. As a result of such individualized de-identification, viewers are asked to explain discrepancies between themselves and Rambo as personal failings rather than systemic flaws. In keeping with the logic of the Reagan hierarchy, any differences between relative successes within the Reagan system must be attributed, not to preexisting racism, disproportionate allocations of social resources, or economic and class inequalities, but to personal inadequacies considered as internal *bodily* failures. In such a system, some men have earned their survival and others have not. And whereas weak men may not be actual enemies, they are nonetheless not entitled to the profits due to those whose strength insures the survival of the nation as a whole.

Rambo does not stand alone as the hard body of the Reagan era. Other Hollywood blockbusters present similar heroes, performing similar bodily feats, overcoming similar wounds, and fighting similar enemies. In the 1984 film *The Terminator*, Kyle Reese (Michael Biehn) and Sarah Conner (Linda Hamilton) overcome wounds, the police, and isolation to defeat a mechanical warrior that threatens to destroy the future of the human race. In the 1987 film *Lethal Weapon*, Martin Riggs (Mel Gibson) uses special-forces training to withstand torture and beatings in order to vanquish an evil ring of drug smugglers. In the 1987 film *Robocop*, Alex Murphy (Peter Weller) survives body transformation and mind erasure to outsmart and physically vanquish drug smugglers and corporate profiteers. And in the 1988 film *Die Hard*, John McClane (Bruce Willis) survives explosions, falls, and injuries to subvert a plot by foreign robber-terrorists. In each of these

John McClane's wounded body. (Die Hard, *Twentieth Century Fox*)

films, the hero is defined and determined by a focus on the body. In each case, the heroic body turns out to be, like Rambo's, superior to those of his enemies, his companions, *and* the audience. In each case, what determines a hero is the possession of a hard body. Though other characters may be quick-witted, charming, experienced, or clever, without the hard body to go with it, they cannot be heroes.

In these films, the hero is pitted against an enemy whose identity and nature makes the hero into an emblem of the national body. What is important to recognize is how, in the process of producing this national body, the nation is reconstructed. These films exhibit some of the ways Reaganism used hard bodies to redraw national boundaries. But what distinguishes these films from the *Rambo* sequence and marks their contribution to the Reagan imaginary is that, where the Rambo films worked out the Reagan foreign policy through battles with the Soviet Union, these films work out the Reagan domestic policy through home-front battles with internal enemies of Reaganism: terrorism, lawlessness, disloyalty, and the deterioration of the family. These later films in effect return to the domestic setting of *First Blood* to trace the alternate trajectory of domestic narratives not pursued by subsequent Rambo films. In addition, these cases extend the themes presented in the *Rambo* sequence which redefine the national body in a manner that does not include all its citizens.

Furthermore, these domestic hard-body films work through in a different way the ambivalences between technology and individualism. Technology was viewed in the Rambo films in two ways: first, in a positive light as a military resource (the "Ram-Bow" with exploding arrows, timed explosives, machine guns, and rocket launchers) and, second, in a negative light as it attempted to circumvent human "freedoms." These domestic enemy films portray technology largely in the second, negative fashion, primarily because it is invariably used as the computers in *Rambo* were, as a way to deny human participation in and control over events. Trying to work through the complex contradictions inherent in an ideology that promotes violence as a foreign policy and tries to suppress it as a domestic option (through the "tough on crime" approach), domestic hard-body films display sophisticated military hardware only in the hands of enemies (antitank weapons in *Die Hard* and *Robocop*, armed helicopters in *Lethal Weapon*, and nuclear explosives in *Terminator*), and used only to deny human "freedoms" (the terrorists of *Die Hard* take hostages and the machines in *Terminator* are carrying out genocide). It is then the task of hard-bodied heroes to thwart these negative technologies by employing and then restoring to others the "freedoms" of human ingenuity. In this way, these films help to resolve some of the contradictions of Reaganism's positions on technology, violence, and militarism by showing how "free-thinking" human individualism can put technology to good uses. These films suggest that any "bad" uses of technology are the result of its employment by "unfree" people (such as East Germans, Vietnamese, Soviets, South Africans, or drug lords). Moreover, these narratives apologize for the use of technology by "free" people (that is, Americans) as necessarily nondestructive and *profitable*.

The enemies in *Lethal Weapon* are, like Rambo and Martin Riggs, Vietnam veterans. They were trained in the same kinds of survival and special-operations tactics used by Rambo and his unit. They *also* represent the elite units of U.S. military forces trained to do covert work during the Vietnam War. In that sense, *Lethal Weapon* presents a different kind of challenge to the hard body than did *Rambo*. Whereas Rambo was pitted against numbers in order to even the odds—

National Guard units, Vietnamese and Soviet troops, Soviet commandos; all men who were less well-trained than Rambo—Riggs fights a
small group of men who have the same training as he, men who knew
or knew of each other during the war. And whereas Rambo's domestic
battles were against products of the Carter years and representatives
of the soft-body syndrome against which Reagan posed himself, these
enemies stem from the same days that generated the hard bodies
Reaganism tries to preserve.

Since all of these men qualify as hard bodies, what makes some of
them heroes and others villains? At the most obvious level, the men
working for General McAllister (Mitchel Ryan) represent enemies
because they are drug dealers, one of the most fully drawn domestic
evils created by the Reagan mythology, a narrative in which evil drug
dealers were ruining the fabric of the nation through attacking the
family, a family that was, like the external body of the nation as a
whole, made vulnerable because of the failures of the Carter years to
uphold a territory the Republicans would successfully claim for the
next twelve years—"family values." *Lethal Weapon* counters this concern both by defeating drug dealers and by portraying the hard-
bodied hero as affiliated with the family, here, the family of Roger
Murtaugh (Danny Glover), Riggs's partner. As in *Rambo,* the hard
body wants to align itself with the family and reap its benefits (Trish
Murtaugh washes Riggs's shirts and he eats family meals there), but
it cannot afford to be burdened by the risks of a family while busy
fighting national enemies. Those risks are shown most clearly when,
in spite of Riggs's having succeeded in stopping the drug trade,
McAllister's men kidnap Murtaugh's daughter Rianne (Traci Wolfe)
and threaten to rape and kill her. It is at this moment that Riggs
establishes himself as the full-blown hero of Reagan domestic policies when, after being tortured by McAllister's Southeast Asian assistant, Endo (Al Leong), he escapes to rescue Murtaugh and Rianne.
McAllister, mercilessly taunting Murtaugh with what he will do to his
daughter, tells him to give up because no one is going to rescue him:
"There are no heroes anymore." (Here, McAllister is echoing *Rolling
Stone*'s assessment of 1987 as a "year without heroes.") At this moment, Riggs comes crashing through the door, defeating not only
McAllister's men but the idea that the heroes are gone. McAllister
must not have been watching the news, because, by 1987, Ronald
Reagan had brought them back.

Riggs's heroism serves a second purpose in this film as well, beyond its support of the American family and antagonism to drug dealing. As *Rambo* showed, it was not enough to have a hard body, such as that of Sergeant Yushin, if it was used unthinkingly in the service of a communist empire. *Lethal Weapon* will make the same argument, primarily through the figure of Mr. Joshua (Gary Busey), except here in terms not of communism versus democracy, but of loyalty to the United States. What truly makes these Vietnam veterans enemies rather than heroes is not simply their drug smuggling efforts, which do seem after all to be rather small time; it is their alienation from the military and government. They have a sense of the law, but one entirely oriented toward their immediate group of veterans and separate from the nation. This is one of the most dangerous internal "enemies" to Reaganism: citizens whose loyalty to a subgroup surpasses their loyalty to the nation as a whole. In such terms, General McAllister's unit is more than simply a group of drug dealers. They stand for any of the increasingly vocal groups whose challenges to the Reagan ideology were being heard across the land, groups whose identifications were increasingly defined not in terms of national loyalty, but in terms of racial, sexual, gender, or ethnic identity.

One of the most compelling scenes of the film shows that its emotional impact does not come from drug deals, which make up only a small part of the plot. McAllister is trying to impress on a potential buyer how he depends on fulfillment of agreements. In order to do so, he insists on the loyalty of his men, who will carry out his orders without question. To display his point, McAllister tells Mr. Joshua to roll up his sleeve. Placing a burning lighter beneath Joshua's arm, McAllister holds it there until the drug seller can smell burning flesh. Throughout this display, Joshua shows no reaction, only intense self-control. He never moves his arm away from the flame. The drug dealer and, presumably, the audience, are sufficiently impressed.

This scene is, of course, reminiscent of the one in which Rambo withholds any response to Yushin cutting his cheek. What's the difference? Rambo's reaction was a sign of his strength and resilience, of how his body could be depended on to maintain itself in the face of enemy assaults; but Joshua's response is depicted as sick, a perverted skill rather than a laudable asset. In case the audience doesn't see this itself, the drug dealer is there to tip viewers off, as he first cringes and then is repulsed by the sight of Joshua's deed. This discrimination is significant to the construction of McAllister as an enemy, for this scene shows that even drug dealers, men who are just criminals, are repulsed by the behavior of McAllister's men, men whose behavior obviously goes beyond that of the merely criminal into the realm of the truly subversive. What makes these men threatening then is not their drug dealing, but their loyalty to McAllister.

John Orman suggests that one of the additional features of a macho presidential style is its adherance to a "loyalty to loyalty" policy, one in which loyalty to the president, especially on the part of members of his staff, is of paramount importance, and, in problematic ways, can create difficulties in leadership if loyalty to the president is seen to take precedence over loyalty to the law. This certainly was the case for some members of the Reagan presidency, such as Oliver North, whose loyalty to the president's desires to help the Nicaraguan contras outweighed his knowledge that such assistance was against the law.[31] As Orman summarizes it, loyalty to loyalty consists of "loyalty to the president, loyalty to the presidency, loyalty to the team, and loyalty to national security."[32] Of this last item, Orman goes on to say that the Reagan administration "has been one of the most secretive and isolated administrations of the twentieth century."[33]

If these principles of loyalty seemed to set a style for the internal workings of the Reagan administration, there is little doubt that they became translated into wider questions of national loyalty as well, questions of the kind that arise in *Lethal Weapon*. It was, after all, during the Reagan administration that former government workers were forbidden to publish and profit from any job-related information, that "national security" was extended from a concept that referred to weapons and diplomatic information to include any information that could be perceived as damaging to the president, and that covert operations that circumvented expressed U.S. policies and laws were taken to be of more value to the "United States" than those laws themselves. Because this form of loyalty to loyalty "trickled down" to the nation as a whole, enemies could be defined, as they had been during the Nixon era, as those whose loyalties seemed misplaced.

Unlike those of McAllister and his men, Martin Riggs's loyalties are never in question. Moving from the military to the police force, Riggs never abandoned the oath to the government that he took on entering the armed forces. There is never any question in the film about whether he would sell drugs, rob banks, or kill without provocation. Though he may not be a model cop, there is no doubt of his loyalty to the police system and the laws it supports. At the same time, one of the most interesting features of Riggs's character and often one of his most appealing behaviors to audiences is his willingness to circumvent the law for the larger goal of stopping criminals or to break rules that he finds tedious and unnecessary. He doesn't read prisoners their Miranda rights because "you already know them." He defies "No Smoking" signs. He flaunts police procedures by encouraging a potential suicide to jump from a building and then jumping with him. He carries his own weapon rather than regular police issue. He sets up his own rescue attempt when Rianne is kidnapped rather than call in FBI agents or other police support. And he shoots to kill rather than to disable. Like so many of the other heroes of 1980s action films, the law is for Martin Riggs something that he can shape to his own needs in his own time. Like his mentors, Richard Nixon, Rambo, Dirty Harry, and Ronald Reagan, Riggs believes that breaking laws in the process of achieving a larger good—stopping drug dealers, protecting the presidency, rescuing POWs, or maintaining a contra supply route—is not only permissible but necessary.

Thus the issue of loyalty is minutely defined. On the one hand, it insists on a loyalty that is focused on national and away from individual interests; on the other hand, the interests of the "United States" are loosely defined in terms of individual figures of national power rather than in terms of the laws or policies that define the state. Ronald Reagan was to be most open about this in 1986, when he commented to reporters that "anything we do is in our national interest."[34] As long as the "larger good" is being served, smaller violations of law are excusable. This "ends justify the means" philosophy explains why it is so important for McAllister to be portrayed as more than a simple criminal out to make a profit. With so little of the film's time devoted to depicting drug activities, it is clear that drug dealing acts as more of a filler than as a focal point for McAllister's status as enemy. It would not serve the logic of Reagan loyalty to depict enemies as exclusively lawbreakers, since so many of the members of the Reagan administration were themselves breaking the law. Instead, McAllister's crime is his creation of an alternate system of loyalties, one that steps outside the bounds of the terms defined by the presidency and invokes a period before the Reagan imprint was placed on policy decisions.

Die Hard makes the same point. The loyalty of John McClane (Bruce Willis) to the values he upholds as a New York police officer bring him to act against a crime being committed in Los Angeles in defiance of orders from superior officers. One of the domestic achievements of the Reagan years was to demonize "big government," and to characterize the welfare state as an intrusive bureaucratic incompetency rather than as an effort to include as many people as possible under a protective state umbrella. Reagan accomplished this task in two ways. First, he attacked the welfare system itself, trying to locate "slackers" and "double dippers," people who were then held up to public contempt and mythification as representative of the welfare system: mothers who would not marry in order to continue to get welfare payments, fathers who would leave the home at the time of a social worker's visit to avoid being counted and forced to get a job, women who were having babies just to get more money from the government; and so on. Second, he shifted the forms of government intrusion away from economic support and civil rights to the body, insisting on government regulation of abortion, sexuality, and child-rearing. In what verges on a New Right rather than a neoconservative critique of these bodies and government operations, *Die Hard* attacks both.

Lethal Weapon focuses on the issue of loyalty and criminality, but *Die Hard* shows more clearly the impediments posed to "justice" by government bureaucracies. When John McClane finds himself in the midst of a terrorist robbery of the Nakatomi Corporation, he sets about methodically combatting the terrorists from within the thirty-five-story company building. His first effort—setting off a fire alarm—is thwarted when the terrorist leader, Hans Gruber (Alan Rickman), former member of a radical German group, calmly calls the fire department and cancels the alarm. When he captures one of the terrorist's radios, he begins transmitting cries for help from the roof of the building, only to be told by a female police dispatcher that the channel he is transmitting on is reserved for emergencies only and that he must find a phone and dial 911 to report a crime; she threatens to report him to the FCC if he continues to use that frequency. When she hears gunshots in the background, she reluctantly assigns a single car to drive by the building and check out the call.

Sergeant Al Powell (Reginald Veljohnson) then enters the scene as the only one to believe McClane's claims about the terrorists. His belief is established when McClane throws a dead body onto the roof of his police car. But even this is not enough to satisfy the deputy chief of police, Dwayne Robinson (Paul Gleason), who continues to think that McClane is making a crank call and that the body was a "depressed stockbroker." Drawing a clear line between the street cop who is in synch with McClane and the bureaucrat who is not, *Die Hard* manages, early in the film, to draw a line not just between McClane and the terrorists but between McClane and police administrators. When Robinson sends in police assault teams to take over the building, McClane tries to tell him that the terrorists are well-armed. Only when numerous police officers are killed and an assault vehicle is destroyed by a rocket launcher is Robinson convinced. Trying to keep any more officers from getting killed, McClane drops a bundle of explosives down an elevator shaft, blowing out most of the lower floors of the building. When Robinson chastises him—"You've just destroyed a building! . . . I've got a hundred people down here covered with glass!"—McClane replies, in the clearest echoes of Reagan attacks on "bureaucracies," that Robinson is "part of the problem." When the FBI takes over, they use the standard procedures for dealing with terrorists, exactly what the robbers wanted them to do. In fact, it is the FBI's act of cutting all power to the building—a predictable part of the FBI program—that finally enables the robbers to break through the last of seven locks on the Nakatomi safe. FBI overconfidence and systematization play directly into the hands of the terrorists. Finally, when the robbers ask for helicopters in exchange for hostages—doing just what the FBI expects—they also plan to detonate bombs that will explode the top half of the building, thus destroying the hostages, the FBI, and, they want everyone to believe, themselves as well, all while they escape undetected. When McClane tries to thwart this plan by sending the hostages back off the roof, the FBI fires at him, believing him to be a terrorist. Finally, when McClane has killed all the robbers and rescued his wife from the building, Robinson confronts him: "You've got some things to answer for. Ellis's murder for one [one of the hostages who tried to buy his life by telling who McClane was]. Property damage! Interfering with police business!" At this moment, one of the criminals rises up to shoot McClane. He is finally protected, not by Robinson or the FBI, but by Sergeant Al Powell, a street cop who has defied the bureaucracy to protect another cop.

While bureaucrats almost cause McClane's death and continually interfere with his stopping dangerous criminals—trying to prevent him, like Congress tried to do with Ronald Reagan, from "doing his job"—it was feminism that put him in the crisis in the first place. McClane's wife, now calling herself by her maiden name, Holly Generro (Bonnie Bedelia), and working at a top position for the Nakatomi Corporation (aligning feminist interests with Japanese takeovers of the U.S. economy—both trying to destroy the fabric of American patriarchal capitalism), has left her husband in New York in order to take a job in Los Angeles. At the opening of the film, they fight again about how she has destroyed their marriage by taking this position and alienating him from his own children. But by the close of the film, after she has watched with pleasure his ability to thwart the robbers, and after he has rescued her, she doesn't fight with him anymore. When McClane comes out of the building and finds Al Powell, he introduces him to Holly Generro. Throwing any remaining feminist sentiments aside, and offering a resounding victory for the New Right/Reagan definition of family, Holly corrects him, "Holly McClane." The simultaneous and two-sided attacks on the "values" of Reaganism have been put to rest by the hard body of one New York cop.

> "Who are you?! Just another American who saw too many movies as a child? Another orphan of a bankrupt culture who thinks he's John Wayne, Rambo, and Marshal Dillon?"
> "I was always kind of partial to Roy Rogers, actually. I really liked those sequined shirts."
> "Do you really think you have a chance against us, Mr. Cowboy?"
> "Yippee-kay-yea, motherfucker."

This conversation between terrorist–bank robber Hans Gruber and New York police officer John McClane captures the challenge posed to the Reagan hard body. Outsiders—foreigners, terrorists, criminals, communist governments, and any U.S. citizens skeptical of the Reagan resurgence—criticize Reagan values as reactionary, harking back to an earlier era in which the United States could effectively play the world's cowboy-hero, wielding guns to stop criminals and evildoers, always on the side of justice, always winning in the end. And as Gruber's comments indicate, those values are posed as childish as well, referring largely to television dramas and Hollywood stars that were the childhood heroes of today's aging combatants. Against Gruber's sophisticated technology, clever planning, and greater numbers, McClane's one-man, barefoot guerrilla fighting seems naive and hopeless.

But this array of external and technologically sophisticated "enemies" is exactly what Reaganism was meant to defy: the threat of economically and technologically advanced countries to U.S. production capabilities (Gruber often speaks German in the film and he is attacking a Japanese corporation), the contrast between highly trained terrorists and inept American law-enforcement agencies, the self-confidence of opponents who outnumber and are better equipped than U.S. forces, and the disbelief of U.S. enemies in the values and beliefs of an American past. In its invocation of an American heritage

*John McClane and Holly Generro, now Holly McClane. (*Die Hard, *Twentieth Century Fox)*

that seemed to leap over the "weaknesses" of the recent past, the Reagan imaginary offered the public a cohesive image of national strengths, accomplishments, and possibilities. And the emblem for these promises was the hard body, whether of the individual warrior or the nation itself. To Gruber's credit, he recognized what many did not, that the foundation for this resurgence of power lay in the images

Die Hard's *foreign terrorists. (Twentieth Century Fox)*

of a mediated past, images produced by earlier eras equally in need of heroes to rely on. Following in the footsteps of those projected heroes, Rambo, Martin Riggs, and John McClane declare themselves to be the new heroes of the Reagan era. Their greatest act of heroism, as it turns out, is in believing that not only their heroic predecessors but they themselves are real.

Fathers and Sons: Continuity and Revolution in the Reagan Years

As the Reagan Revolution got underway, it became apparent that it would not be sufficient for Ronald Reagan merely to introduce the ideas that were to mark his presidency and philosophy as radically different from those of Jimmy Carter. He would have to construct a mechanism for insuring that those philosophies and policy changes—military buildup, moral conservatism, patriotism, a tough anticommunism, and economic deregulation—would continue past his own tenure as president, a concern tellingly brought home to Reagan supporters with the 30 March 1981 attempt on the president's life and the subsequent recognition that the "revolution," barely begun, could be over with the death of its leader. Consequently, and somewhat paradoxically, a question of continuity underlay the narrative of revolution that characterized the heady conservatism of the early years of the Reagan era. In short, *who* would carry the revolution forward?

Many of the films that came out of Hollywood during these years portrayed the anxieties of this cultural dynamic—continuity/revolution—through what Robert Bly would later identify as the key issue for manhood in the 1980s—the relationship between fathers and sons. Whether as actual fathers and sons, the central defining narrative for the universe according to the *Star Wars* series, or as symbolic fathers and sons, as in *Platoon* (1986, Oliver Stone), many Hollywood films about men would take this relationship as a key dynamic. Because so many films of the 1980s came down to this often "hidden" father/son relationship, it is clear that the poles of continuity and revolution were not to be seen as opposed, as might have been the case with equally matched figures of good and evil set against each other, but as *intimately* related, with each dependent on the other and any successful resolution of the plots dependent on the activities of both.

In the *Star Wars* trilogy, for example, Luke Skywalker's personal quest to learn about his father is intertwined with the rebellion against the dictatorial rule of the Emperor, who is out to destroy not only the democracy that the rebels represent but fathers and sons as well, as he knowingly orders Darth Vader to kill his own son. It is finally only the reconciliation of Skywalker and his estranged father, Darth Vader, that enables the rebellion to succeed, as Vader chooses to kill the Emperor rather than sacrifice his son. And though Vader had gone over to "the dark side," it is his blood that guarantees that Skywalker will become the Jedi Knight who would lead a revolution throughout the universe. Without this genetic continuity, there would be no rebellion; without the rebellion, there would have been no chance for Skywalker to learn about and enact his genetic influences.

Just as it was for Vader and Skywalker, so it would be for the Reagan Revolution: without an opportunity to extend his influence beyond his own generation, Reagan's ideas would have no chance to take hold. This is one of the reasons for the many narratives of father/son continuities and revolutions that characterized the eight years of Reagan's presidency, films that were, most tellingly, portrayed as sequels, highlighting in their serial repetitions the questions of continuity: simply put, how long can this go on? Among these films were some of the biggest box office draws of the 1980s: *Star Wars* (1977), *The Empire Strikes Back* (1980, Irvin Kershner), and *Return of the Jedi* (1983, Richard Marquand); *Raiders of the Lost Ark* (1981), *Indiana Jones and the Temple of Doom* (1984, Steven Spielberg), and *Indiana Jones and the Last Crusade* (1989, Steven Spielberg); *First Blood* (1982), *Rambo: First Blood, Part 2* (1985), and *Rambo III* (1988); and Robert Zemeckis's *Back to the Future* (1985), and *Back to the Future 2* (1989) and *3* (1991). The cultural emphasis placed by the rising of the New Right on the continuity of its own "revolution" (a revolution that many characterized as biblical, thereby invoking one of the most effective continuity and father/son narratives of all time) led to greater attention paid in the 1980s to questions of extended and extending narratives, which reinforced the conservative movement's concentration on "family values" as a mechanism for asserting the primacy of the father/son relationship to the operation of the culture as a whole.

*Father and son. (*Indiana Jones and the Last Crusade, *Paramount Productions)*

As the following discussions will indicate, the tensions surrounding father/son relationships and the abilities of the son adequately to replace—though not to overturn—the father increased in the years approaching the end of Reagan's second term of office, with the questions of whether George Bush could first win the presidential election and then succeed in carrying on the Reagan Revolution. These transition films, in which the son learns to operate independently of the father and in which he in turn protects the father, externalized the deep-seated anxieties for those in the conservative movement (speaking here in the broadest terms) about the passage from Reagan to Bush. They capture as well anxieties about whether the apparent successes of the revolution—enhanced U.S. world power; increased military strength; the significant influence of moral conservatism in education, politics, abortion debates, social programs, and media; deregulation; and the expanding incomes of the wealthy—could be sustained in a post-Reagan era.

The three *Back to the Future* films (all directed by Robert Zemeckis) figured anxieties about the continuity between the past and the present explicitly as a father and son relationship, as Marty McFly (Michael J. Fox) travels to the past to meet his own father, to the future to meet his son, and to the Old West to meet his great-grandfather. In doing so, the films enabled Marty McFly's personal excursions into the past and the future to symbolize large-scale social and economic changes that took place between his father's generation, his own, and that of his future children. What makes these films more than a humorous story about an individual's family history is that the plots tie Marty's life to the character of the entire community in which he lives; on his successes or failures depend the fate of all who live in Hill Valley. Underscoring the themes of continuity, Marty's actions take place in relation to his father/great-grandfather/son. Underscoring the theme of revolution, the *Back to the Future* films insist that, indeed, one man *can* change the world.

And change is precisely what these films are about, as Marty works both to change some events and to prevent others from changing. In keeping with this dual purpose, these narratives pose change as a source of both profit and fear. "Doc" Brown (Christopher Lloyd), the inventor of the time-travel machine, is always reminding Marty that any action they take in the past could have drastic effects on the future (their present). Not only could they literally change the world they return to, but one of them meeting "themselves" in the past or

The fate of all the people in Hill Valley rests with Marty McFly. (Back to the Future, *Universal City Studios)*

future could, he hypothesizes, tear apart "the fabric of the universe" and destroy all life. Marty's actions in the past threaten his very life; as the possibilities for his parents' relationship diminish, Marty's family photograph begins to fade, suggesting that he and his brother and sister are being eliminated altogether, losing all chance of being born (this is the most extreme anti-abortion message of the decade—if your mother believed in abortion, you couldn't return to the past to rescue her). And yet at the same time, Marty profits from changes in the past, as his own poor and dysfunctional family becomes, through his intervention, the perfect, wealthy family of his dreams. Both messages converge in determining how, during the Reagan era, change was to take place. By insisting that not *all* change is good, these plots delineate not only what changes were to occur but, and perhaps most important, for whose benefit and at whose direction they were to take place.

When Marty McFly returns accidentally to the year 1955 in *Back to the Future,* he changes the course of time by intervening in his father's relationship with his mother, thereby risking his own future existence. Trying to save his father from an oncoming car, Marty takes his place in the affections of Lorraine (his future mother played by Lea Thompson), who takes him in, instead of George McFly, to nurse him back to health after his accident. The remainder of the film follows Marty's efforts to reunite his father and mother and make them fall in love. But while he is successful as a matchmaker, Marty alters their relationship by enabling George McFly to come to Lorraine's rescue (rather than the other way around) as she is being attacked by the brutish Biff Tannen (Thomas F. Wilson). Consequently, the George McFly who became a doormat for Biff, a failure at his job, and a weak role model for his children, now, in the alternate future that Marty has created, becomes Biff's superior, a best-selling author and community leader, a loving husband, and a well-rounded father. The film's opening showed a McFly family in which the father was a wimp who delighted in *Three Stooges* comedies, the mother was an alcoholic, the uncle was in jail, the brother worked at a fast food restaurant, the sister could not get any dates, and the house was a cramped collection of junk and trash. But after Marty's intervention in the past, he returns home to find an immaculate and well-furnished house, his parents returning from a morning tennis game, his brother dressed in a suit and tie and heading for his office, his sister not able to keep track of the many boys who call her, and himself with the truck he had coveted parked in the garage.

In contrast, the destructive nature of change is shown in the plot of *Back to the Future 2*, when the McFly family nemeses—the Tannens— acquire a copy of a sports history almanac that Marty purchased in the future, a magazine that detailed all of the sports scores during the twentieth century. Returning from 2015 to 1955 to give the magazine to "himself," Biff Tannen manages to change the entire course of time by becoming, through the assistance of the magazine, "America's greatest living folk hero," according to the "Biff Tannen Museum" erected in Hill Valley in his honor. The world that Biff has created is governed by gambling, overrun by criminals, and violent beyond repair. Schools have been burned down, housing developments have been allowed to deteriorate, and even Marty's mother, now Biff Tannen's wife, has been forced to succumb to Biff's wishes by having her breasts surgically enlarged to distorted proportions. But perhaps the most telling sign of how bad the future world has become is that Marty's father, George McFly, was killed in 1973. Only by returning again to 1955 and retrieving the magazine does Marty manage to return the "present," not to its orginal form in the beginning of *Back to the Future*, but to its altered and happier form that Marty brought about through his first return to 1955.

Consequently, change in these films is both good and bad, depending on the direction it takes and whom it benefits. Although Doc is concerned that any change in time may put the universe itself at risk, and Biff's acquisition of the magazine produces a future full of terror and abuse, Marty's minute actions in the past have improved not only his own life but that of his family as a whole. What's the difference between the change that brought about these dystopic and utopian worlds? Biff Tannen's desire for personal profit and the power that he accrues because of it produce a world that is violent, racist, ignorant, and depraved, in which the personal desires of one man have taken precedence over the interests of the community as a whole. In contrast, Marty's efforts to reunite his parents are not self-serving in material terms—his only desire is to ensure his own future birth—but altruistic: he works throughout the film to help his father develop a stronger character. And in spite of the fact that he does profit from his efforts, he has no idea at the time that he will; he is as surprised as anyone when he wakes up to a changed world. The message? Change for personal gain is bad, but change for the improvement of the family—especially the father—is good.

At the opening of the first film in the series, Marty is confronted by his school disciplinarian, Mr. Strickland, with his fate as his father's son: "You remind me of your father. He was a slacker too. . . . You're too much like your father. You don't have a chance. No McFly ever amounted to anything in the history of Hill Valley." Marty's reply—at the time an empty retort—is prophetic for the film's plot: "Yeah, well, history is gonna change." The plot of *Back to the Future* turns around Strickland's edict so that not only is Marty a success but his reconstructed father is as well. Now, in the altered world of the future, Strickland's insult—"You're too much like your father"—turns out to be praise.

This is one of the strategies of Reagan America—to rewrite the recent past so that the charge "You're too much like your father" is turned from an insult—"America in the 1980s is too much like the 1970s and doesn't have a chance"—to a compliment. To accomplish this, heroes must return to the time before things went wrong—the 1950s, before the Democratic vision of the Great Society took over the government—and reinvent the characters who would shape the future. As Marty coaches his father from a wimp to a rescuer, Reagan set

Marty McFly watching his dad be a wimp. (Back to the Future, *Universal City Studios*)

out to coach America from acting the part of the "wimp" of the Carter years, being the doormat for communism and fundamentalist Islamic revolutions, to becoming the economically and socially successful international father of the Reagan years. From the man/country who gave his children/citizens only shame, George McFly and the America he figures is turned into a father who can give his children just what they want—a well-rounded family and material success.

A second key date in the films is that of George McFly's murder at the hands of Biff Tannen in *Back to the Future 2*. George is killed in 1973, the year in which the United States withdrew its final troops from Vietnam. That is the year, this film seems to be saying, in which the nation lost its direction and was given over to a period of destructive liberal values, in other words, the year in which the nation lost its father. As a result of George's death, Uncle Joe is back in jail, his sister is in debt, and Marty himself has been sent to boarding school in Switzerland. Biff and Lorraine live in a penthouse at the top of his gambling casino, where Biff entertains women in his hot tub. Lorraine, physically and verbally abused by Biff, has resorted again to drinking. She has been turned from a nurturer to a sex object; her children have

*Marty McFly coaching his dad from a wimp to a hero. (*Back to the Future, *Universal City Studios)*

been abandoned; their home has been turned into a business venture. All of this is the result of the family being cut off from its rightful father.

As goes the McFly family, so, the dates of this film would suggest, goes the nation. With the "father" gone, American children/citizens have been abandoned to lead lives of self-indulgence, addiction, and crime, all because they have been severed from their "family" by a leader who cares nothing for "family values." The home has been taken over by a "false" father who was never intended to have a family at all. All of this began in the devastating year of 1973, when an otherwise happy and thriving family/nation was cut off from its source of guidance and leadership by an untimely death. That George McFly was murdered by Biff suggests as well that the nation's troubles were brought about by an unjust assault on the father. It is, according to *Back to the Future 2*, the job of faithful and dutiful sons to retrieve not only their father's memory but his very body from the grave, and in so doing, to save the community from a future full of misery.

In this context, and because the future can be altered for the worse as well as for the better, Doc's edict never to disrupt history takes on a qualified meaning. Biff Tannen has falsified history, and it is up to Marty and Doc to do everything they can to return history to its rightful path, the path in which Hill Valley is still a pleasant and peaceful community, one that honors writers like George McFly and not criminals like Biff Tannen. But the "history" to which Doc and Marty want Hill Valley to return is in fact itself an altered history, the one in which George McFly is a hero rather than a wimp. Consequently, these narratives suggest, changing history—and risking the fabric of the universe—is worthwhile, not for personal profit, but only for the good of the father, because, as Marty's story makes clear, what is good for the father is good for the family and the community as a whole. Only Biff Tannen profits from the information in the sports magazine from the future, but everyone profits from Goerge McFly's enhancement.

This is "trickle-down" historiography with a vengeance. Like these films, Reaganism would argue that changes in the tax structure, in corporate regulations, in government support of social service programs, and in the size of the federal deficit were not meant to benefit just the wealthy few—not, in other words, to create a Biff Tannen future—but to benefit the many, the family and community as a whole, as everyone would profit from this restructuring of the role of the father to produce a heroic future. But in order to create these benefits not only the present but the past itself has to be changed. This was to be one of the key insights of the Reagan ideologues: they could sell their vision for the present if they could invent a version of the past that validated it. For a president apparently incapable of distinguishing Hollywood from history, this proved to be a snap. From commemorating a tomb for an Unknown Soldier from the Vietnam War to put an "end" to that troubling part of the nation's past, to refiguring the mercenary Nicaraguan contras as "freedom fighters," to vilifying the actions of the Carter presidency, Reagan reworked history in order to produce, like Marty McFly, the happy "present" he desired. And, like Marty McFly, he hoped that a present full of poverty, failure, and social dysfunction could be mended, not by offering social programs to assist those bearing these burdens, but by waving the magic wand of "history" over such scenes and thereby manufacturing a rosy image of those same lives.

When Marty and Doc first discover, on their return to 1985, the disastrous world that Biff has created, Marty wants simply to return to the future and put back the sports magazine that would lead to Biff's wealth. But Doc warns that the future, from which they had just returned, is now closed off for them, since it was the future of another time line that now has been realigned through Biff's intervention. With urgency in his voice, he explains to Marty:

> *Our only chance to repair the present is in the past*, at the point where the time line skewed into this tangent. In order to put the universe back *as we remember it* and get back to our reality, we have to find out the exact date and the specific circumstances of how and where young Biff got his hands on that sports almanac. (Italics added)

By articulating this Reagan strategy of rewriting history, Doc acknowledges that there are alternate possibilities not only for the future but for the past as well, and that it is the job of faithful sons and ethical technologists to make sure that the "right" time line is adhered to. Without consulting any of Hill Valley's citizens, Doc and Marty "know" which time line is "right," which future will be the best for the entire community, and they take it on themselves to secure that future for everyone. This paternalistic attitude, in which "national security" was offered as a screen of trust behind which presidential actions and decisions that would determine the futures of entire countries were to be made without consultation with U.S. citizens or their congressional representatives, proved to be the hallmark of the Reagan administration. As in the case of Iran-contra, the president simply *knew*, regardless of congressional restraints, how to "correct" the flaws of history (such as a successful Marxist revolution) and get back to the world "as we remember it."

Back to the Future 2 even figures Reagan in its future scenarios. To follow changes in history, Marty and Doc frequently have recourse to newspapers and historical records. It is in fact a newspaper headline that prompts Doc to take Marty to the future, where he is to save his son from a jail sentence. As evidence of the bad future that Biff Tannen has created, Doc shows Marty a copy of the *Hill Valley Telegraph* with a headline that reads, "Emmett Brown Committed," above a story about how Doc has been declared insane under Biff's direction, presumably in order to prevent Doc Brown from revealing the source of Tannen's wealth. As part of this negative future, beneath this headline is a story with the lead, "Nixon to Seek Fifth Term, Vows End to Vietnam War by 1985." After Marty retrieves the magazine from the 1955 Biff, thereby restoring the "true" history of the film, these headlines change. The feature story now shows Doc Brown being honored for his inventions, but what is more interesting is how the Nixon headline has been rewritten: "Reagan to Seek Second Term, No Republican Challengers Expected." The negative and destructive future is associated with a continued Nixon presidency and an endless war in

Vietnam; the positive future puts Ronald Reagan back in the White House, unopposed. But over which "future" is Reagan presiding? The one in which George McFly is a wimp? or the one in which he is a celebrated author and successful businessman? When Doc triumphantly declares, "The future is back," to which future is he referring? Because Marty returns home again to the altered McFly residence, audiences can only conclude that it is the second, heroic "future" that will elect Reagan president and over which his unchallenged image will reign. The prosperity of the American future is associated with a continued Reagan presence, one that will make it possible for him to seek a second term as president, unopposed, because he, like the new future he represents, was the author of the nation's "true" history all along.

Back to the Future showed the son rescuing his community from the shameful world produced by a weak father; *Back to the Future 2* shows how the successful father can be put at risk by a society that denigrates "family values"; but *Back to the Future 3* abandons any interest in biological fathers and focuses on the symbolic father of all three films—Doc Brown, the inventor of the time machine, the savior of the future, and the man who taught Marty how to take control of time. Although George McFly's character and its development are instrumental to the plots of the first two films, they are more significant as factors in Marty's own narrative of personal improvement; but it is Doc Brown's presence that impels the stories along, as he originally sends Marty back to 1955 and then compels him to visit 2015 to solve his son's dilemma. As with the *Rambo* series, in which the third film is finally about Rambo's rescue of his own symbolic father, Colonel Trautman, *Back to the Future 3* propels Marty into the past, to rescue not his father or his son but Doc Brown. And as the year in which the story takes place, 1885, would indicate, the stakes here are much higher. Whereas the failure of Marty's parents to fall in love threatened the lives of their future children, and the intervention of Biff Tannen in his own past threatened Hill Valley, the death of Doc Brown, the embodiment of American ingenuity, inventiveness, and curiosity, and the triumph of Buford Tannen, the embodiment of self-interest, corruption, and ignorance, could doom not only the McFly family and Hill Valley but, coming at a key time of U.S. expansion and national development, the entire country. No longer accidentally thrust into history, or dragged there by someone else, Marty now knowingly enters time, not to save himself or his children but to rescue the nation itself.

Marty McFly and his symbolic father, "Doc" Brown. (Back to the Future, *Universal City Studios*)

Back to the Future 3 offers the ultimate justification for changing time—to rescue Marty's symbolic father, Doc Brown. When Marty learns by reading a gravestone in 1955 that Doc died in 1885, he returns to that year, against Doc's orders, to save him from being shot by Buford Tannen. And, as in the first movie, Marty achieves his goal by himself becoming a part of a time narrative in which he does not belong. By antagonizing Buford Tannen, Marty manages to redirect Tannen's wrath to himself, just as he had redirected his mother's affections away from George and toward himself in 1955; but in this film, as in the first, his actions are undertaken for altruistic rather than selfish reasons, in this case, saving Doc's life. The message is very much the same: by inserting himself into time, Marty can improve history.

But in both cases, such interventions are undertaken at the cause of sustaining the father—both the actual father in George McFly and the symbolic father in Doc Brown. For it is finally Doc Brown, and not George McFly, from whom Marty learns some of his most important values: that the community has precedence over the self, as when Doc makes Marty throw away the sports magazine, cautioning him that his personal gain is not worth risking altering everyone's future; that anything, given perseverance and work, can be accomplished, as when Doc completes the time machine after three decades of effort; and that it is the individual who finally counts in the making of history. And his final lesson may be the most important of all—that history is what we make of it. It is Doc and not George who molds Marty's identity, improves his life, and opens his future. This, according to the film, is not only a man worth saving but a man without whom history itself would seem to come to a halt.

But the outcome of *Back to the Future 3* indicates a change in the series' attitudes toward the perils of handling time. Whereas Doc insists in the first two films of the trilogy on the risks of "tearing the fabric of the universe," here, he is himself the chief architect of changes in history. In one of his first acts in the film, he rescues a woman in a runaway carriage, only to discover that she was supposed to have died, giving her name and her story to Clayton Ravine, the site of her crash. By the end of the film, Marty has returned safely to his altered present in 1985, keeping fairly within the parameters of "history" as the films have established it. In contrast, Doc has gone beyond history. Having married Clara Clayton, Doc, Clara, and their two children, Jules and Verne, have embarked on a free-ranging travel through time, not simply tearing but reweaving the fabric of the universe. As Doc advises Marty at the film's close, "Your future hasn't been written yet. No one's has. Your future is whatever you make it. So make it a good one."

In the first film, Doc instructs Marty not to alter time in any way; at the end of the second he orders Marty to destroy the time machine; but by the end of the third film, Doc is himself a freewheeling time traveler. In contrast to the restricted version of time Doc offered in *Back to the Future*, in which change brought about death, Doc tells Marty at the end of *Back to the Future 3* that the future is full of possibility and that time is unwritten. But it is so now only because time, no longer the manipulator of people, is their servant.

Whereas time seemed a potential enemy for the Reagan Revolution in its early years—with the memories of the Vietnam War still not put firmly to rest, with Reagan's own age a possible deterrent to the continuation of the revolution, and with the U.S.-Soviet conflict at its potentially worst state in decades—by the end of the 1980s time seemed to have embraced the Reagan version of history with open arms, sanctioning its rewritten narrative of American prowess and progress with the defeat of communism, the founding of a Republican dynasty, the increased political influence of the religious right, the defeat of the Sandinistas in Nicaraguan elections, and the final placement of the United States as the lone superpower in the world. Having seen his version of history triumph in progressively larger circles of time—from 1985 to 1955 to 2015 to 1885—Doc Brown, like Reagan, is now able to see time as his ally, not his enemy. "The future is," he intones, "whatever you make of it," indicating that time, which had once controlled him and Marty, is now in their hands. This may have been, in the long run, one of the chief accomplishments of the Reagan Revolution—to have made history a tool of social control, to have pressed the past into service to one of "history's" newest sagas, "The Reagan Revolution."

For who is Doc Brown other than Ronald Reagan himself? He has allied himself with technology in the name of progress; survived an assassination attempt (at the hands of one of Reagan's chief targets, Libyan terrorists!); acted as a surrogate father; turned to science fiction tales for his inspirations (Doc's childhood reading led him to want to build a time machine; Reagan's viewing of *The Day the Earth Stood Still* led him to envision his own "Star Wars" program); fought a future filled with crime, drugs, and idleness; enabled a dysfunctional lower-class family to improve its wealth and social status; returned an American family to its values of nurturance and success; and found his own personal history not in the hothouse parlors of the east but in the open spaces of the Wild West. Ranging over history, apparently in control of time, Ronald Reagan and Doc Brown come to stand as surrogate fathers, supplying symbolic leadership to a generation of youth whose futures seemed to have been opened up by their visions of technological wizardry and moral instruction. Both, by the end of the decade, seem to have gone beyond time itself, to have left the limitations of history and entered into the realm of fantasy, glory, and dreams.

Whereas the *Back to the Future* films displayed the relationship between an actual father and son in order to demonstrate the father's importance in controlling history, the *Rambo* series traces the same paths through a symbolic father/son relationship in order to demonstrate the father's importance in constructing images of masculinity, the characters of those who would act in history. The three films, *First Blood, Rambo: First Blood, Part 2,* and *Rambo III,* display different stages in the historical development of a reconstructed U.S. masculinity through the symbolic father/son relationship between Rambo and his mentor, Colonel Trautman. These films sequentially display the rejection of various forms of masculine identification, progressively triumphing over traditional middle-class roles (*First Blood*), institutionalized forms of paternity in the military and government (*Rambo: First Blood, Part 2*), and finally global/international political authorities (*Rambo III*). But more important, the Rambo films do more than reject received models of masculinity. They rewrite masculine relations in terms of a father/son dynamic that confirms masculinity as the relevant framework for subjective and social relations in U.S. culture. Not only does Rambo reject the U.S. government and the military as paternal figures but he also confirms his relationship to his actual mentor and teacher, Colonel Trautman.

First Blood shows Rambo struggling unwillingly against a town sheriff who is a Korean War veteran. Sheriff Teasle is shown to have middle-class concerns and prejudices. He decides that Rambo is a hippie and acts to keep his town of Hope, Oregon, a quiet and safe place for its citizens. The ease with which Rambo disrupts that quiet and destroys that town are only the most superficial evidence that Teasle's masculinity and the middle-class ethic he represents are no longer sufficient in a post-Vietnam, New Right world. But in spite of this easy rejection of Teasle, Rambo's character at the close of the film is firmly subordinated to that of Colonel Trautman, Rambo's leader and teacher in the Army. Rambo walks away from what could have been his final battle under Trautman's protective arm. It is clear that Trautman is the only man—the only type of masculinity—that still has control over Rambo.

In the second film, Rambo must work against Marshall Murdock, a government representative. Murdock is a technologically sophisticated, bureaucratized professional and a powerful, paternalistic figure whose influence and abilities far surpass those of Sheriff Teasle. A World War II veteran, Murdock is politically astute and economically clever.

But again, as in *First Blood*, Rambo triumphs over this adversary, returning with the POWs Murdock said did not exist, destroying Murdock's computers, and threatening to return and "find" him if Murdock fails to find other POWs. As in the first film, Rambo closes with his relation to Trautman, though here Rambo is moving out of the subordinate position that confined him in *First Blood*. Instead of accepting Trautman's offer to "come home," Rambo turns away and walks off into the jungles of Thailand.

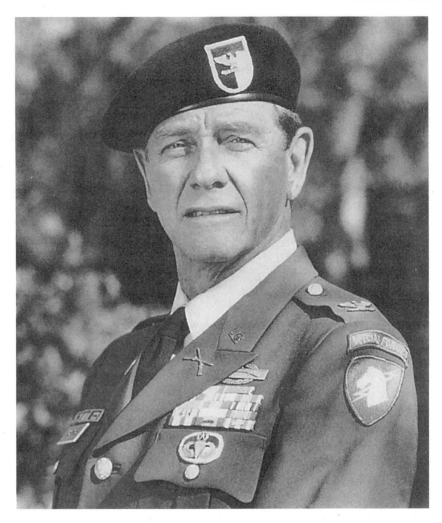

*Colonel Trautman. (*Rambo III, *Tri-Star Pictures)*

In *Rambo III*, Rambo's entire mission is defined by a now clearly altered paternal relationship with Trautman. The early advertisements for the film make this shift clear. Rambo's motivations are declared, in bold print, without context or ascription (as if everyone must by now know the context for their meaning): "The first time was for himself / The second was for his country / This time is for his friend." Naming Trautman as Rambo's "friend" suggests the distance between this film and *First Blood*, where it is clear that Rambo and Trautman are not on a level to be "friends." Here, though Rambo refuses to accompany Trautman on a mission to help Afghan rebels, he quickly offers to rescue Trautman when he is captured by Soviet soldiers. The incentive for action here is straightforwardly linked to this paternal tie, with masculine roles reversed; now Rambo, like Marty McFly in *Back to the Future 3*, must save the "father" who first saved him. The enemy here, Colonel Zaysen, represents a power that does not respect national boundaries, has no interest in justice or politics (he excels at his job so that he can be promoted out of Afghanistan), and is focused on destroying the family unit and traditional way of life that "subvert" his enforcement of power.

To mark the clear shift in the father/son dynamic that has taken place, Rambo not only succeeds in rescuing his "father" but then proceeds to fight beside and outdo him on the battlefield. And at the close of *Rambo III*, Rambo does not walk out to a waiting police force under the protection of Trautman's raincoat and sheltering arm as he did in *First Blood*, Rambo and Trautman drive away from the celebrating Afghan tribes, exchanging quips about their military successes. They are no longer father and son but buddies.[1] Rambo has taken the place of the father (he is "adopted" by a small Afghan boy as evidence of his own ability to stand as father) and the father has been "wounded," infantilized, and has to depend upon the son for his own survival.

Rambo, a film about the rescue of U.S. POWs, of "lost men," records the story of the son's recognition that the father is not all-powerful, and of the son's exchange of power with and in support of the father. Trautman, who taught Rambo how to survive in war, who rescued Rambo from his first "battle" at home, and who promises Rambo a pardon for volunteering for this mission, is shown in this film not to be in charge. Instead, he is subordinated to Murdock. As the film progresses, Trautman's remaining power is increasingly cut away by Murdock, until he finally is unable to help Rambo at all. When Rambo and a POW are unexpectedly sighted by the rescue helicopter, Murdock aborts the mission and recalls the ship. Though Trautman orders, "We're going down," the door gunner, one of Murdock's assistants, points a gun at Trautman and replies, "You're not going anywhere." When Trautman screams, "There's men down there! Our men!" the gunner answers coolly, "No. Your men. Don't be a hero." As the helicopter flies away, Rambo calls out, "Colonel! Don't leave!"

The violence of the film's combat scenes increases in direct proportion to the decline of Trautman's power. More specifically, the most extended and violent scenes of the film—Rambo's single-handed

*Rambo fighting beside and outdoing Trautman on the battlefield. (*Rambo III*, Tri-Star Pictures)*

defeat of his numerous Soviet and Vietnamese pursuers—occur immediately following Murdock's emasculation of Trautman, when he tells him, "I'm in charge here. You're just a tool." And though the film's narration is set up in such a way that we are to see the death of Co Bao, Rambo's Vietnamese female guide, at the hands of a Vietnamese officer as Rambo's motivation for this rampage, there is not a continuous narrative line between Co Bao's death and Rambo's actions. Instead, the death and burial are interrupted by a scene of Trautman demanding that Murdock gather a rescue team to help Rambo. It is here that Murdock declares that he, not Trautman, is in charge. The film then cuts to Rambo's hands on Co Bao's grave and his return to exact revenge upon his pursuers.

Framing the final emasculation of the father, Co Bao's death and burial become diversions from the film's narration of the reconstruction of masculine identity. The immediacy of the physical and emotional

*Rambo and Trautman as buddies. (*Rambo III, *Tri-Star Pictures)*

ties between Rambo and Co Bao seems at first to outweigh the bond between Trautman and Rambo. And the brevity and inaction of the intervening scene between Trautman and Murdock would make it appear incidental in comparison to the lengthy and action-filled scenes with Co Bao. But the placement of these scenes reveals where the weight of the film's tension lies, as it is Trautman's "death," not Co Bao's, that immediately precedes the celebrated combat sequence. The grave at which Rambo kneels could just as well be the grave in which Trautman's father-image has been laid to rest. It is finally the tension of Trautman's emasculation, not Co Bao's death, that must be relieved and reoriented by the elaborate violence that follows.

After the combat scene, when Rambo has defeated the Soviets and the Vietnamese, Rambo announces over a helicopter radio that he is returning with POWs. As the men in the receiving room begin to cheer, they halt and look questioningly at Murdock, waiting for his response. When Murdock leaves the room in silence (supposedly escaping from Rambo's threat to come back and "get" him), Trautman takes over, saying "You heard him! Let's go!" Though again in charge and in a position superior to Murdock's, it is only through Rambo that Trautman has regained his power. Indeed, even his "orders" only restate Rambo's own orders to prepare for their arrival. And when Rambo returns to the base, Trautman only follows him as he first destroys the computers, threatens Murdock, and then walks off toward Thailand. Though Trautman is still the significant figure in relation to whom we are to view Rambo, he is no longer the powerful mentor of *First Blood*. Now he is a product of Rambo's own strength and activity.

The most spectacular scenes of violence in *Rambo III* (a film that is almost entirely combat scenes of various kinds, a result of the father's kidnapping—the threat of his disappearance and death) are the culmination of this exchange of power between father and son, and the confirmation of Rambo's reconstruction as father-figure. After having rescued Trautman from his Soviet torturers and apparently evading their pursuers, Rambo and Trautman find themselves surrounded by a large and technologically sophisticated Soviet force. When they are told to surrender, and Trautman asks Rambo what they should do, Rambo replies, "Fuck 'em," and they decide to fight. When it seems that they will be killed, Afghan rebels ride to their rescue on horseback, and they collectively defeat the Soviet soldiers.

The triumph of Rambo and the Afghan rebels in the ensuing scenes validates the value of the personal versus the impersonal, the individual versus the corporate, and the paternal versus the bureaucratic line.[2] Rambo's valiant but hopeless desire to fight the Soviet army is evidence of his commitment to the paternal and masculine characters that define him. Having gone to such lengths to rescue the father—to insure the father's "survival"—Rambo would rather die than relinquish that image. More to the point, without the figure that represents and insures that system, without that system itself, Rambo would himself be powerless, "defeated." What saves him is his own portrayal as father-figure to the Afghan soldiers, emblematically shown in the boy who is drawn to Rambo. It is finally as if the Afghan rebels are fighting not for political, national or religious independence from the Soviet occupation forces (there is no discussion in the film of reasons for rebellion other than to protect wives and children from Soviet torture and murder, again constructing the Afghan characters in a solely patriarchal vocabulary) but for the possibility of confirming that a father-figure—a "savior"—exists. As in *Rambo*, before this final threat to the father's power, the rebels were prepared to evacuate the area and seek safety elsewhere. But the threat of emasculation, here so much stronger because both white father-figures will be eliminated, brings the "rebels" back to the battlefield and to victory.

The plot of these films is in many ways the successful narrative the

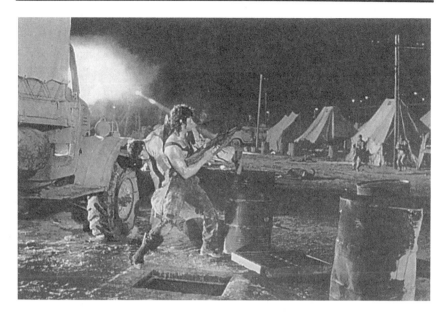

*Rambo is a father-figure to an Afghan boy. (*Rambo III, *Tri-Star Pictures)*

conservative movement would like to record about the Reagan/Bush transition. As Rambo was in *First Blood,* Bush was clearly the subordinate in the early years of the Reagan presidency, especially given Bush's own vice-presidential philosophy of never disagreeing with or upstaging the president. Even when Reagan had been shot and his health was still in question, Bush reprimanded aides who wanted him to fly directly to the White House on his return from Texas by saying, "Only the president lands on the south lawn."[3] But by the time of *Rambo III,* Bush was campaigning for his own tenure in the White House, and he became less Reagan's subordinate than his "buddy," the one who would need to rescue his "friend" from any situations in which hostile forces of evil—whether godless communists or antagonistic Democrats—would attempt to hold him captive. Wounded by Iran-contra and a failing memory, Reagan was no longer able to pilot his own jeep and would now need to leave the driving to George, a task this "healthy" son (both physically and politically, in the sense that he had successfully evaded being linked to Iran-contra) was happy to undertake. The violence that marked the transition of power from Trautman to Rambo would take place, not in 1988, the year of the campaign, but in 1989, with Bush's inauguration as president and the military invasion of Panama.

The *Rambo* and the *Back to the Future* films are representative of many of the sequels of the 1980s in their reliance on relationships between fathers and sons (or men and their symbolic fathers) as not only the chief determinants of masculine identities but, through those identities, of a national narrative as well. As I suggested earlier, the *Star Wars* films provide the earliest of these scenarios in which the fate of the entire universe depends upon the successful reunion of a father and son. *Star Wars* suggests that knowledge of the father is such an important part of an individual's identity that, without that knowledge, the individual cannot realize his true skills and abilities. Until Luke Skywalker knows that his father was a Jedi knight he remains a frustrated farmer. And because it is he, using the powers that he has inherited from his father, who finally saves the universe from the evil Emperor, the plot suggests that if Luke had stayed a farmer and if he had remained unaware of his parentage (there is no suggestion that he could have inherited these skills from his mother), the universe would have been doomed to misery.

But one of the key features of this and other father/son stories in the 1980s is the gradual transformation of that relationship. Rambo, once trained by Trautman, is rescuing him from the Soviets in the final film of that sequence. Similarly, Marty McFly, initially awed by Doc Brown's knowledge and at the mercy of Doc's inventions, finally rescues Doc from his own death in 1885, enabling him to go on and become a father to his own time-traveling family. In the *Star Wars* series, Luke is initially tormented by and divided from his then un-known father. But by the final movie, Luke has rescued his father from the "dark side" and returned him to the heavenly world of the "force." And the final *Indiana Jones* film reunites Indiana Jones with his long-estranged father, whom he must rescue from his Nazi jailers. This list comprises a substantial selection of Hollywood's blockbuster film series of the period. Why? What does it mean when a group of films so diverse in plot content—from fighting intergalactic wars to rescuing Vietnam POWs to traveling through time to recovering an-cient artifacts—should be so similar in the structure of their plots and in the sequence of their narratives?

It is not possible to say that the Reagan Revolution *caused* such stories to be written or to be so popularly viewed. What it is possible to suggest is that both the Reagan Revolution and these film se-quences captured in some sense the concerns of American audiences and offered a resolution to their anxieties through the restoration of a

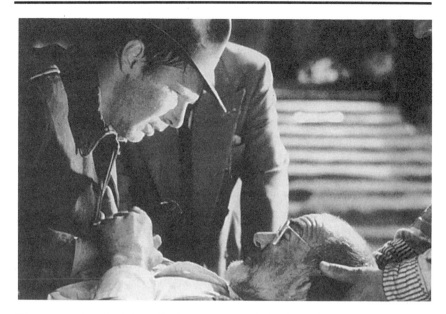

The son rescuing the father. (Indiana Jones and the Last Crusade, *Paramount Productions*)

happy father/son relationship to the benefit of the community/nation/ universe as a whole. It is not hard to conjecture about such concerns. It is a commonplace of discussions of the Vietnam War that it brought the United States its first military defeat (the Korean War is seen in such analyses as a standoff). Coming a few years after the final, igno- minious withdrawal of American forces from Vietnam was the hostage crisis in Tehran. During this same period, the United States experi- enced several recessions (the most significant of which was during the Carter presidency) at the same time that increased international com- petitiveness became a source of concern for U.S. manufacturing. With all of this, it is not hard to imagine how narratives of continuity could well capture the attention of large sectors of the American public, concerned as they were with the central question of whether U.S. power, ascendant after World War II, would be able to continue in the future. And, in the face of signs that that power was diminishing, what kind of "revolution" would be needed to restore that power?

Invoking the days before that power waned, Ronald Reagan, Colo- nel Trautman, Doc Brown, Dr. Jones, and Obi-Wan Kenobe all stand as emblems of a personal and national identity that could be recap- tured. But because those men seemed themselves too old or too weak to bring that time back, it became important to put forward younger men who could, through rescuing these elderly mentors, rescue the nation that needed them as well. (The extent to which such stories are historically specific will be brought out in Chapter 6, where those old men are themselves brought back to fight, without the aid of younger men.) For a while, Reagan was himself that "younger man," with his image of vitality, health, and agelessness. But, throughout the Reagan presidency, George Bush stood waiting to take on the role he would adopt in 1988 of the son who would receive his inheritance from his acknowledged father.

All of the plots of these films present a successful father/son relationship as essential to the defeat of evil and the triumph of good. In *Indiana Jones*, that evil is one of the most readily acknowledged demons of twentieth-century western history—Nazism. In *Star Wars*, the evil emanates from a similarly despotic ruler who is attempting to crush all freedoms from the universe. In *Rambo*, the evil is the overtly communist enemy who has made Americans hostage to their own freedoms. And in *Back to the Future*, the evil of the small-minded and greedy Tannens represents not just a bad family but a crime-ridden and lawless future world. In each case, the ability of good to win out over evil depends absolutely on the dedication of a son to a father and all he represents. Such apparently simplistic terms are exactly the terms in which Reagan carried out his own narrative of American history. Externally, the Soviet Union was an "evil empire"; Marxist revolutionaries in Latin America were merely surrogates of that evil. Internally, non-normative families and peoples were bringing about the decline of the nation as a whole.

Because the relationship between a father and a son automatically invokes time, these films all take the spans of time as their subjects, with Indiana Jones an archaeologist who explores artifacts from early biblical to ancient Indian religions, with Luke Skywalker as the last in a long line of Jedi Knights, with Rambo fighting the wars of America's recent past, and with Marty McFly traveling through time itself. Consequently, one of the keys to the success of these films is not only their resolution of father/son relationships but their appropriation of time. In each case, a "happy" ending depends upon the ability of the hero to overcome the limitations of time, to rewrite history, to restructure the future, or to rescue the father from the burdens of time itself. Indiana Jones literally holds time in his hands, or rather carries it in his knapsack in the form of the artifacts of lost civilizations. Luke Skywalker's success as a Jedi depends on his ability to see what no one else can—the ghosts of his past: Obi-Wan Kenobe, Yoda, and, finally, his own father, Darth Vader, as they join the afterlife of the "force." Rambo transforms the first American military defeat into a victory with his resounding defeat of Vietnamese and Soviet armies. And, while Marty McFly turns his own dismal life into one of prosperity, Doc Brown moves beyond his own lifetime to become a master of time itself.

This link between the father/son narratives and the control of time is not merely coincidental but necessary. For if stories of American decline and loss are to be rewritten, and the emblems of previous times are to be retrieved, then history must come under the control of the present. In other words, the father and all he represents cannot be brought back unless the son controls time.

All of these films present masculine models that rewrite the pasts they have inherited. In successive battles Rambo rejects narrow middle-class economy, bureaucratic government leadership, and a self-serving multinational corporate mentality. Marty McFly rejects the unambitious and self-defeating image of his economically incompetent father and his own middle-management future to become the author of his own open life. Luke Skywalker rejects his uncle's limited agrarian goals as well as Darth Vader's service in the authoritarian empire of evil to align himself with the forces of rebellion. All these films insist on the value of the father to the health of the community, but they also caution that restoring the father will not be enough, that the habits of the father will not ensure a successful future. Instead, in each case, the son must develop his own individualized characteristics, under the mentorship of the father, to produce a set of abilities that are appropriate for his future. Continuity must be combined with revolution to produce a happy ending.

But this combination of continuity and change indicates an important qualification of the Reagan ideology. Many criticized Reagan for wanting to return to the past, for retrieving the images, characters, and values of an earlier time; but Reagan's procedure was much more complex. He did indeed invoke those earlier times for many of his agendas—a heterosexual and domestic family unit, a triumphant international police officer, or a simpler sexual model—he also combined those nostalgic images with an up-to-date technology and a "new" economic theory. And, perhaps more than anything, Reagan himself stood paradoxically for continuity *and* change, continuing images and narratives of earlier decades at the same time that he lobbied for immediate change from a Democratic leadership and a social service agenda.

Consequently, these narratives of father/son relations help both to make change possible (the son replaces the father) and to prevent change from taking too radical a form (the son models himself after the father). They serve largely to justify a conservative agenda that can be adjusted to accommodate different economic and political policies while still maintaining the general framework of the narrative of continuity. "Family values" thus comes to mean a great deal more in the Reagan era than simply which parent works and whether teenagers abstain from sex until marriage; it provides the ideational paradigm for the very structure of mainstream social narratives in the 1980s, as fathers and sons pass on the stories of national identities, agendas, and futures.

By the late 1980s and early 1990s, the moviegoing public's fascination with the father/son plot seemed to have dwindled, with the appearance of many popular films celebrating brother and buddy films again over father/son narratives. *Twins* (1988, Ivan Reitman) and *Rain Man* (1988, Barry Levinson) are the most explicit examples, though interracial buddy films—*Lethal Weapon, Die Hard, Diggstown* (1992, Michael Ritchie), *White Men Can't Jump* (1992, Ron Shelton), *Flight of the Intruder* (1991, John Milius), and so on—are among the most popular of these narratives (though white men are invariably constructed as somehow "superior" to their black buddies, the relationship has more to do with interracial dynamics than father/son positionings). Perhaps the growing recession, increasing joblessness, and decreasing U.S. economic standing have led some viewers to feel less concern about continuity than about the need for a "revolution" in their own economic positions, a tendency that the presidential campaign of Bill Clinton successfully recognized and capitalized on as a political strategy. That the Clinton/Gore ticket negated any expectations for a presidential/vice-presidential father/son relationship by emphasizing their shared youthfulness is yet another indication that the father/son narrative, so much a part of the Reagan era and perceived "revolution," may, in the 1990s, no longer be a dominant narrative for the construction of U.S. masculine subjectivities.

The Bush Style

G eorge Bush faced a difficult task when he took office in January 1989. He was succeeding a president with the highest end-of-term approval ratings of the previous forty years. As Ronald Reagan's vice-president, he could be expected to continue many of Reagan's policies, to enact phase two of the Reagan Revolution. And yet, as an individual politician whose own opinions had been subordinated to Reagan's for eight years—who had, for example, once called Reaganomics voodoo economics; and who had been, before 1980, more moderate on abortion—Bush must have wanted to place his own mark on the presidency. Haynes Johnson suggests that Bush began this latter process in the first days of his presidency:

> On his inaugural day the new president sent a subtle but strong signal that he was in fact attempting to distance himself from his predecessor. He made known to congressional leaders that he would not continue to press the ideological battle to support the contras. . . . John Tower let it be known publicly that another cherished Reagan goal—"Star Wars" . . .—was both too costly and impractical.[1]

The presidency shifted in 1989 from the single-imaged and hard-bodied style of the Reagan years to what might be seen as a sort of schizophrenia as Bush tried to balance his Reagan inheritance with his own interests.

A 1988 film, *Twins* (Ivan Reitman), addresses this issue of "inheritance" directly, in its story about identical twins who inherited the same genes from their fathers but who look and live differently. Julius Benedict (Arnold Schwarzenegger) is the perfect human being. The product of a "top-secret experiment designed to produce a physically, mentally, and spiritually advanced human being," an "experiment conducted by the American government," he is stronger, more intelligent, more cultured, and more loving than other people. Raised on a remote island by a scientist, Julius has led a perfect life, sheltered from the violence, confusion, and deception of the rest of the world; he has grown into a self-confident, skillful, honest person. The experiment blended the sperm of six exceptional scientists who had each donated their genetic patterns to the forthcoming child. Artificially inseminated into the body of an exceptional woman, Mary Ann Benedict (Bonnie Bartlett), their sperm coalesced to produce Julius. But, to the surprise of the scientists, their sperm also produced a second child, Vincent (Danny DeVito). Though the brothers were identical twins, having been formed from the same egg, they did not split equally. While Julius received all the "good" genetic materials, Vincent got all the "garbage," everything that was left over from what went into Julius. And whereas Julius was raised on an idyllic island, Vincent was sent to a Los Angeles orphanage, where he became a juvenile delinquent, seduced one of the nuns working there, and distinguished himself as a loser. In his adult life, he steals cars, seduces women, lies, and scams. He is considered by almost all who know him to be worthless.

As the film goes on, however, the audience learns that the differences between Julius and Vincent are only superficial. Though Julius is tall, strong, and just, and Vincent is short, weak, and deceptive, they share what come to be seen as "instinctive" likenesses: the way they scratch their backs, the way they put their napkins under their chins, or the way they arrange their food. At bottom, audiences are instructed, Julius and Vincent really *are* twins.

This is the story that the Republican party wanted to tell at the end of Reagan's second term about Ronald Reagan and George Bush. Both products of a blending of Republican "fathers"—men like Richard Nixon and Barry Goldwater—they represent the different sides of the Republican party: Reagan, the populist individualism in which the economic policies of the Republican party are really working for the people of the country and in which military action is an expression of the nation's moral uprightness; and Bush, the party's corporate elitism, in which economic policies are designed for the health and welfare of business interests and in which foreign policy is an art of coversion, surveillance, and international control. And although it was certainly one of Ronald Reagan's successes that he embodied both of these aspects of the Republican party while appearing to represent the average American, it is nonetheless the case that throughout his presidency and at the time of transition that Reagan and Bush seemed to carry different banners of that party and to be interested in different sectors of its constituencies (George Bush, for instance, was largely unable to retain the support of the New Right during the 1992 election, a support that was key to Reagan's election and legislative successes).

In such terms, it is possible to see Reagan as the "golden twin," superior physically, mentally, and spiritually, and Bush as the "garbage twin," manipulative, deceptive, and evasive. Bush seems more like Vincent than Julius. When it is said of Julius that "he wasn't equipped to deal with the outside world," there is a certain echo of Reagan's own apparent childlike innocence, in which he seemed to have approached the presidency, not as a vehicle to enhance his own power, but as a way to help the American people. When it is said of Vincent Benedict that "you'll probably find him in jail," there is an echo of Bush's own tainted role in Iran-contra and his approach to the presidency as an inevitable privilege of his social and political history. Bush's association with the CIA, his experience in the oil industry, and his shifting political positions mark him as representing the darker side of the Republican party in contrast to Reagan's role. And yet the Republican party hoped to persuade the U.S. public that Reagan and Bush were really "twins" at heart, that they shared the same behaviors, habits, and "instincts" in ways that would make it possible for voters to see Bush as a continuation of Reagan rather than a divergence from him.

Like the Reagan philosophy, *Twins* is very much about family. Not only are Julius and Vincent rejoined, they find their lost mother as well. Told by the scientists that she died at birth—the same scientists who told Mary Ann that her baby died—they are able to reconstruct a coherent family unit as part of the film's happy ending, a family unit whose happiness depends finally upon the retrieval of the mother. The evil forces in this film are the scientists who believed that they could manipulate the family, change its composition, and decide who should be its proper members. *Twins* argues that the family cannot be so controlled, that its members are tied together by a kind of unconscious bond that surpasses scientific intervention and social control. It argues, in other words, that the family is *natural*.

Twins shows the destruction brought to the family through social manipulation, precisely the kind of social determination the Republicans had accused the Democratic party of creating, in their efforts to "engineer" family structures through institutional oversight of the family. Placing Vincent in an orphanage because he is the inferior twin is seen in the film as a tragic injustice done to Vincent. He suffered the trauma of abandonment and the anxieties of loneliness, both of which were manufactured through scientific intervention. (In a nod to another piece of the Reagan family puzzle, it is almost as if Vincent were an aborted son, a consequence of scientific birth control). In the flip side of the genetic determination of the narrative, the film asks audiences to believe that Vincent would have been a different person if he had been raised, as Julius had, in a perfect environment. Arguing for the importance of family nurturing, it is suggested that Vincent's criminal behavior is less a product of his genetic makeup than of his unhappy childhood. When Julius finally intervenes in Vincent's life, Vincent becomes caring, open, and honest. The film concludes that a good family is able to turn around such social maladjustment and produce a "good" son.

Most important, the real bond of the family here is not that of mother and child, for Mary Ann Benedict fails to recognize her sons when they come to see her. It is only when she reads their story in a newspaper that she believes what they have said. Julius and Vincent, however, believe in their relationship beyond all surface contradiction. Even Vincent, who at first thinks Julius is crazy, comes at the end to sacrifice money—what had been the sole driving force of his life—to save Julius. When they are in trouble, they "sense" each other's whereabouts and rescue each other. Mary Ann Benedict exhibits no such "homing signal" for her sons.

But, for Reagan and Bush, this is as it should be. It is not the bond with their "mother"—the Republican Party—that counts so much as their bond with each other. For all that Bush may hold the tenets of the Republican party platform and support its main positions, it is his bond with Ronald Reagan that finally won him election. It is this bond that lies at the heart of the rising strength and power of the conservative movement throughout the 1980s. And, the conservative movement hoped in 1980, Ronald Reagan would be able to take this "maladjusted" Republican child—George Bush—and turn him, through the force of a family environment, into a good conservative son.

At the movie's close, Julius and Vincent have married two sisters, Marnie and Linda Mason (Kelly Preston and Chloe Webb), each of whom is quite different in her own right, yet they are sisters nonetheless. They are all shown together at a family outing, along with their rediscovered mother, Mary Ann Benedict. The last scenes of the film pan to Julius and Vincent pushing two baby strollers, each holding twin babies. These distinct yet similar twin brothers have won the hearts of two sisters and reproduced two more sets of twins, suggesting somehow that their discovery of each other has improved not only both of their individual lives but has fruitfully produced a new happy family. This happy ending is thus one of wealth and propagation, as the reunited Benedict family can become the source for the development of a whole new happy family in defiance of scientific control.

Similarly, the Reagan/Bush partnership was seen in 1980 as the start of an alliance within the Republican party that would yield a numerically larger future Republican "family," one in which Americans would be like sisters, mothers, and brothers to each other. In 1988, such an image helps to create the sense that George Bush's election to the presidency would help to carry on such a family.

Some of the most popular films of 1989 continued to carry this theme of dual or ambivalent masculinities. *Rain Man,* for example, depicts two brothers—one "normal" and the other autistic with a singular ability to remember numbers—who discover that each alone is less than the two of them together. Three other films on the top-ten list were about less-than-heroic fathers whose children learned to love them nonetheless: *Honey, I Shrunk the Kids* (1990, Robert Zemeckis), *Parenthood* (1989, Ron Howard), and *Indiana Jones and the Temple of Doom.* The resolutions of these plots center around children coming to recognize that their fathers—none of whom has a hard body or the escapades to go with it—have instead other skills that are finally appreciated by their once-disillusioned children. In each of these films, masculine heroics are downplayed in favor of family commitments and love. In the themes of Bush's inaugural speech, "We as a people have . . . a purpose today. It is to make kinder the face of the Nation and gentler the face of the world."[2] The difficulty with achieving this "kinder, gentler" image was that it brushed perilously close to appearing, in the aftermath of a hard-bodied preesidency, weak and soft. George Bush would struggle throughout his presidency to straddle the images of himself as a man who "cares" about people and as a tough commander-in-chief.

The best-selling film of 1989 in what proved to be a record year for box office receipts articulated this Bush dilemma. The movie, which is about a children's fantasy character turned real on the screen, is

Timothy Burton's *Batman*. This movie exhibits better than any other the difficulties of masculine identity in the immediate post-Reagan years. For Batman, played by the less-than-heroic-looking Michael Keaton, has been turned from a knowledgeable and confident comic book figure into a troubled and uncertain film character. In *Batman*, Bruce Wayne/Batman presents the divided masculine ideals of external strength and internal goodness that Ronald Reagan had seemed so seamlessly to embody, and that George Bush seemed so perilously to split apart, and in doing so tips toward the films of the early 1990s, in which internal emotions would take the lead over muscles and violent spectacles in defining masculine heroics. But in 1989, like George Bush's new presidency, masculinity seemed as yet unsure of its direction and divided about its performances in a post-Reagan, post–hard-body era.

In the opening scenes Batman captures two criminals who have just robbed a family (an echo, as audiences will later discover, of how Bruce Wayne himself was orphaned). Batman at this point is still scarcely known in Gotham City. When one of the robbers looks fearfully at his captor and asks, "Who *are* you?" the reply is terse, husky, and sure, "I'm Batman." With a vigilante heroism that seems almost to harken back to Dirty Harry, Batman then drops the criminal to his death over the side of a skyscraper. Batman's brand of rough justice leaves all Gotham unsure whether he is a good guy or a bad guy.

Shortly after this, a reporter who has been following the stories of the mysterious "bat," accompanied by international photographer Vickie Vale (Kim Bassinger), attends a gala benefit at the mansion of the wealthy Bruce Wayne. Vale approaches Wayne and asks if he knows which one of the men in the room is Bruce Wayne. He replies, "No, I don't," and only introduces himself to her later while she is viewing his collection of ancient warrior costumes. When he invites her to dinner, they dine in a dark-paneled room at a long dining-room table. When Vale asks him if he enjoys eating in that room, he replies "Yes," and then, after looking around, admits that he has never been in that room of the mansion before. The scene shifts to them finishing their meal in the pantry, as the butler, Alfred, tells stories of Wayne's childhood. Still later, when Wayne decides to tell Vale who he really is, he stands in front of her, stammering explanations about how "normal" people have "normal" jobs and lives, but how some people have other parts of their lives that are rarely shown. While she answers the door, he rehearses the words, "I'm Batman," the same words he had delivered so forcefully and clearly at the beginning of the film.

Here, they're whispered hoarsely and uncertainly and, because the Joker has arrived, are never said.

The contrast between these two personas could not be clearer. Batman is confident, muscular, invulnerable, decisive, and strong. Bruce Wayne is uncertain, isolated, and vulnerable because of the early death of his parents. He is slight and retiring. In a revelation that earlier hard-body films would have been terrified to admit, *Batman* shows that the muscular body that repels bullets and defeats criminals is nothing more than a suit of body armor—highly sophisticated body armor, but body armor nonetheless. And yet, when in this costume, the vulnerable Bruce Wayne becomes the crime-fighting, villain-stopping Batman. In addition, there is never any explanation offered about any of Batman's paraphernalia or about any of his martial skills. How is it that the average-looking Bruce Wayne can be turned into the supernormal Batman? The answer seems to be the costume itself, as Wayne seems to acquire these skills the minute he puts on the bat suit. There is something about *being* Batman that transforms an average man into a superhero.

Batman shifts the focus on masculine identity away from hard-bodied heroism to a manhood divided and troubled. Where the *Rambo* films use violent spectacle to distract audiences from the potentially ambivalent parts of Rambo's character—combining, for example, his invulnerable body with his tearful confessions of loneliness in *First Blood—Batman* exteriorizes that ambivalence by dividing the body and the emotions, depicting that body as something to be put on and off at will. And yet, it proves to be no less essential to the well-being of society than Rambo's strength was to the survival of Afghanistan. As in the Bush presidency, the hard body is being both rejected and embraced, recognized as a burden and as a necessity, as something to hide at the interpersonal level and as something to display in the public arena, as a source of fear and of attraction, of goodness and destruction.

Part of the solution for this troubled manhood would be to capitalize on and deny hard-bodied externality at once by considering the hard body itself as a role whose power is conveyed to the "average" man when he is playing the role, as, in the case of *Batman*, it is conveyed to Bruce Wayne when he is wearing the costume. In other words, the hard body is enacted as a performance that is independent of any particular history it may have (as, for example, audiences never learn how Bruce Wayne acquired any of his unique skills; nor do they learn what part George Bush played in the Iran-contra operations). For

*Bruce Wayne in his hard-bodied Batman costume. (*Batman, *Warner Brothers)*

Bush, the presidency seemed more a role to be put on and taken off than, as it was for Reagan, a person one became.

One of the difficulties in discussing the image of George Bush's presidency in relation to Ronald Reagan's is not simply to contrast it to Reagan's but to determine what that image was. Bush seemed often to struggle, as did his mentor, Richard Nixon, with projecting an effective public persona. Bush was trained not in the arts of public speaking and acting like Ronald Reagan but in the quiet arts of diplomacy (his service as ambassador to China), secrecy (his brief tenure as director of the CIA), and boardroom camaraderie (his success as an oil-company executive, achieved largely through his father's business contacts). Even after four years as president, his gestures—the characteristic hand slicing the air, or exaggerated fist-pounding when he wanted to achieve emphasis—still seemed stilted or, after Dana Carvey's effective impersonation of him on *Saturday Night Live*, even self-parodic. His well-noted failure to complete sentences, to leave verbs dangling and prepositions unattached, often left him appearing to stumble through a press conference or to waffle on an answer.

Bush's campaigns tried to paint an image of him as a warm and loving family man and as a tough and unrelenting commander-in-chief. For Reagan these dual presidential poses merged seamlessly in his image as "father" to the nation. For George Bush they never merged, as became explicit in the 1992 Republican National Convention, when Bush's efforts to promote himself as the leader of Desert Storm and a partner in bringing about the end of the cold war were quickly and disastrously overshadowed by the "family values" wing of the Republican party, which clearly viewed its issues as more important than matters of foreign policy. The division of the Republican party that took place under Bush's watch—a division so extreme that the leaders of the Republican party in Oregon considered in late 1992 ways to separate themselves from their party's most active and most conservative members, the Christian Coalition—is evidence of a sundering not only of national and domestic issues but of the very definition of the national body that Bush's image was not able to solidify.

Part of the problem of Bush's image stems from the very reason for his success—Ronald Reagan. It was very much Bush's association with Reagan that won him the support of the most conservative and active members of the Republican party (Bush had not been able to secure the Republican nomination on his own in 1980), but it was also the power of Reagan's image that made him, quite literally, a difficult act to follow. In order to establish his own presidential image, Bush needed to differentiate himself from Reagan. In doing so, he chose, from the day of his inauguration, to articulate that difference as one of "kindness" versus, by implication, meanness, of "gentleness" versus harshness. And by giving up Reagan's most cherished dream—Star Wars—Bush gave up as well any claim to toughness or vision.

This "generational" split leads to the kind of duality present in *Batman*, where the hard body is needed to enforce social order but is irrelevant to the character of a "family man." This division will become more explicit in later years; the hard body will come to seem not only tangential to the family but antithetical to it. Yet when George Bush was inaugurated and *Batman* was released, there was still some effort to have it both ways, to continue the association between hard bodies and families that Reagan had underscored.

The impetus for Batman's persona is seen to spring from the destruction of the family by a crime-ridden social order; street robbers kill Wayne's parents. Consequently, in contrast to *Rambo* or *Die Hard*, *Batman* shows audiences that the generation of the hard body is not a response to external threats but the result of the disintegration of the American family, which, presumably, the hard body was manufactured to protect. The film also shows that the hard body may protect the family, but it cannot be a part of it. The place where the bat suit is kept and where all of the bat technology rests is not in Wayne's mansion, but in a cave. And Batman is himself always isolated from society in the film, posing in those haunted shots perched above Gotham City (this is the closing shot of the film).

So here was the problem for Bush: if he rejected the Reagan hard body in order to differentiate himself from his predecessor, he would be forced to be Bruce Wayne instead of Batman, to be, by necessity, a non-image. As Bruce Wayne makes clear, he must be nondescript in order to hide his association with Batman. He cannot know himself, he must be able to hide at his own parties, and he must play the lesser role to his hard-bodied alter ego. So it is not simply that Bush never had the public personality that Reagan did, or did not know how to play up to audiences as Reagan did (though both of these are certainly true enough), but that his choice to differentiate himself from Reagan left him in the position of having no real image at all.

Whereas Reagan celebrated his body and his actions—his personal strength, his survival of an assassination attempt, his confrontations with Congress, his showdowns with the Soviet Union—Bush promoted his performances and the image that they created, relegating the body to an ambivalent role that would later be expressed in Hollywood films through a male body that betrayed its internal integrity. As journalists Michael Duffy and Dan Goodgame put it, Bush has been a president who "substitutes frenetic movement for lasting action. . . . Bush is more than half-serious when he says, paraphrasing Woody Allen, that '90 percent of life is just showing up.' "[3]

As would happen in some of the best-selling movies of 1989 and 1990, the Bush presidency worked to repudiate the images of its predecessor.

> What Bush intended . . . was to act as custodian of the Reagan movement, while reining in what he considered its unsightly excesses. . . . Less open acceptance of bigotry. Less braying insensitivity to the less fortunate. Less grasping and petty corruption. Less celebration of greed and gaucherie. Less indolence and inattention in the Oval Office. Less of a "lone cowboy" style in world affairs.[4]

Bush tried to tone down the externalized features of the Reagan years and replace them with a "kinder and gentler" image of internal goodness and caring; Bush attempted to label the Reagan style "bad form," pulling rank on him with Bush's elite Andover/Yale breeding that became public policy through his "thousand points of light," a kind of national noblesse oblige.

Bush entered the presidential lists in 1980 less because he had a list of policies he wanted to put forward or a set of crises he felt he could resolve than because he wanted to "be" president: "[Bush] has always been less interested in doing anything specific as president than in just *being* president. He had entered politics without a desire to accomplish anything, but rather just to *serve*. He had wanted the job, as he once said, because he was taken with 'the honor of it all.' " As Duffy and Goodgame go on to say, Bush "simply craved the adventure and honor of holding office and would embrace whatever policy positioning and media imagery he deemed necessary to win." His erstwhile chief of staff, former governor of New Hampshire John Sununu, when asked what was to be the goal of the Bush presidency, captured the Bush emphasis on performace rather than action when he answered, "a 'successful presidency' that would bring reelection in 1992."[5]

Bush wanted voters to evaluate his presidency not on the number of bills he has passed or the rate of unemployment or inflation (with a predicted recession in 1989 that came into being in 1990, these would hardly be among the items of a "successful presidency") but instead in terms of "how many places he has just shown up," or, as he articulated the issue in the 1992 presidential campaign, as a question of "character" rather than record or actions. Equally, "Bush often talks not about his convictions on difficult issues, but about how he wants to be 'positioned' " on them.[6] The public was asked to judge Bush on his contemporary performances—his character—and not his past record or accomplished deeds. George Bush cast his presidency in terms of his current expressions of sympathy for victims of disasters, his current outrage about international terrorism, or his current lament for individual laid-off shipyard workers, rather than in terms of his record on taxes, his service as ambassador to the U.N., his brief tenure as CIA director, or his response to the Tiananmen Square massacre. This is why Bush's campaigns, far more than Ronald Reagan's, have consistently been about "values" rather than "issues," since values are statements that express immediate feelings and sentiments (allowing Bush to alter, for example, his stance on abortion in 1980), whereas issues might raise specific questions of consistency, decisiveness, or accountability. (Where *was* he during Iran-contra? What *did* he know about the Banca Nazionale del Lavoro?)

Bush also tended to evaluate others along similar lines, viewing world leaders less in terms of their actions than in terms of their "style" or character. "Because," Duffy and Goodgame explain, "Bush sees diplomacy through a prism of personality, he tends to see evil people, not evil systems or governments."[7] Consequently, Saddam Hussein was Hitler-like, but Bush had no negative feelings toward the Iraqi people and encouraged a takeover of the Iraqi government by Saddam Hussein's next-in-command. Manuel Noriega was an outlaw and terrorist, but the Panamanian government was worth preserving. Individual single mothers may be neglectful and lazy, but the family system of mothers as primary parents is a mainstay of American life. Because George Bush sees performance as not only immediate but necessarily personal, he considered individuals and individuals alone to be responsible for actions, no matter how widespread or damaging the consequences of those actions might be. But because he judges individuals by how they perform in the present, even the guiltiest individuals are capable of reevaluating, or, to be more pragmatic, forgetting their actions (Richard Nixon is George Bush's primary advisor and mentor).

At the beginning of his 1988 presidential campaign, George Bush declared, "We don't need to remake society, we just need to remember who we are."[8] Whereas the heroes of *Rambo*, *Die Hard*, *Lethal Weapon*, and other male action films implicitly or explicitly criticized through their own actions the U.S. government, the legal system, the FBI, or working women, George Bush declared that the system seemed to be working just fine and that all that was wrong was how Americans were acting in relation to it. This is why so much of his philosophy of domestic policy was based not on an economic or social agenda but on popularizing voluntarism and a revival of a class-based American spirit of obligation toward others and commitment to helping those "less fortunate." In such terms, remembering who "we" are required not a grand shifting of the social system or reform of malfunctioning institutions but a mere reminder that it is performance that counts, the kind of reminder that would produce heroes, as the next chapter will discuss, out of white men who would ally themselves with institutions in films such as *Casualties of War* (1987, Brian DePalma), *Mississippi Burning* (1988, Alan Parker), and *The Accused* (1988, Jonathan Kaplan). George Bush, in putting forth this philosophy of internal expression as performance, in contrast to the Reagan emphasis on external action, hoped that it would make a hero out of yet one more white man, George Herbert Walker Bush.

The Movies Are Looking for a Few Good White Men

O ne of the most consistent themes of Hollywood films of the 1980s, as pointed out in Chapter 2, was one that pitted human values against the presumed non-values of technology and mechanization. Films such as *Alien* (1979, Ridley Scott), *Blade Runner* (1982, Ridley Scott), the *Star Wars* series, *Terminator* (1984, James Cameron), and *Robocop* (1987) depicted not simply individual humans but humanity itself at stake in battles against mechanized corporations or computer-production systems that held human life as at best insignificant in relation to profits and at worst as an impediment to machine domination of the world.

> The machines were ubiquitous. . . . People were approaching a time . . . when they were spending more time relating to machines than they did to each other. Many even saw their machines more than they saw each other. Their machines held more possibilities than could be fathomed, and yet by lessening human contact, they left many feeling controlled or plundered by them.[1]

It is these voices that echo in Rambo's declaration in 1985 that "the mind is the best weapon," and in his triumphant destruction of a bank of computers and monitoring devices as his first act after his successful rescue of POWs. Even the 1987 comedy *Crocodile Dundee* (Peter Faiman) creates a hero out of a man whose defeat of international drug smugglers depends upon his very ignorance of technology.

Coproduced then with-the hard body is a complementary theme of anti-mechanization that reinforces the sense of the male hard body as "natural," not manufactured, and individual, not mass-produced, both qualities on which a Reagan philosophy—whether of economics or family values—intimately depends. As Michael Ryan and Douglas Kellner summarize these values in their discussion of films that portray "technophobia": "From a conservative perspective, technology represents artifice as opposed to nature, the mechanical as opposed to the spontaneous, the regulated as opposed to the free, an equalizer as opposed to a promoter of individual distinction."[2] In such terms, *Terminator,* for example, represents not only the more overt anti-nuclear messages that its plot professes but it also works to put to rest fears about the logical extensions of a hard-body mythology—that that body would become so hardened as to forget that it was human, or "natural," at all. In this sense, Rambo and the Terminator are necessary complements, one portraying the hard body at its best—reviving strength and individualism in foreign policy—and the other starkly portraying that body's dark underside of hardened brutality as a destructive force directed against humanity itself. The *Star Wars* films come closest to depicting this relationship explicitly, with the "good" individual body of Luke Skywalker set against the literally "dark" technologized body of his father, the evil Darth Vader.

What saves the hard-body mythology during this period from its own logical implications of hardened destructiveness is the projection of that hardened body onto an outside, even alien, force. What *Rambo* shows in the character of Sergeant Yushin—a taller and more muscular Soviet version of Rambo's body who has no mind of his own—is drawn out more straightforwardly in the completely mechanized and machine-made Terminator, an object with no feelings, only a programmed target that it will go to any lengths to eliminate. The crossover between Sergeant Yushin and the Terminator is very smooth, as both are portrayed as forces that could potentially destroy all freedom for human beings. In the Reagan anticommunist ideology, the evil of the Soviet Union is not only its drive for world domination but its desire to place all humans under what Reaganism, and decades of anticommunist rhetoric before it, described as the severe repressions—the "programming"—of a communist system. In Richard Nixon's words, "If the Soviets win, all will become slaves and satellites."[3] The destruction of human freedom was not then a simple science fiction fantasy but for Reaganism a concrete consequence of Soviet domination. Those machines who imprisoned humans and methodically set about killing them were, in the minds of Reagan ideologues, no different from Soviet communists. So, while the hard-body mythology might have been subverted by fears about its development into the hardened body, those fears were, in these films of the mid-1980s, diverted through the presentations of those hardened bodies as foreign, alien, or nonhuman.

The intimate connection between the hard body and its mechanistic dark side is not simply a means to construct an anticommunist narrative but the means for constructing, in a Hegelian sense, a story of the nation as well. Reagan's pro-technology militarism—one of the three consistent features of his political agenda (along with tax cuts and decreasing government bureaucracy)—was justified exclusively in terms of a "missile gap" that presumably existed between the Soviet Union and the United States. It is why Reagan's demonization of the Soviet Union as an "evil empire"[4] was not merely a revived form of an antiquated McCarthyism but a necessary component of his efforts to restructure a post-Carter America. But just as the American hard body needed the external negative body of the Soviet Union against which to define itself, it would require a domestic version in order to transcribe itself at home.

In 1987, that foreign body came home. In *Robocop*, Paul Verhoeven brought the Terminator and Rambo together in a plot that revolved around the transformation of a dying police officer's mutilated body into a fully computerized, titanium-shielded, law-enforcement officer, who has only his face and brain remaining from his human body. He is, according to his creator, Robert Morton (Miguel Ferrer), "the best of both worlds: the fastest reflexes modern technology has to offer, an on-board computer-assisted memory, and a lifetime of law-enforcement programming." Robocop (Peter Weller) is literally the hard body that Rambo represented, both personally and nationally. Neither emotions nor bullets can penetrate his titanium exterior, and he has the strength and determination that made Rambo a hero. Robocop is able to meet any kind of criminal—from the small-time robber to the rapist to the major drug dealer—and bring them all to justice. After Robocop's appearance, Morton predicts that crime will be eliminated from Detroit in forty days because "there's a new guy in town. His name's Robocop." This is, of course, the kind of claim that Reaganism wanted to make for its revived U.S. military—that communism could be eliminated with the appearance of the "new guy in town."

But there's trouble in paradise. Robocop doesn't eliminate crime,

"There's a new guy in town. His name's Robocop." (Robocop, *Orion Pictures*)

primarily because he discovers that crime doesn't exist just on the streets but in the board rooms of the largest corporation in Detroit, OCP—Omni Consumer Products. In the representational constructs of this film, OCP is no ordinary corporation but one that has, in addition to taking over hospital, prison, and space-exploration markets, now taken over the police force and governance of Detroit itself. OCP controls all of the services citizens in the 1980s have come to expect government to provide. More than this, through contracts and the manufacture of weapons, OCP's CEO, Richard Jones (Ronny Cox), can boast, "We practically *are* the military." Unlike the Rambo films, which blamed Congress and interfering governmental bureaucracies for preventing victory over communism—a constant Reagan theme—*Robocop* portrays that governmental bureaucracy in the guise of the biggest beneficiary of Reagan economics, the conglomerate corporation.[5] Yet this corporation, like the mechanized terminators, sees humans only as instruments of corporate interests and profits, not as individuals. As the OCP official, Johnson (Felton Perry), says of Alex Murphy, the police officer whose body is transformed into Robocop, "He signed the release forms when he joined the force. He's legally dead. We can do pretty much what we want to."

But it is precisely the services of OCP—health care, law enforcement, administration, and so on—that were targeted by the Reagan agenda as features of a government bureaucracy that had grown too large and had interfered in too many areas of people's lives. OCP is called a corporation, but it clearly functions in Detroit as a government. Indeed, it has displaced any elected authorities and plans to build a whole new city that it will own outright. This is certainly not the kind of corporate model that Reagan believed would enhance and strengthen the U.S. economy, nor the kind of model that he proposed as the resource for privatizing many of the very services Reagan wished government to cut. By characterizing OCP as a quasi-governmental body, one that is decidedly bureaucratic, *Robocop* holds out for its viewers the possibility of a different kind of corporation as well as a different kind of government, ones that would keep to their own arenas and not overextend their mandates for services, whether consumer or social.

Ryan and Kellner offer a clue why the hard body seemed so ambivalent in the late 1980s:

> As conservative economic values became ascendent, increasingly technical criteria of efficiency came to be dominant. In addition, conservative economic development emphasizes the displacement of excessively costly human labour by machines. . . . One antinomy of conservatism is that it requires technology for its economic programme, yet it fears technological modernity on a social and cultural plane.[6]

Thus at the international level, the hard body seemed to mobilize nationally desired strengths and abilities against communist threats, and therefore seemed appropriate when used against "other people," but at the domestic level, the hard body veered into the threatening arenas of automation and regimentation that were antithetical to the very conservative values of individual freedom and deregulation that the Reagan administration was instituting as government policy. This was occurring not only at the level of public mythologies but at the level of daily economic production, as, on the one hand, increasing numbers of jobs were given over to computerized automation, and, on the other hand, increasing numbers of jobs were being lost to foreign competitors or oversees investment sites that offered fully automated factories or cheaper labor. As early as 1980, stories began to appear about the pending job losses from automation. In October of 1980, *Omni* magazine asked the question: "Can you earn a living after the Robot Revolution?" Their answer was largely negative: "If we don't change our present patterns, the inevitable and widespread use of robots will come at the cost of high unemployment, high inflation, social unrest, and violence both physical and psychological."[7] This is precisely the picture that *Robocop* paints.

There was a none-too-subtle dovetailing between the characterizations of communism as nonindividualistic and inhuman—qualities that made the Soviet Union the "evil empire"—and the effects of changing factory production techniques during the 1980s. Yet, although these characterizations seemed continuous, leading to the conclusions that increasingly conglomerated—and therefore nonindividualistic and inhuman—corporations were themselves part of an "evil empire," Reaganism celebrated corporate development as the panacea for U.S. economic difficulties in the face of increasing Japanese and German dominations of international markets. The hard-bodied solution to U.S. economic problems—making factories as financially strong and determined as Rambo's body—came, to many citizens, to seem more akin to a hardened body, a threatening rather than a protective one.

Out of this contradiction between the foreign and domestic aspects of Reaganism came films like *Robocop*, in which the hard-bodied hero fights a domestic corporate enemy. The extent to which that enemy epitomizes fears about automation is shown in the CEO's preferred law-enforcement product, E(nforcement) D(roid) 209, a fully automated and fully armed robot, "a twenty-four-hour police officer, a cop who doesn't need to eat or sleep." To show that this product is not

OCP's CEO with ED209, the fully mechanized police officer. (Robocop, *Orion Pictures*)

designed for the safety of Detroit's citizens but for corporate profit instead, Jones goes on to explain to OCP's board of directors, "After a successful tour of duty in Old Detroit, we can expect ED209 to become *the* hot military product for the next decade." But, he later admits, profit is all that matters: "I had a guaranteed military sale with ED209. Renovation programs! Spare parts for twenty-five years! Who cares if it works or not!" The failure of ED209 underscores the characterization of OCP as an "evil empire." When it is first brought out for display, a board member volunteers to act as a criminal that ED209 will disarm. Though he complies with ED209's orders to throw down his weapon, ED209 kills him. What Jones calls a "glitch, a temporary setback," is exactly the fear presented by automation to many U.S. citizens—that a nonhuman product will first, not listen to you, and second, eventually kill you.

There is one "product" in this film that audiences can rest assured will not kill them, as long as they are not criminals—Robocop. His prime directives are to "Serve the public interest. Protect the innocent. Uphold the law." Even when in pursuit of his own murderer, Clarence Bodicker (Kurtwood Smith), Robocop cannot kill him. As Bodicker reminds him, "You're a cop!" and Robocop holds his fire and arrests him. Throughout the film, and in sharp contrast to earlier heroes such as Martin Riggs, Dirty Harry, and Rambo, Robocop fulfills his programming and "upholds the law." Even when other members of the police force are on strike for better working conditions, Robocop is on duty, because "somewhere, there is a crime happening." Whereas Rambo and Riggs were heroic because they could see beyond the bureaucratic details that impeded their pursuit of justice, Robocop is heroic because he remains loyal to the law in the face of rampant crime and corruption. In this film, adherence to the law is opposed directly to the interests and behaviors of the corporation. Robocop's secret fourth prime directive compromises his ability to fulfill the third, "Uphold the law." His instructions are that "any attempt to arrest a senior officer of OCP results in shutdown." The corporation thus knowingly plans to break the laws its own services have been hired to support.

The corporation is then the site of privilege, corruption, insensitivity, profit-seeking, inhuman values, and elitism. But the film's commentary goes beyond simply condemning corporations for their values by linking street crime, drug-dealing, prostitution, gambling, and death to corporations. In his darkened vision of late 1980s America, Verhoeven shows the systemic ties between corporate operations and criminal operations, all finally linked by their disregard for human life and emphasis on profit. The chief drug-dealer of the film, Clarence Bodicker, works for OCP's Jones, and they are cooperating on OCP's new venture to build a "New Detroit," completely serviced by OCP. In exchange for killing Robocop, Jones offers Bodicker access to the two million workers who will be hired to build Delta City, all of whom will need, according to Jones, prostitutes, drugs, and gambling, "virgin territory for a man who knows how to open up new markets." But what truly links Bodicker and Jones is not simply their shared sales habits but their stated philosophy that each repeats during the film: "Good business is where you find it." Holding such a position, "good business" can include drug-selling, bank robbery, prostitution, and murder, as long as a profit is turned. For Verhoeven, the crime that occurs on the streets and the crime that occurs in corporate board rooms are continuous. And Robocop is heroic because he stops both.

But he needs more than a hard body to do it, and this is where *Robocop* indicates a move away from the *Rambo* and *Lethal Weapon* films. As long as Robocop's hard body follows his original programming, he is an oddity, not a hero. It is only when Robocop rediscovers his identity—that he is/was Alex Murphy, that he is/was human—that he moves from being a mere hard body to being a hero. And that discovery hinges not on file information that his computerized brain can absorb but on his emotions. After operating successfully as a police officer, Robocop is back at the police station processing information and undergoing tests, when he suddenly has a flashback of Bodicker shooting Alex Murphy. Robocop's readouts go haywire, and he walks out of the station, uncommanded. Later, when he learns that he was Alex Murphy, he goes to his former home, only to find it deserted and for sale. Walking through the house, he has more flashbacks, this time of his wife and son.

It's only at this point that Robocop and OCP begin to come into conflict, suggesting that the moment of crisis that separates people from corporations, that divides the law from crime, is a moment of human emotion, when people remember that they are humans and not machines or products. Full of anger, Robocop goes after Bodicker, only to find that Bodicker leads him to Jones and OCP. When Jones orders the police force to destroy Robocop, he is finally isolated completely from the corporation and free to act on his own. In one of the key moments in his transition from hard body to hero, he removes his helmet and reveals the human face of Alex Murphy, which he continues to show for the remainder of the film. In this new presentation of the human machine, he defeats Bodicker, destroys the ED209, and successfully circumvents directive number four to kill Jones. At the film's close, the "Old Man" (Daniel O'Herlihy), the founder and head of OCP, compliments Robocop on his killing of Jones: "Nice shooting, son. What's your name?" Showing the triumph of human individualism over technologized replication, Robocop replies, "Murphy."

For this is really what *Robocop* is finally about—the effort to work out a new identity for the masculine hero in the post-Reagan presidency. The mythology of the hard-bodied hero John Rambo, who was celebrated in the White House and emulated by U.S. allies, was revealed to promote the very problems plaguing U.S. jobs and citizens' relations to increasing corporate power. *Robocop* shows the insufficiency of that body in a domestic context when it is unaccompanied by masculine memories of family, pain, and love (Rambo never does come home again). When he is able to "rediscover" his human side, Robocop becomes the hero of the post-Reagan years and the man who

Robocop after he remembers he's Alex Murphy. (Robocop, *Orion Pictures*)

can stop both ruthless corporations and brutal criminals. The message of *Robocop* for the new masculine hero is clear: only by remembering who you really are—the feelings that identify you as an average human male—can society as a whole be saved.

There's a lot going on here. First, there is a shift away from the exceptional man—"Rambo was the best" (*First Blood*)—to the

Alex Murphy's maimed and wounded human body. (Robocop, *Orion Pictures*)

average man—Alex Murphy is just another cop who happens to get killed at a time when OCP needed an available body. Second, this means that there are no more wound scenes, moments when audiences, especially male viewers, are asked to see themselves as inferior to the heroes on the screen. Because his body is made of titanium, Robocop does not feel the same kind of pain Rambo felt when he was wounded. In fact, after being pierced through the abdomen by a steel rod (an exaggeration of Rambo's wound in *Rambo III*), all Murphy can say is, "I'm a mess." Instead, Murphy's pains are redefined to include those that any man could feel. The loss of his wife, love for his son, hatred for the man who killed him—these are recognizable emotions that would cement rather than disintegrate male audience identifications with Robocop. Consequently, the achievement of the hard body no longer seems the goal of such films, but instead an effort to redefine that body as meaningful in emotional rather than physical terms.

This reconfiguration of the hard-bodied hero away from the unemotional imprint of the externalized macho presidential style to an

This hard body can't be wounded. (Robocop, *Orion Pictures*)

emotionally defined and internally motivated character like Alex
Murphy marks an important shift in the articulation of masculine
heroism in the 1980s. Both Rambo and Robocop defined themselves
as antitechnological (Rambo's mind as the best weapon, and Robocop's self-identification as Murphy) primarily to position themselves
as individuals opposed to mass-produced and mechanistic systems.
But whereas Rambo's heroism could, as discussed in Chapter 2, be
defined through an externalized weaponry that could be safely used
against foreign enemies, Robocop's heroism was by necessity defined through a more internalized set of features. But part of the
tension that yields the spectacular scenes of violence in *Robocop*
springs from the ambivalence such a domestic heroism poses for
Reaganism, as the emotional hero comes perilously close to reviving
the imagery of the "soft" Carter characterization that Reaganism so
closely depended on as its own negative image. The antimechaniza-
tion theme of Reaganism that was coded as a straightforward anticommunism thus brought about a kind of heroism that came close to
contradicting one of the very foundations of that anticommunism in
the Carter soft body. The films that are discussed in this chapter

resolve this dilemma through their domestic positioning of white masculine heroism.

The deteriorating economy and subsequent decline of U.S. international prestige contributed to this Hollywood redefinition of masculinities. As American citizens watched other nations—particularly Japan, Germany, and the oil-rich countries of the Middle East—gain increasing control over international markets, locate factories on U.S. territory, and invest in U.S. banks and properties, the hard-bodied nationalism touted by Ronald Reagan seemed to be missing the mark somehow. The increased weapons production that put the United States back on track to stand up to the "evil empire" did little finally to prevent German and Japanese products from dominating U.S. consumer outlets, or to lessen U.S. dependence on Arab oil, or to bolster the dollar in international trading.

Consequently, the nation needed a mechanism for reasserting its superiority over its international competitors. Whereas U.S. superiority over the Soviet Union could tap into a wealth of imagery and rationalization left over from decades of old anticommunist rhetoric, this same anticommunism did little to elevate the country's status over some of its most important noncommunist allies. But another feature of the Reagan ideology could be of use here—the rhetoric of American values. To be able to show that Americans were still superior in values to their international competitors could help to sustain a disintegrating national ego and a deteriorating job market. What made Robocop a hero—his ability to use his memories of and love for his family to defeat corrupt criminals whose sole interests were to gain control of Detroit's *financial* operations—could make any U.S. male a hero as well, as he could use his status in relation to his family to combat his decreasing status in the economy. (Thus, the increased emphasis on abortion as an issue, not just of moral debate, but of male control—would men have the "right" to force their female partners to deliver babies women wanted to abort? Would daughters have the right to have abortions without the consent of their parents? Would wives have the right to have abortions without the consent of their husbands? Connecting these emphases to mounting figures of domestic violence and rape only begins to tap into some of the various ways in which such a return to "values"—values based, as discussed in Chapter 3, on a paternalistic system—was worked out in terms of personal relations.)

Finally, Robocop's simple relation to the law—"Somewhere, there is a crime happening"—resuscitates as well a sense of individual

"Somewhere, there is a crime happening." (Robocop, *Orion Pictures*)

power. In the face of corporate manipulations, criminal harassment, and bureaucratic mixups, the law remains as a constant resource for the average citizen, who, if the law can be enforced, will be adequately protected by it. Access to social power seems to rest then only in knowing the law and being able to implement it. Where the Rambo films were structured to leave audiences desiring the externalized strength of Rambo's national hard body, *Robocop* invites audiences to desire a protective figure who not only can enforce the law (a repaired ED209 would do if this were the only requirement) but who can wield it fairly and faithfully, without corruption or compromise. The system, such desires whisper, is already in place. All we need are a few good (white) men to make it work.

There are three films I want to look at here to sketch out the parameters of these revised heroes: Brian DePalma's *Casualties of War* (1987), Alan Parker's *Mississippi Burning* (1988), and Jonathan Kaplan's *Accused* (1988). All three turn on the heroism of white men. All three work to resuscitate that heroism through an adherence to values and an effective system of justice. All three are grounded in "true" stories, which shifts masculine heroics from the world of fantasy and daring to the world of history and courage. And all three respond in some way to the chief challenges offered to white male authority in the preceding decades—the loss of the Vietnam War, the civil rights movement, and feminism. They attempt to resolve the tension generated by the narrative solution of *Robocop*—the tension caused by producing an emotional domestic hero who does not appear to revive the presumed Carter legacy.[8] The resolution offered by *Robocop* to the problems of mechanization has thus produced its own "new" problems that these and the films discussed in subsequent chapters struggled to address. Collectively, these films worked to create an image of white male heroism on which the successful achievement of each of these social changes comes to depend. In order, these films say, for women and people of color to be happy, there must be white male heroes.

If Hollywood masculinity was going to construct a character who was superior in internal if not external strength to his foreign counterparts, then one source for that redemption was to return to the place where masculine integrity, ethics, and strength were presumably lost—the Vietnam War. Even contemporary assertions of masculine integrity could not erase the admitted failures that surrounded the Vietnam War. The only recourse was to return to that war and rediscover white male heroism there. But whereas *Rambo* returned to Vietnam to show that Rambo's strength and fighting skills were truly superior to those of the Vietnamese, *Casualties of War* concentrated not on these hard-body issues, which would eventually remind audiences of the proofs of American "weaknesses," but on issues of behavior, morality, and character. To do so, DePalma returned to a 1969 story of a single soldier,

Private Sven Ericksson, whose testimony exposed the abduction, rape, and murder by U.S. soldiers of a Vietnamese woman.

Like the *Rambo* films, *Casualties of War* begins with an emphasis on the male body. But in contrast to the shots of bulging muscles and sweating torsos that marked Rambo's dramatic entrances, *Casualties of War* introduces audiences to a body cultural representations have made familiar over the past fifteen years—the weakened and helpless Vietnam veteran. In the first combat scene of the film, the Vietnam War is given its accepted 1980s look of confusion, disorientation, death, and helplessness, as Ericksson's platoon is mortared by a Vietnamese unit. An explosion launches Ericksson (Michael J. Fox) into the air and lands him with his head protruding from a Vietcong tunnel, his legs dangling in the tunnel beneath him. As he cries for help, a Vietnamese man in the tunnel crawls toward Ericksson's legs. With knife in hand, he stabs at Ericksson's groin, just as Sergeant Meserve (Sean Penn) returns to pull Ericksson out of the tunnel. Later, during the patrol's first visit to a Vietnamese village, Meserve and his friend, Brownie (Erik King), are discussing their immanent departure from Vietnam, when Brownie comments that "maybe it's about time we stop balling these slant-eyed bitches. Otherwise we might end up with a disease, you know?" With Meserve's assent, they reveal their bodies as vulnerable, not only to enemy fire, but to sexually transmitted diseases as well, showing that the sites of both combat and pleasure are potentially dangerous. Shortly after saying this, Brownie is himself shot by a sniper. Trying to affirm that he will live, Brownie shouts out, as the medevac helicopter takes him to the hospital, the motto of the hard-bodied hero: "I'm an armor-plated motherfucker!" But in 1987, this slogan and the mythology that accompanies it do Brownie no good, and he dies that afternoon.

In the film's opening scenes then, the male body is depicted as extremely vulnerable, to castration by Viet Cong men—a literal manifestation here of what had become established as a metaphor in general narratives about the war—to infection by Vietnamese women, and to death at the hands of unseen enemies. Having established the unreliability of the male body as the source of narrative resolution, the plot then shifts away from combat scenes to closer and more isolated interactions among the men themselves, allowing for investigations of the psychological dynamics of this small group of soldiers, investigations that will eventually yield a heroic figure that exists apart from and in defiance of the hard bodies that had come before.

In frustration at being denied access to Vietnamese prostitutes outside the base, Meserve decides to kidnap a Vietnamese woman from a nearby village and take her on their next patrol, "a little portable R and R" to "break up the boredom" and "keep up morale." After forcing Oanh (Thuy Thule) to carry their packs and walk miles in the heat without food or water, Meserve rapes her. Out of the five men on the patrol, only Ericksson refuses to follow Meserve's command that they will all "take their turn" with her. Later, when an encounter with the Viet Cong exposes their patrol to other U.S. soldiers, Meserve orders his men to kill Oanh so that there will be no evidence of their deeds. Though several refuse, one finally stabs her with a hunting knife, rather like the one Rambo films made famous. When she still tries to escape, all but Ericksson join in shooting her.

Ericksson's defiance of Hatcher's defense that "this is what armies do!" takes him from the level of the patrol to that of the Army itself. When he refuses to rape Oanh, Meserve threatens to kill him, insinuating that Ericksson is a "VC sympathizer" who "could get killed real easy" without the support of his fellow soldiers. He threatens as well to rape Ericksson, accusing him of being homosexual and telling him, "Maybe when I'm done in there, I'm gonna come after you! Maybe when I'm done humpin' her, I'm gonna hump you!" When he tells his story to his immediate superior, Lieutenant Reilly (Ving Rhames), Ericksson is told to "forget the whole thing." When he goes further, to his company commander, Captain Hill (Dale Dye) reminds him that Meserve saved Ericksson earlier, and "now you're gonna ruin his life!" Only when Ericksson tells his story to a chaplain does anything get done. Formal charges are filed, and each man in the patrol is convicted and sentenced.

The length and detail of this section of the plot, in contrast to the opening scenes of combat, emphasize that the film is more intentionally "about" the questions of morality, ethics, and principle that underlie Ericksson's dilemma than it is about combat or the Vietnam War per se. More to the point, because of the star quality of Fox, the omission of subtitles for Oanh's speeches, the frequent use of point of view camera for Fox, and the introductory and resolving scenes focusing on Ericksson outside the war, *Casualties of War is* finally about Ericksson's "dilemma" and not Oanh's. And his dilemma, unlike Rambo's, *and unlike Oanh's,* is a decidedly internal one. Where Rambo was deciding whether to assist the Afghan rebels or not, Ericksson is deciding whether he can keep silent about Oanh's death. Where Rambo expresses his decision in spectacular physical clashes with the Soviets, Ericksson manifests his in speaking quietly to a chaplain.

And where Rambo was a hero because his body was strong and he could defeat Soviet soldiers to rescue (an) America(n), Ericksson is a hero because his conscience is strong and he can defeat the hard-bodied men around him to rescue (an) America(n).

For there is no question that the men around Ericksson are more in the mold of Rambo than of Ericksson. Sergeant Meserve is a tough and seasoned fighter who knows how to survive in Vietnam. As his trial record shows, he has been on numerous successful operations and has trained many new recruits; during the time of the film, audiences see him fearlessly return to a mortared position to rescue Ericksson, and then quickly save Ericksson's life again when a Viet Cong soldier tries to kill him. He is loyal to the men around him and is willing to risk his life for them. Corporal Clark (Don Harvey) is Rambo gone over the edge, as he takes pleasure in killing Vietnamese and believes that "soldiers like Tony Meserve and me belong out in combat, not in the stockade." Private Hatcher (John C. Reilly), the other new guy in the platoon, "can't figure out why [Meserve] never thought of [the kidnapping] before." He envisions himself and Meserve to be like Genghis Khan, great warriors who fight by their own plans and take what they want. Private Diaz (John Leguizano), though he reluctantly participates in the rape of Oahn, finally succumbs to the pressure of the group, needing to prove that he is not the "queer" and "faggot" Meserve is ready to label him as being if he does not.

The dynamic of Ericksson's "dilemma" is laid out here in relation to these men and the army they represent, not in relation to Oanh. The resolution of the plot is not simply for Ericksson to prove that he has some moral or ethical stance that others lack but that he can differentiate himself from the men who surround him, that he can, in other words, differentiate himself from the hard-bodied image that seems to dominate the lives of the men in this movie. Standing as he does, with Robocop, at the point of transition to a revised masculine image, Ericksson must prove that the hard-bodied model that preceded him and that once seemed to work so effectively for "survival," is no longer viable. He cannot simply offer an alternative; he must oppose the hard body to show that the strength of the hero of conscience is finally greater than that of the hard-bodied heroes who can defeat armies.

How can Ericksson, a small man who, as the film shows, could easily be killed by his fellow soldiers, possibly defeat these muscular, seasoned soldiers? How can he prevent them from raping him, treating him like the woman they have already assaulted, insisting that his

Sergeant Meserve as the hard-bodied enemy. (Casualties of War, *Columbia Pictures)*

Ericksson must differentiate himself from the hard-bodied image to become a hero.
(Casualties of War, *Columbia Pictures*)

strength to resist them is no more than hers? He does so with the help
of the Army system of legal justice. Alone in the woods, Ericksson is
in danger. But with the weight of the Army behind him, Meserve and
the others are sentenced for their crimes. This is the other key shift in
these films: from a hero who succeeds by defying the system to one
who survives by aligning himself with it. Like Robocop, it is finally
the law that wins out for Ericksson, enabling justice to occur and evil
to be defeated.

Ericksson's allegiance to the military system is not an opportunistic
one that arises out of his need for protection, but instead one that has
defined him from the beginning of the film, suggesting that his heroism arises out of this allegiance, and not vice versa. When, after the
rape, Meserve challenges Ericksson, "You probably like the Army,
don't you? I hate the Army." Ericksson replies, "This ain't the Army,"
suggesting that Ericksson holds a truer and less brutal model of the
Army than the one held by men like Meserve. And later, when he
tries to help Oanh escape, he cannot go with her, because he does not
want to be a deserter. And when it seems that the Army hierarchy is
going to ignore the behavior of Meserve and his men, it finally acts
quickly and effectively when the attention of officers out of the field

is brought to bear. Even Captain Hill, who doesn't want to pursue formal charges, admits that "these men fucked up good."

Because the national hard body was no longer enough to defeat enemies, especially those who seemed to be challenging U.S. supremacy in areas other than the military, these films offer in its place a system of justice and morality that underlies U.S. society, one that has, presumably, been present all along but was usurped by the rogue warriors and congressional bureaucrats who have defied it or used it for their own purposes. All that is needed to revive this dormant system is a man who is willing to stand up for it, to represent its values and espouse them in the face of opposition. Such a man is offered as an alternate hero to figures like Oliver North, whose own manipulation of the system was so highly popularized in the last years of the Reagan presidency. To redeem the military after its loss in Vietnam, to revive faith in a system of justice that had failed to prevent the war crimes committed during Vietnam, to resuscitate an ailing hero image that had become either useless (the national hard body) or tainted (Oliver North), and to reassert a U.S. superiority of strength in an area that did not yet seem to be claimed by the Soviet Union, Germany, or Japan—all of these goals are achieved in Private Sven Ericksson's quiet assertion of moral law and a system of justice.

Because it is clear that both the hero and the victim *and* the enemy here are American men. This is a struggle that takes place among American men, *for* American men. When Captain Hill tries to get Ericksson to back down, he presses, "But you bringing formal charges against [Meserve and the others]. Is that going to help her?" Obviously not. By the time of this conversation, Oanh is already dead, and her family will not be compensated for her loss even if Meserve is convicted, nor will other Vietnamese necessarily be safer because of Ericksson's actions. So what is Ericksson actually fighting for here? For the ability of U.S. definitions of manhood to claim the territory of justice and law for themselves, and not to have it taken away by the image of a single-minded warrior who rules by his own laws.

And why 1987? Because those laws seemed to have been taken away from them, seemed to have been put to the use of women and men of color, seemed to have deprived white men of *their* justice and their ability to determine what is right and what is wrong.[9] Ericksson works on behalf of a woman of color, and is willing to support a man of color, Diaz, who resists the coercions of white masculinity. Both Diaz and Oanh finally prove unable to fight these hard-bodied men on their own. It is only Ericksson—the white man—who has the strength to resist other white men's orders and threats, because Ericksson, the white man, is laying claim to the law, something neither Oanh nor Diaz can effectively do. And now, as the conclusion of the film shows, the law is going to work for men like Ericksson. They are back on the same side, fighting the same enemies, and declaring the same winning character. They have ceased to be "casualties" of war.

After redeeming the Vietnam War for white men, showing that there were good white boys in that war and that audiences simply didn't hear about them, there remained another battle to fight for white male redemption, another place of loss, another image of villainy—the civil rights era. Appearing in the year following *Casualties of War,* *Mississippi Burning* answered that need. Taken from the story of the murders of James Chaney, Michael Schwerner, and Andy Goodman by Ku Klux Klan members in Neshoba County, Mississippi, in 1963, Parker's film focuses on the work of the FBI in uncovering the murderers and bringing justice to a racist society. This time, the heroes are Robert Anderson (Gene Hackman) and Alan Ward (Willem Dafoe), two white FBI agents who enter the state of Mississippi, where law again seems to have been taken over by someone else—in this case, the local police department and the Ku Klux Klan—and reclaim that law for the United States government, in the process offering justice to black Mississippi citizens. And, in the process, defining themselves as heroes.

All three of these films—*Casualties of War, Mississippi Burning,* and *The Accused*—capitalize on the historical referentiality of their plots, using well-publicized trial cases to validate the existence of both a system of justice and the men to uphold it. Because the topics of these films—racism, sexism, violence, murder, and rape—are among the most vitriolic of the past three decades, and because so many of the popular images of white men have been constructed in defiance or neglect of these issues, it would seem almost a fantasy, something akin to *Star Wars*'s interplanetary open-mindedness, to offer them as defenders of justice rather than its defi(n)ers. Recourse to the historical record absolves these narratives of this fantasy element, offering "real" white men who were "real" heroes and whose actions led to "real" justice. In such terms, the existence of a historical record itself becomes part of the tale.

In the case of *Mississippi Burning,* that record is, as many film critics at the time suggested, somewhat skewed. From the opening scene, in which Mickey Schwerner is shown driving a car in which James

Chaney rides in the back seat (Chaney, the more experienced civil rights worker, was driving the car that night), to the confessions that were forced out of Mayor Tillman by a black man threatening to castrate him (the bulk of FBI information was obtained from an anonymous informant who was paid $30,000), *Mississippi Burning* has altered the script of the historical record to emphasize the actions of Anderson and Ward, and to deemphasize the presence and influence of two other groups important in resolving the Mississippi crimes—civil rights workers, predominantly black, and the Justice Department, headed by Robert Kennedy. Why?

In order to manufacture Anderson and Ward as independent heroes realizing the potential of a system of law, they need to be portrayed as taking the initiative in solving the murders and defying the white society that condoned them. The *individual* quality of their initiative would be lessened if the actual, documented work of the Justice Department on this case had been shown: how the department pressured Mississippi's governor to restrain white violence, how it invoked the "Lindbergh Law" and redefined the murders as kidnappings so that federal action could be taken, how it sent Allen Dulles as a special envoy to assess the situation in Mississippi, how it had many years earlier convinced Herbert Hoover that the Ku Klux Klan was a worthy object of FBI investigation, how it had offered the National Guard to assist in the search, how it had promoted and actively lobbied for the Civil Rights Act, and how it had supported voter registration drives for blacks throughout the South. Robert Kennedy's personal and intricate involvement in the search for Schwerner, Goodman, and Chaney's bodies as well as the indictment of their murderers is well known.[10] Without Justice Department action, the murders probably would never have been investigated at the federal level. Left to work with local law enforcement officials, in Neshoba County a notably close-mouthed and loyal group, little would probably have come of the investigation of these deaths.

Mississippi Burning makes little mention of this work. When, after finding scant information, Ward tells Anderson that he has been given "full authority" to do what he must to solve the crimes, this authority is not attributed to the Justice Department or to Robert Kennedy. The only mention of Kennedy at all in the film is in an early conversation between Anderson and Ward that figures the dichotomy between their two styles. Anderson, the former Southern sheriff and "good ole' boy," is opposed to Ward, the Northerner whose formal style alienates anyone he talks to. Ward is a former Justice Department member,

*The only ones who defy the Ku Klux Klan are two white men. (*Mississippi Burning, *Orion Pictures)*

what Anderson calls "a Kennedy man." But what audiences see of that "Kennedy" influence in the film amounts to a certain degree of intensity and commitment coupled with naïveté and a preference for procedure that will, the audience is meant to believe, never be able to solve the murders.

At the same time, the only civil rights workers shown in the film are the three men who die in its opening moments. In these scenes, the black civil rights worker is silent, sitting frightened in the back seat of the car while the white driver confidently says that he can handle the pursuing police car and the sheriff's men who approach. For the remainder of the film, none of the courageous and influential civil rights workers who were present during the investigations and who continually put pressure on local and national bodies to solve the murders is shown. The only ones who truly defy the sheriff and the Ku Klux Klan are Anderson and Ward, two white men.

There are only two important roles given to black actors in the film. The first is that of Aaron, the boy who is not afraid of the sheriff or the Klan and who convinces another boy, witness to a house-bombing, to identify the men he saw throw the Molotov cocktail. He is also the first one to tell the FBI agents that they should be looking to the sheriff's department for their culprits. He is depicted as strong, defiant, and not afraid to stand up for his beliefs in justice for Southern blacks. But he is only a boy and therefore poses no real challenge to the authority of the white FBI agents as the representatives of justice in Jessup County. The second role is given to another FBI agent who is brought in to help coerce Mayor Tillman into giving information about the murders. With Tillman tied to a chair, this agent poses as a black man who has been castrated by a white lynch mob. After offering graphic details of the story, he shows Tillman a razor blade and paper cup like those used in the story, unbuckles Tillman's pants, and prepares to reenact the castration on him. Tillman confesses immediately. While the scene certainly is loaded with the dramatic irony of having the tables turned on a white KKK supporter, the FBI agent disappears immediately afterward, brought in secretly by Anderson to play this part and then leave. He is not part of the FBI "team" that investigates and solves the murders, nor does he seem to have the same authority and status attributed to other agents. His work is clandestine and, as Ward immediately points out, produces a clearly illegal confession. In addition to his holding this marginal status in the film, audiences also never know whether the story he tells about a lynching and castration are true or not, leaving the impression that, as powerful and effective as this man seems, he may not really be a "man" at all, leaving him desexualized in comparison to the white agents, Anderson and Ward.

For one of the key efforts of this film is to reinstate, in a way that *Casualties of War* simply could not, the sexual desirability of this new male hero. One of the caveats of the hard-bodied hero was that that body was fascinating and desirable, that, whether he willed it or no, people would be attracted to the hero's muscular physique and hardened torso. But when heroism is internalized and portrayed by actors such as Michael J. Fox and Gene Hackman, there is a question about whether such desirability can still be maintained. What is it that people, women in particular, would be attracted to? *Mississippi Burning* resolves any anxieties about the sexuality of these new bodies by introducing a romantic subplot between Anderson and Deputy Pell's wife (Frances McDormand). Recognizing her early on as a possible source of information and then targeting her as the weak link in Pell's alibi for the night of the murder, Anderson seduces her. But he does so in a way that highlights his habits as a "new" man. He offers her flowers, chats with her about her day, compliments her on her appear-

*Aaron, strong but infantilized. (*Mississippi Burning, *Orion Pictures)*

ance, talks with her about her Southern childhood—all things that her hard-edged and commanding husband never does. It is this she finally finds attractive—a man who pays attention to her and is kind—and not Anderson's appearance (he is balding and pot-bellied) or his sexual come-ons.

And the payoff of this new attractiveness? It is Mrs. Pell who tips Anderson off to the location of the buried bodies, the break in the case that the FBI was unable to crack. This event contrasts sharply to the $30,000 payment to an undisclosed informant who revealed the burial site to the FBI during the actual investigation. Such a payment would negate the personal effectiveness of agent Anderson, both through his seduction of Mrs. Pell and through his set-up of Mayor Tillman's confession. The film's plot shapes Anderson into the sole catalyst for solving the crimes and does it in a way that positions him as the more authoritative figure in relation to a white woman and a black man.

Mrs. Pell's role serves another function in the film, as the final motivation for Anderson to solve the case. Throughout the first half of the film, Ward has been in charge of the investigation, often giving orders that Anderson criticizes. It is only when Mrs. Pell is brutally

A white woman's beating as the motivation for white male anger. (Mississippi Burning, *Orion Pictures*)

beaten by her husband and his friends that Anderson's outrage reaches a pitch of fury that cannot be controlled by Ward's adherence to FBI rules. More than this, Ward himself capitulates to Anderson's way of doing things after Mrs. Pell's beating, asking Anderson to teach him how to get these men and promising to run the investigation Anderson's way. Here, Anderson brings in his own people, stages the castration scene, physically threatens Pell, and coerces a confession from Lester Cowans by pretending they are Ku Klux Klan members about to lynch him for a supposed betrayal of the Klan. Anderson's methods are unorthodox, brutal, and often illegal, but they produce convictions. In these scenes, he is portrayed as decisive, commanding, and authoritative, though never through the use of his own muscle or physical prowess. He achieves results because he is committed to a cause, to achieving justice in any way necessary.

In 1988, only the FBI, or what *Mississippi Burning* represents as its "true" character, could get away with this. After the scandals of Iran-contra and revelations throughout the 1980s of CIA covert activities around the world, there remained little public trust in the CIA's commitment to justice. The shock waves of Iran-contra that ran throughout the Reagan administration left little confidence in the government's position on questions of justice. And in the wake of increasing accusations of police brutality, especially against people of color (the series of beatings and killings in Miami throughout the 1980s would be in many viewers' cultural memories, and remember, this film was released before *Cops, Most Wanted,* and other "live-action" police shows had begun to heroize police departments), the sheriff's office of Jessup County could only seem all too real in the 1980s. The FBI was involved as well in breaking a spectacular insider trading scam in the Chicago futures market in 1987. Only the FBI, which had been shut out of Iran-contra activities when it objected to weapons transactions, and which seemed to be committed to solving the kinds of domestic problems citizens were coming to be more concerned about, had the kind of public image that would make it a believable defender of justice and a credible arena for the discovery of a new kind of white hero.

The use of the FBI helps to reinforce the alignments of white men with justice, since the FBI seems both untainted by foreign covert activities and has the task of addressing domestic crimes, an issue the Reagan adminsitration had highlighted throughout its years in office. Consequently, the FBI seemed to offer a national system of justice that, in the hands of good white men, could protect the country from its internal enemies.

In 1983, six men gang-raped a woman on a pool table in a New Bedford, Massachusetts, bar, while onlookers failed to stop them. Raymond Veary, the prosecutor on the case, concluded, "This is a story without heroes."[11] By 1988, when Jonathan Kaplan released *The Accused,* a film loosely based on this event, a hero had been found.

Much of the plot of *The Accused* follows the events of March 6, when an unnamed woman went into Big Dan's Tavern to buy cigarettes. Like her, the film's character, Sarah Tobias (Jody Foster) went into a local bar unsuspectingly. Like her, she was gang-raped, this time on top of a pinball machine, while other men in the bar looked on and cheered. And like her, she escaped and was picked up by a passing motorist. But the first shots of the film let audiences know that there will be another character whose presence will affect the narrative. The quiet opening shots of "The Mill" are suddenly interrupted by Sarah Tobias, running and screaming from the bar's front door. As she tries to flag down a passing motorist, holding onto her torn clothing, a voice is heard to explain, "There's a girl in trouble." As the camera follows Sarah from a distance, audiences are shown a young white male in a pay phone, talking to the police: "It's a rape. There's three or four guys. I don't know. A whole crowd. . . . Just send somebody!" As he runs after Sarah, presumably to help her, she is picked up by a truck driver who takes her to the hospital. From the beginning then, *The Accused* is never just Sarah's story, since the audience already and always knows that there is a white man whose presence is important. In many senses, because audiences "know," both from generic clues and from the factual case, that the rapists will be convicted, the suspense and tension of the film, and therefore the audience's narrative focus, is not on whether Sarah's rapists will receive the justice they deserve but whether or not and when that white man will speak again. As in *Casualties of War*, the film's pressure is on Kenneth Joyce's "dilemma."

Like Sven Ericksson and Rupert Anderson, Kenneth Joyce (Berni Coulson) must differentiate himself from the men who would rape or watch a rape take place without trying to stop it. The film's camera work helps him to do this, as Joyce is consistently shown isolated from the men around him. When his close friend and fraternity brother Bob Joiner (Steve Antin) is arrested for the rape of Sarah Tobias, a long shot reveals Ken watching from behind a closed window as Bob is taken away in a police car. Later, when Bob's lawyer is shown on television, declaring that "there was no rape. The so-called victim consented enthusiastically to all of the alleged acts," Bob is cheered by his surrounding fraternity brothers. Ken is shown at a distance, watching them. When Ken visits Bob in prison, they are separated by a glass barrier, through which the camera repeatedly shows Ken's expressions. When Bob insists, "Did you see me rape her, Ken? You didn't, did you?" Ken replies through that wall, "Yes, I did, Bob."

These camera shots and framing devices, combined with Coulson's slight build and blond hair, continually distinguish him throughout the film from the rapists, all of whom are dark-haired, and most of whom are muscular or heavy. In contrast to the men whose physical size overshadows Sarah and holds her on the pinball machine, Joyce's height is closer to Sarah's. When they are finally shown together in the district attorney's office, it is as if they are two small people who have both been victimized by the hard-bodied men of that bar. When he admits to Sarah that he is afraid, he becomes more closely aligned with her than with any of the brazen men who did not even bother to leave the bar after the rape, assuming that what they did was not a crime.

Much of the film's overt plot is centered around the barriers that separate its two female protagonists—Sarah Tobias and Kathryn Murphy (Kelly McGillis). Divided by class, education, background, language, and access to the law, Murphy sees Tobias as a counter in her "win/lose" column as a district attorney. Only when Tobias confronts her after the plea bargain and later ends up in the hospital after her anger leads her to stage a head-on collision with one of the onlookers from the bar does Murphy realize that she "owes her" an opportunity to tell her story in court, to tell everyone that she was raped and not "assaulted." From this moment of conscience, Tobias ceases to be just a case number for Murphy and becomes instead a crusade, one that she is willing to defy her boss and risk her career to fulfill. This is why she initiates the second trial, of the men who cheered on the rape.

By the film's end, Tobias and Murphy have established a bond, a connection forged between women who are insistent that men not get away with rape or with standing by while other men rape. The glue that seals them together is the justice system, as the courts have vindicated both of them, against the rapists and against those in the district attorney's office who do not want to try cases like these. Like Ericksson and Anderson, their power at the end of the film comes from the power of a legal system that has supported their claims and interpretations of justice. But this closure would seem to contradict the earlier pattern by placing two women and not a man in the position of heroes who defy custom and expectation to "do the right thing."

At the same time that Murphy and Tobias are connecting as women, Kenneth Joyce is disconnecting from men. But because Murphy comes to her moment of conscience at the midpoint of the film, the only remaining tension concerns not what happens between women but what happens between men. Will Kenneth Joyce betray his best friend and the other men in the bar in order to support a strange woman's accusations? The suspense is sustained up to the moment he testifies, when he tells what he saw at the bar. And there is no doubt in the film: it is his testimony that sways the jury and brings justice to Sarah Tobias. As Murphy tells Tobias after the first court session, the case could go either way, based only on Tobias's testimony and that of her friend, both of which appear questionable to the jury. The defendants' lawyer, Mr. Paulson, even tells the jury in his summation that "the people's case depends on Kenneth Joyce," not on Sarah Tobias or other witnesses. Consequently, Sarah's vindication in the courtroom depends less on her newly formed bond with

Tobias and Murphy bonding as women. (The Accused, *Paramount Productions)*

another woman than upon the willingness of a white man to defect from his community of men to align himself with Tobias.

This is what makes Joyce a hero. When Murphy first approaches him about testifying, he seems uneasy about prosecuting men who just watched and didn't rape: "Those guys didn't do anything. . . . It was like a show. They just watched. I bet if you asked a thousand people, 999 would watch. It's no crime!" In fact, as his own testimony reveals, Kenneth Joyce himself watched for some time before he left the bar to make that phone call. But he finally proves himself to be the one man out of a thousand who would make the call, the one man out of a thousand who would stand up for what's right and what's wrong, the one man out of a thousand who could be a hero. He makes the phone call, he testifies at the trial, and he dissociates himself from the men who surround him.

But this begins to sound like Rambo's wound, a moment in the film when the hero's behavior elevates him so far above the behavior of the viewers, particularly the male viewers, that the distance effectively negates those men from identifying with that hero and possibly emulating his moral and social position. Murphy's summation helps work this through. She asks the jury if Joyce seemed different from other men, more sensitive or observant. The rhetorical form her questions take implies that he is not, that he is an average man who was simply telling the truth. In an important logical distinction, Murphy argues that Joyce, though he too watched, was different from the men around him because he remained silent and watched. He did not participate in the cheering and jeering that encouraged others to commit rape but finally left the bar and phoned the police.

This is the move that allows white male viewers back into the narrative. Even if they're among the 999 who would watch, they can be among those who did not commit a crime by being in the group who remains silent and not the group who rapes or encourages others to rape. They're allowed to expiate their guilt about rape through inaction, something that, by this point in the film, viewers would have experienced. Because as Joyce offered his testimony, the cameras show, for the first time in the film, what happened in the bar that night. Sarah's testimony consisted only of her voice and face in the witness box. Only Joyce's story is given that added credibility and impact of a visualization of the crime. Through Joyce's eyes then, viewers are offered the opportunity to witness a rape without having to be present at one, in a way that is far less powerful than the same story if shown from Sarah's point of view. If the camera had offered Sarah's vision of three men on top of her, of the men behind them cheering, of the pinball machine, of the ceiling of the bar, the focus of the scene would not have been on *watching*, which is what Ken and the audience are doing at that point, but on being the object that everyone else was watching. When the jury convicts the three who cheered and, in the process, absolves Ken of responsibility for the rapes, the jury is acquitting the audience as well, especially the male viewers of the audience who might have found the rape scene titillating or exciting, certainly appealing enough to watch. This could help to explain why the film rewrites the events of 6 March 1983 to include two trials instead of one. The rapists in the New Bedford case were convicted, and it was later concluded that there were not as many bystanders as originally thought. But *The Accused* takes as its focus not the rapists but the watchers, those men whose position is more like that of the audience, and offers a mechanism for separating those men from each other, allowing the male members of the audience to enact their disgust with the rapists and the cheerers while still not seeing themselves as implicated in the crime, while being able to see themselves as heroic men.

After the trial is over, Murphy and Tobias embrace, solidifying their bond as women who have triumphed over violent men. Kenneth

Joyce is also standing in the back of the courtroom, again separated from the other men. Murphy and Tobias smile at him, showing their approval of his decision, and he smiles in return, showing that he is satisfied with what he has done. Now fully separated from the men who surrounded him earlier—the rapists in the bar and the fraternity members—he is free to bond with Tobias and Murphy, aligning himself happily with them against violent men and in the process aligning himself with the law against criminal men. Here is his true moment of triumph, for the women have accepted him as a different man. They have acknowledged him as a hero.

No one made that phone call in 1983. As *Newsweek* tells it, "Many of those present said they were too scared to call for help."[12] And while one patron apparently spoke up after a while (the gang rape took one and a half hours), telling the men to "knock it off—this is getting out of hand," no one listened. The bartender and another customer later said that they tried to call the police, but one of the rapists stopped them. But these efforts would not have made an effective story, and would not have worked in 1988 to do the job of revising the conception of masculinity and heroism that Hollywood films were undertaking at the time. They would not have served as a fulcrum against which men could repudiate their pasts as embodied in other "guilty" men, and thereby see themselves as cleaner and more worthy than they. While all three of these films use the historical referentiality of their narratives to underscore the validity of white male heroism, they stray from those parts of the historical record that would show that "real" men failed to enact those heroic deeds. *The Accused* finally creates a character out of whole cloth, indicating that, while other events of that night might have been sufficient to the story being told, the absence of a heroic man was not. The creation of such a man is the task of these films and the work of mainstream cultural representations of the immediate post-Reagan years.

There are several changes in masculine imagery that have taken place between the hard-body films of the Reagan and the immediate post-Reagan years. The hard body that emblematized a renewed national and international strength has been repudiated, not for a return to the soft body of the Carter years, but for the creation of a body in which strength is defined internally rather than externally, as a matter of moral rather than muscle fiber. This body is then positioned as a domestic rather than as an international hero, defending the rights of women and people of color across the country. Rejecting the male

The white male defending people of color. (Mississippi Burning, *Orion Pictures*)

bonds that typified many films of the 1970s, these heroes prove themselves through their isolation from other men, deriving their power not from male solidarity and communication but from alliances with the larger institutional systems of justice to which they turn for the solution of social problems. In the process, the distances that separated hard-bodied men from their viewers/citizens have collapsed to suggest that any white man can be a hero such as these, if only he is willing to commit himself to federal laws rather than local loyalties.

Is this a conscious repudiation of Reaganism as well? Did the decline of Reagan's popularity, the aftereffects of Iran-contra, and the turnover of power to George Bush indicate a rejection of Reagan's key policies, images, and ideologies? The deteriorating economic situation of the nation, combined with the rapidly changing events in Eastern Europe, suggested that a turn to domestic concerns was inevitable. Consequently, one of the key strengths of the Reagan administration—its emphasis on international status—seemed less relevant and less heroic. This is why, for example, George Bush's Willie Horton campaign worked so well, focusing as it did on internal anxieties about racial difference, safety, violence, and the effectiveness of the legal system, all correlatives for an underlying anxiety about "justice"—who had it, who "deserved" it, who defined it, who needed it, and who controlled it. Bush's election suggested that the definers and distributors of justice would continue chiefly to be white American men such as he. This is one reason why the blockbuster male heroes of the late 1980s are almost exclusively white men, because mainstream America was not prepared to perceive African-American men in the position of controlling and defining justice.

In the face of the increasing popularization of concepts of cultural diversity and multiculturalism during this time, it could seem reassuring to many citizen/viewers to acknowledge white male heroes who affirmed rather than rejected institutional structures underlying U.S. social operations and provided a source of stability by retaining control of those institutions. Most important, these were men who were willing to uphold the values of those institutions in the face of those who would opt for their own separate systems of values and laws. This is why it is so significant that the men who raped Sarah Tobias would stay in the bar afterwards, not expecting to be arrested, because they did not perceive themselves to have committed a crime; in other words, they had their own definitions of crime and community. Similarly, the sheriff, deputies, and Ku Klux Klan members who killed Goodman, Schwerner, and Chaney had their own system of law and their own definitions of crime, which did not include the murder of civil rights workers or black men and women. And Tony Meserve makes it very clear to Sven Ericksson that out in the jungles of Vietnam he *is* the law, and rape and murder are not crimes. In all three cases, the men who need to be repudiated are those who take into their own hands the definitions of social law, community, and justice. What is on trial then in each of these stories is not so much these individual men as the concept of individual definitions of criminality and behavior. Where Rambo's individual determination of what was right and wrong—rescuing POWs against direct orders from a government representative or shooting at the National Guard—made him a hero, the heroes of these later films are exactly the men who acknowledge that, without the larger system of law that surrounds them, *they are nothing.* More directly, without access to an operating system of law, they are at the mercy of the rogue lawmakers who surround them: Ericksson is almost killed by Clarke, Mrs. Pell is nearly murdered by her husband, and Kenneth Joyce was helpless in the presence of the rowdy men in the bar.

Do these films then directly represent public anxieties about rape, lynching, and murder? Admittedly, the three scenarios of these plots seem remote, both in time and place, from the experiences of most viewers, especially most white male viewers. But the fears about small, independent groups of people taking the law into their own hands, determining what is just and unjust, and punishing those who disobey these laws—these are fears that could well be more available to U.S. audiences, audiences who see their social networks increasingly challenged by communities of color, communities of gays and lesbians, communities of women, communities of the poor, communities of refugees, communities of the disabled, gang communities, communities of the aging, and so on—what the Reagan and Bush administrations labeled as "special interests." Hinted at in the construction of Colonel McAllister's loyal group in *Lethal Weapon,* these films offer the more threatening, because less exotic, images of citizens who stray from the center in establishing their own systems of values, laws, and actions. In such a context, the only true heroes are not those who defeat these groups (there are too many of them) but those who reaffirm that these groups are outside the norm, that they are what Francis Ford Coppola once called in *Apocalypse Now* (1979) "off the boat." Additionally, these films pinpoint an even more fundamental anxiety, simply that there is a struggle for equal justice in which white men do not figure, and in which they are no longer the active or receiving agents of a legal system.

In what may well have been a prophetic comment for the 1980s, Captain Willard (Martin Sheen) declared, as he was going up the river in pursuit of the rogue warrior, Colonel Kurtz, "Never get off the boat. Absolutely goddamn right." For these films of the late 1980s, the heroes are not the Colonel Kurtzes who go out to set up their own fiefdoms in the jungle but those who can captain the ship safely through the treacherous waters of difference that surround them. "Absolutely goddamn right."

Terminal Masculinity: Men in the Early 1990s

The films discussed in the previous chapter worked toward clearing white men of charges of racism and sexism. Repudiating the hard bodies who perpetrated these oppressions, white male heroes stepped forward to champion the causes of men of color and women, aligning themselves with a system of law and justice that would ensure both the institution of justice and white men's continued control of it. In 1991, the hard bodies of the 1980s seemed to have been successfully rejected in mainstream Hollywood films, but not, as the films of the late 1980s might have suggested, for the values of justice. The interest in "justice" was a cover for an alliance with the law, a crucial component for a national social order that seemed, by the late 1980s, to be disintegrating. Justice was never a conservative issue, only the law. As the economy grew worse (the national debt doubled under Bush's first two years), as the threat of communism grew less (Gorbachev, the leader of the "evil empire," was named "Man of the Decade" by *Time* magazine in 1990), as many on the right became increasingly outspoken and independent (Randall Terry's "Operation Rescue"), as reports of drug use increased, as AIDS moved clearly out of the "closet" and into white heterosexual homes, as the Iran-contra scandal refused to disappear, as George Bush came under attack for his relationship to Manuel Noriega, as the Reagans were accused of abuse and neglect by their daughter, Patty Davis, U.S. mainstream citizens began to worry that the social order that had seemed to be so smoothly instituted under Ronald Reagan had begun to deteriorate.

The need for a reinstatement of the law as under the control and for the discretionary use of mainstream white America (part of the function of the "war on drugs") became narrativized in Hollywood films.

But by 1991, Hollywood's interest in justice had waned and been replaced by a less socially troublesome topic—commitment to the family. The only real addition Ronald Reagan made to the Nixon agenda for the 1980s was a focus on the family and the moral values that for those on the far right defined the family. But whereas Reagan was able to balance the disparate and potentially contradictory interests of a hard-bodied militarism and a warm-hearted familialism, largely through the force of his personal image, George Bush could not manage the same feat. The Republican ticket for 1988 revealed the divisions between these elements of the right, as Bush campaigned on his experience as vice-president, as former CIA chief, as former U.S. ambassador, and as personal friend of foreign leaders, and Dan Quayle campaigned on his defense of family values and moral principles. This evidence of a splintering of the conservative movement was supported by other divisions, particularly the "gender gap," as Republican women began to become more vocal about their support of choice on abortion and women's rights in the work place. But with the economy declining, the national debt skyrocketing, and the reasons for many military expenses disappearing, the Reagan emphasis on family seemed to provide the only secure legacy of the Reagan ideology. At the same time, it provided a popular and facile site for retaining a sense of American superiority in the face of Japanese and European economic competition.

In such a context, it would seem quite logical that the hard body that had been so closely affiliated with the foreign policy imaginary of the Reagan era would now shift toward domestic policies, emphasizing the family and personal values over market achievements. With a good deal of bravado, these new male heroes would thumb their noses at an economic superiority that they did not have and return to the families they had neglected before. Leonard Reitman's 1990 film, *Kindergarten Cop*, starring one of the hardest hard bodies of the 1980s, Arnold Schwarzenegger, shows how the transition from law enforcer to family man was to be sketched out.

At the beginning of the film, John Kimball *is* the eighties man, the lethal weapon *par excellence*. He is a tough, unshaved, brutal, determined police officer single-mindedly pursuing the goal of imprisoning Cullen Crisp, an expert drug dealer and murderer who is backed up by his evil, overprotective, single mother. When legal police procedures prevent his partner from detaining the only witness to Crisp's crime, Kimball chases after her on his own, breaking down doors, blowing away furniture with his customized shotgun, and brutalizing anyone who comes between him and his witness. For Kimball, as for all eighties action-adventure heroes, the legal system is only an impediment to getting things done and putting criminals away. In the mold of Martin Riggs or Dirty Harry, Kimball is a loner who writes the rules as he goes along, a tough guy who needs no family or partners, and a brutal, violent, and unfeeling man. He is, in other words, the typical eighties action hero.

But by the end of the film, Kimball has given up being a police officer in favor of teaching kindergarten. He has broken through his emotional barriers to tell Joyce, another teacher, that he doesn't want to lose her or her son, Dominic. He feels guilty when he punches an abusive father and promises from now on to let the law punish such men. His life is most threatened not by another super-macho, special combat male enemy (like Mr. Joshua in *Lethal Weapon*) but by a determined mother who is out to avenge the death of her son. And his life is saved not by a fancy weapon or an effective body blow but by his partner, a short woman with a baseball bat. What happened to turn a brutal cop into a nurturing, playful, and loving kindergarten teacher?

It takes only one word: family. John Kimball, the cop, had a wife and child, but his wife left him many years ago and has since remarried a "nice man" who now raises Kimball's son. One of the reasons Kimball devotes his life to police work is simply that he has no other life to go to. He has, audiences are invited to psychologize, used the violence and confrontation of his job to block out the pain he feels about the loss of his family. It is only when he is reintroduced to children (who are coincidentally about the age of his son when they were separated), that he begins to remember this pain and realize how the loss has affected his life. When his police assignment invites him not only to have contact with another mother and son but to guard and protect them from the sadistic drug-dealing Crisp (the quintessential domestic Reagan enemy: a drug-dealer who is *also* an abusive father), Kimball's emotions are given full play, and he learns that he does not want to lose yet another opportunity to have a family. Consequently, when all the bad guys are caught and Kimball's battle wounds have begun to heal, he returns, not to the police station to tag yet another criminal, but to his newfound family and the life of a full-time father, both as parent and as kindergarten teacher. The message? The emo-

Instead of arresting hardened criminals, the new man punches abusive fathers. (Kindergarten Cop, *Universal Studios)*

tionally and physically whole man of the eighties would rather be a father than a warrior.

Kindergarten Cop anticipates the endings of many 1991 films that are resolved through a man's return to his family. When the character played by Billy Crystal in *City Slickers* (Ron Underwood) finds himself on a cattle ranch and discovers the meaning of life, the "one thing" he learns is that he must return to his family, accompanied by his own "child," a calf that he birthed on the trail and subsequently saved from the slaughterhouse. Michael Keaton's character in *One Good Cop* (Heywood Gould) is excused for the theft he committed and is welcomed back onto the police force because he took the money in order to provide a house for his family. Steve Brooks gains a pardon for his sexist treatment of women and entrance into heaven when s/he gives birth to a daughter in *Switch*. Even the Terminator "dies" in *Terminator 2* to ensure the survival of its new family, Sarah and John Connor. In these films, families provide both the motivation for and the resolution of changing masculine heroisms.

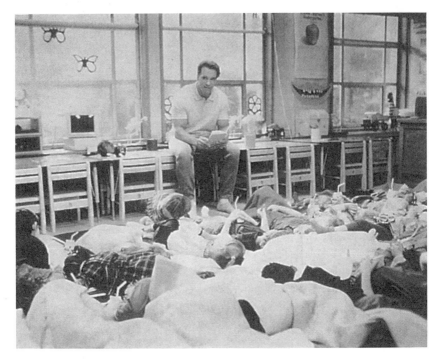

*The hard body is now a kindergarten teacher, reading books rather than Miranda rights. (*Kindergarten Cop, *Universal Studios)*

In addition to laying the outline for the male transformation of the nineties, *Kindergarten Cop* identifies how the issues of manhood are to be addressed and defined in the next decade. One of the clearest messages to come out of *Kindergarten Cop* is that the tough, hard-driving, violent, and individualistic man of the eighties was not that way by choice. Kimball was, like the police officer of *One Good Cop*, the radio call-in show host of *The Fisher King* (Terry Gilliam), the lawyer of *Regarding Henry* (Mike Nichols), or even the Terminator, trying to do his job, and doing it the way the job had been defined by a social-climbing, crime-conscious, techno-consumer society. The problem all these men confront in their narratives is that they did their jobs too well, at the expense of their relationships with their families. Spending so much time tracking criminals and making money left little time for having, let alone raising, children or meeting, let alone relating to, women. And, as *Kindergarten Cop* makes so clear, while these men were doing their jobs, they were unhappy, lonely, and often in pain.

Retroactively, the men of the 1980s are being given feelings, feelings

The hard body can be happy as a new family man. (Kindergarten Cop, *Universal Studios*)

that were, presumably, hidden behind their confrontational violence. And whereas 1980s action-adventure films gloried in spectacular scenes of destruction, 1991 films began telling audiences that these men were actually being self-destructive. (The extent to which audiences responded to this message can be seen in the difference between many female viewers' reactions to Mel Gibson's character in *Lethal Weapon.* In 1988, they spoke of his sex appeal; in 1992, they were touched by his expressions of pain at his wife's death.) At the cost of their personal and family lives, hard-body heroes were rescuing armies, corporations, and ancient artifacts. Now, they're out to save themselves.

But didn't they bring all this loneliness and suffering on themselves? Were *they* not the ones who picked up the guns and went for the high-powered jobs? Were *they* not the ones who spent time at the office (or firing range) instead of at home? According to these films, not exactly. To return to the *Rambo* films, at the beginning of each narrative, Rambo is minding his own business when someone else—either government or local law enforcement—forces him to engage in his heroic acts. In *Rambo III* he even refuses, until the Soviets make the issue, as they say in *Lethal Weapon 2* (1989, Richard Donner), "personal," situations in which the heroes cannot turn their backs on their friends and family. So even the narratives that these nineties films are challenging had already carved out a space for their heroes that allowed them always to be reacting to some outside force rather than acting from their own internal needs for violence or action. (Reagan was always "defending" the United States against Soviet agression.) In each case, it was their jobs, their nations, or their friends who made it necessary to enter into these violent confrontations. It was not, these films conclude, the wishes of the men themselves.

But these films go even further than this, suggesting that it wasn't just the jobs or social obligations that brought these men to betray their own feelings and families. It was, in an odd way, their very bodies themselves, these heroic exteriors that made it possible for them to do what other people could not. One of the plot features of a number of 1991 films is a discovery by the male lead that this body has failed him in some way, whether through wounds, disease, or programming. The body that he thought was "his," the body he had been taught to value as fulfilling some version of a masculine heroic ideal—suddenly that body became transformed into a separate entity that was betraying the true internal feelings of the man it contained. *Robocop 2* (Irvin Kershner) led the way in 1990 by showing the distress brought about in its hero's life by the conflicts between Robocop's bullet-proof exterior and his memories of his family. The indestructible body that was to make Robocop invincible led not to a machine-like insensitivity but to deep pain and isolation at the loss of love. *Robocop 2* makes clear that behind the tough bodies of these male heroes lies, not cheap insensitivity and lusty brutality, but a caring, troubled, and suffering individual. In 1991, though the Terminator had been reprogrammed to protect John Connor and had been ordered not to hurt humans, it had to destroy itself, not because it was afraid that its "feelings" for humanity would change, but because a piece of its body—a computer chip—could be used to rebuild Skynet and destroy all human life. And though the Disney Beast wanted love and companionship, its horrific body and mystical curse doomed it to live alone and unloved until someone could see past that body to the "true" man inside. But what 1991 films provide that *Robocop 2* did not is a happy ending, where the betrayed body is transformed, either back to its "original" loving owner, or into a body that is now in tune with the internal goodness that the film's narrative has revealed.

Transformations are certainly nothing new in Hollywood cinema. From vampire movies to alien takeovers, movies have been populated by people whose bodies have ceased to be their own and whose minds are being controlled by external forces. In most cases, much of the horror these films produce is that these possessed bodies look no different from the "normal" ones that people inhabited before. From *Invasion of the Body Snatchers* (1956, Don Siegel) to *Alien* (1979, Ridley Scott), much of these films' suspense surrounds the effort to try and tell whether and when someone had been transformed.

But while women in those earlier horror films were just as subject as men to being taken over by a pod, or infested with an alien creature, these new transformations happen almost exclusively to men.[1] To be even more specific, to heterosexual white men, the men whose profit from traditional masculinities seems most threatened by the changing economic and social marketplace that typifies this period. These "white boy adventures," as Elayne Rapping calls them,[2] suggest that it is largely white men who have suffered from the burdens of traditional masculinities, and white men who have to be given this extra help in learning how to change themselves into "better" people.

And although many 1991 films by black male directors about black men's lives emphasize families and masculinities as well—*Boyz n the Hood* (John Singleton), *Straight Out of Brooklyn* (Matty Rich), *Jungle Fever* (Spike Lee)—the thematics of internalization and bodily betrayal are not present as they are in Hollywood films about white male leads, largely because the action-adventure heroism of the 1980s was never meant to figure black men's bodies in the first place.[3] Whereas, for example, Martin Riggs (Mel Gibson) *is* the "lethal weapon" in the films named for his body, Roger Murtaugh's body (Danny Glover) is never depicted as "lethal" at all. Audiences first see him in a bathtub, surrounded by his loving family, all of whom tell him he looks old. And Riggs has to insist that Murtaugh shoot, not to maim, but to kill, since the enemies you maim always come back to haunt you. Under Riggs's tutelage in *Lethal Weapon 2*, Murtaugh is able to fire point blank and kill the chief enemy of the film, Argen Rudd (Joss Ackland), a South African diplomat whose immunity, Murtaugh declares, has just been "revoked." The safe, nonlethal, aging image of an African-American police officer who kills only when provoked by true evil is an appealing screen character for white mainstream audiences who can be assured that assimilated black men will enforce rather than challenge the system. Murtaugh does not have to "discover" his feelings for or through a family, since he has an intact family at the beginning of the film. Neither his job nor, more pointedly, his masculinity has taken him away from his family, largely because, such films imply (the *Die Hard* films are another example), he has not been out saving countries, artifacts, or corporations. He has not, in other words, been carrying the white man's burden or, by implication, his masculinity.

There is, consequently, a dangerous racial subtext to all this Hollywood body shifting and internal reform. As has historically been the case in dominant U.S. cultures, masculinity is defined in and through the white male body and against the racially marked male body. Action films of the 1980s reinforce these assumptions in their characterizations of heroism, individualism, and bodily integrity as centered in the white body. And though 1991 films repudiate many of the characteristics of that body—its violence, its isolation, its lack of emotion, and its presence—they do not challenge the whiteness of that body, nor the "special" figuration that body demands. If, these films suggest, there is a body that has been betrayed, victimized, burdened by the society that surrounds it, it is not the body of color, the body that has been historically marked by the continuous betrayals of a social, political, and cultural system that has marginalized and abused it. It is, instead, the body of the white man who is suffering because he has been unloved.

No one, certainly, seems to have been less loved than the hero of the Walt Disney Corporation's 1991 success, *Beauty and the Beast*, bringing to the screen an updated version of Marie de Beaumont's eighteenth-century tale. Whereas animated film versions of classic fairytales have been a Disney staple for decades (*Snow White* [1937] and *Cinderella* [1949], for example), the Disney corporation has also had success in recent years with animated features that develop new characters, such as *Rescuers from Down Under* (1990). But in a time when children's animated features are one of the sure markets of the film and, more pointed, the home video industry, why would Disney return to a 250-year-old fairy tale? Because that tale helps to forward the image of unloved and unhappy white men who need kindness and affection, rather than criticism and reform, in order to become their "true" selves again.

In this context, it's worth looking at the changes Disney made to the original "Beauty and the Beast" story. Briefly, in its earlier versions, the beautiful daughter of a merchant is asked to take her father's place as the prisoner of a horrible beast as punishment for the father plucking a rose from the beast's garden. Her every whim satisfied at the beast's enchanted castle, Beauty is soon more impressed by the beast's generosity, kindness, and intelligence than by his animalistic appearance, though she continues to refuse his nightly request to marry him. When Beauty discovers that her father is ill, the beast allows her to return home under the provision that she will return voluntarily in a specified time. When Beauty fails to return, she learns of the Beast's suffering through a dream (or enchanted mirror) and returns to the castle, only to find him (and there's never any question that the beast is male) dying. Beauty declares her love and agrees to marry the beast, only to find that the beast has disappeared and a handsome prince has taken his place. The prince then explains that a wicked fairy cast a spell over him that could be released only when a beautiful woman would love him for himself and agree to marry him (equally, there is never any suggestion in any of the stories that the spell could have been broken by the open-hearted affection and love of a man, Beauty's father, for example). The prince is restored to his wealth and power, and Beauty lives happily ever after.

In the Disney version this plot is changed in several key ways. First, and most important for the subject of masculinity, the curse is altered. In none of the other versions of the story that I read was the curse explained anywhere except at the end, when Beauty had already vowed her love for the Beast. In some versions, the Beast is even forbidden to tell of the curse before it is broken. The Disney version does keep the Beast's enchanted state from Beauty, but it doesn't hesitate to tell the audience what's at stake at the very beginning of this picture. As the opening scenes of the film explain, a selfish young Prince refuses shelter to an old beggar woman. An enchantress in disguise, the woman condemns him for his selfishness: "I have seen that there is no love in your heart. . . . That makes you no better than a beast—and so you shall *become* a beast!" And, she goes on to explain, "The only way to break [the spell] is to love another person and earn that person's love in return."[4] To heighten the tension of the narrative, she adds that he must do so before his twenty-first birthday, after which time he will remain a beast forever.

The most important consequence of this change is that this movie becomes the story of the Beast, and not of Beauty—or Belle, as she is called in the film—at all. The older tales only introduce the Beast well into the story, when the father has trespassed on the Beast's property, and he is only seen then *as* a Beast, as a horrible and frightening creature and a danger to those around him. The story throughout is Beauty's, telling of her goodness and kindness, her love for and devotion to her father, and her ability to transform through her love even the most miserable of circumstances. In contrast, Belle's equal kindness and love for her father are made secondary to the young Prince's dilemma. Will he learn to love someone before his twenty-first birthday? How can someone love him when all are frightened by the sight of him? Who will break the spell?

Belle is less the focus of the narrative here than she is the mechanism for solving the Beast's "dilemma." And in case the audience doesn't understand this narrative setup from the plot arrangement, some of the most appealing characters in the film offer this information straightforwardly.

These new characters are the next major difference between the traditional and movie versions of the tale. The older versions isolate the Beast in his castle, and all of Beauty's needs are met magically. Disney adds its own trademark to the tale—inanimate objects come to life, the objects that are the direct descendants of *Snow White*'s talking mirror, *Cinderella*'s dazzling pumpkin, and *Fantasia*'s (1940) dancing brooms. In this updated *Beauty and the Beast*, all of the Prince's servants share his plight, having been turned themselves into household objects: clocks, candelabras, teacups, pots, feather dusters, and wardrobes. The audience must be concerned not only about the Beast's impending twenty-first birthday but also about the fate of all of those innocent servants. The Beast may deserve his punishment, but must all these people be condemned to lives of confinement as well? Consequently, when they remark, after first seeing Belle, that "maybe, just maybe, the Beast could make Belle fall in love with him. And if he did the spell would finally be broken," the audience is to share these dreams.[5]

Another important change is in the curse itself. The older versions condemn the Prince to live as a Beast until someone can see past his exterior ugliness to his interior beauty; the Disney curse requires that the Prince also learn to love someone else. In other words, he must change if he wishes to be readmitted to human society. This change in the curse reinforces the plot focus on the Prince and away from Belle, since the audience now anxiously awaits his changes as well as her insights. Will he be able to overcome his beastly temper and terrorizing attitude in order to learn to love?

This focus on the Beast makes possible one of the key emphases of this 1991 *Beauty*, the Beast's helplessness. In the earlier versions, the

Beast commands the enchanted powers of the castle, and uses them to make Beauty comfortable. In one version, for example, the Beast anticipates all of Beauty's wishes, supplying magical trunks laden with gifts for her family, as well as the books and musical instruments that she enjoys. But for the Disney writers, the Beast is as much a prisoner in his castle as is Belle. He has no special powers, and the only services he can provide for her are at the hands—or the teapot spouts—of the equally enchanted and helpless servants who surround him.

Some of the earlier Beasts were good men unfairly cursed by an evil fairy, but it seems that this Beast actually deserves his punishment. But the wording of the opening description of the Prince is important here: "He had grown up with everything he desired, yet his heart remained cold. He was selfish, spoiled, and unkind. Yet because he was the Prince, no one dared say no to him. No one dared try to teach him a lesson."[6] As an anticipated character shift would require, the Prince was not innately selfish but had been made that way through, audiences can only surmise, bad parenting. Those who failed "to teach him a lesson" may be more at fault for his behavior than he is himself. In this scenario, he simply didn't know any better. And although a man might be blamed for being knowingly cruel, can audiences fault one who had "no one" to teach him anything different?

Again, enter Belle to solve the Beast's problem. She becomes that "some one" who can and will save him from the curse, for she will teach him all he needs to know in order to return to—or perhaps enter for the first time—humanity. For another of the key differences between the earlier versions and the Disney tale is that Belle is consistently cast as the Beast's teacher, positioning him again as powerless, as awaiting her decisions to accept and love him: "He didn't know how to eat with a fork and knife, so she taught him. He didn't know how to read, so she read to him. She taught him how to feed birds and how to play in the snow."[7] One of the key romantic scenes of the earlier tales is when the Beast finally feels comfortable enough with Beauty to ask her to dance. She is impressed with his grace as a dancer and begins to forget about his beastliness and think of him as human: "Firmly, lightly, the creature danced with her, gently guiding her across the balcony. Beauty was astonished at the skill of his movement, the strength of his grasp and tenderness of his touch. She closed her eyes and released herself. Her heart pounded, and she was filled with an inexpressible happiness."[8] But in the Disney *Beauty*, the Beast takes Belle in his arms and "whirled her into a dance position.

He lifted his huge, hairy foot and took the first step—and practically mashed her toes." Belle's reaction to the "clumsy" Beast typifies the shifts in their relationship in this story: "She gave him a warm smile and did what she had been doing for the last few days—she taught him."[9]

Why does this matter? Because in contrast to the commanding, sophisticated, and intelligent Beasts that frequent the other tales and that finally make them so deserving of Beauty's love, this Beast seems childish, blustering, "clumsy," petulant, and untutored. As with his upbringing and his initial acquisition of his selfish personality, the Beast does not have to take responsibility for his behavior. It is the work of other people, especially women, to turn this childish Beast into a loving man. This message is clear: if the Beast has not changed before, it is not his fault, but that of those around him who failed to show him otherwise.

The less-than-attractive character of the Beast explains one of the other Disney changes to the tale—the addition of the arrogant and beautiful Gaston, Belle's suitor. Beauty's beauty and goodness had made her the object of other men's affections in the earlier tales, but none played as prominent a role in the plot development as Gaston. From the second scene, where he declares that Belle "is the lucky girl I'm going to marry,"[10] to the climactic scene where he stabs the Beast with what seems to be a death blow, Gaston figures throughout the film as an antagonist in the clearest sense of the term. He thwarts all of Belle's desires: he tries to force her to marry him, arranges to have her father locked away in an insane asylum, and rallies the village to kill the Beast. He is, clearly, the external social version of the Prince's flaw. At large in the world, Gaston seeks to gratify only his own interests and epitomizes the quality of selfishness.

But, unlike the Beast, he is beautiful, as Gaston himself is the first to inform the audience. Belle's credentials as heroine are established early when she is the only one of the town's single women not to swoon over Gaston. With his cleft chin, broad shoulders, brawny chest, wavy hair, and towering height, Gaston fulfills the stereotyped image of male beauty, the hard body that populated the films of the 1980s. And with his pastimes of hunting, drinking, and male-bonding, he fulfills as well a stereotyped image of masculinity. Gaston does not simply look the part of the hyper-masculine male, he holds all the opinions that are supposed to go along with it. Not only does he decide to marry Belle without asking her opinion, he paints this picture of their wedded bliss: "A rustic hunting lodge. My latest kill roasting on the fire. And my little wife massaging my feet while her little ones play on the floor—six or seven of them."[11] He operates through terror and bullying, intimidating those who do not succumb to his good looks. He condemns himself irrevocably when he tells Belle that "it's not right for a girl to read."[12] But while Gaston serves both as comic relief and plot motivator, he functions as well as a contrast to the Beast. Only the purely and self-consciously self-centered Gaston could possibly make the petulant and childish Beast seem appealing. Once Disney replaced the dignified and wordly Beast with a spoiled brat, Belle's choice to love the Beast could only be made reasonable by making the alternative even worse.

The film admires Belle for refusing Gaston. But she is, as the audience's introduction to her reveals, an exception in her town. In fact, in one of the longest production numbers of the film—requiring a cast of voices, elaborate animation, and complex movement—the townspeople call her "strange" and not "normal," principally because she spends all of her time reading. The earlier Beautys were also avid readers, but the Disney film marks Belle's interest as more of a social than a character feature, and uses it to mark her as better and less provincial than the rest of the townspeople.

This is the clue that Disney's *Beauty and the Beast* is not just another "don't judge a book by its cover" morality play typical of Disney productions. For Belle is, for all intents and purposes, a Disney feminist. And Gaston is the kind of male chauvinist pig that would turn the women of any talk-show audience into beasts themselves. And the Beast—where does this new gender scenario leave the Beast?

He is the New Man, the one who can transform himself from the hardened, muscle-bound, domineering man of the eighties into the considerate, loving, and self-sacrificing man of the nineties. His appearance is more than a horrific guise that repels pretty women; it is instead a *burden*, one that he must carry until he is set free, free to be the man he truly can be. The body that is strong (he fights off a dozen snarling wolves), protective (he shelters Belle from their attack), imposing (he frightens Belle's father), domineering (he growls every order he gives), and overpowering (he is even bigger than Gaston)—this body is not, as it was for Rambo, a gift but a curse. It is as if, the Beast's story might suggest, masculinity has been betrayed by its own cultural imagery: what men thought they were supposed to be—strong, protective, powerful, commanding—has somehow backfired and become their own evil curse.

But whose fault is this? Presumably, men bring this curse on themselves by acting so self-centeredly and deriving pleasure from the power it gave them. But those opening descriptions of the Prince put a halt to such an easy interpretation. For men, like the Prince, are only doing what they had been taught. If no one stops them from terrorizing the household, how are they to know that they should act any differently? With the film's emphasis on teaching, it's clear that such ugly and repulsive men are not *really* to be shunned; they're to be nurtured until their "true" goodness arises. For as the ever-reliable servants tell Belle, "The master's really not so bad once you get to know him"[13] (this from the people he probably terrorized during all those selfish years). To reinforce this nurturing theme, the Beast's curse becomes permanent at age twenty-one, implicitly apologizing for all adult men who have remained Beasts, because they simply were not properly educated in time.

And why should the audience care at all about this transformation? Because, like the helpless servants who are also suffering under the enchantress's curse, the audience is to believe that they too are implicated in this burden of hyper-masculinity, captured, like it, in a false and confining objectification that can only be reversed when the Beast is released from his enchantment. In other words, this plot suggests, no one can be free until men are released from the curse of living under the burdens of traditional masculinities.

Kindergarten Cop shows that men can change and that they are really loving and kind beneath those brutal exteriors; *Beauty and the Beast* explains men's aggressive behaviors and suggests that they should not only be forgiven but helped along toward revealing their "true" inner selves. The Disney film, like so many of its 1991 companions, pinpointed the problems in the very place that the earlier successes of men had been located—in the hard bodies that made them heroes. But for the Beast and his friends, those bodies are not resources but burdens, the exterior images that they must overcome in order to be happy. And the weight of this task lies less with the men themselves than with those who must learn to look past the hard body to the loving interior (Robocop is more than a machine; John Kimball is not just a cop; the Terminator is not a killer; and so on) in order to achieve their own real happiness. Without changing direction, only course, these films continue to suggest, as did the films throughout the 1980s, that the happiness and well-being of society as a whole depends on the condition of these men, whether that happiness be defined as national security, social justice, or familial bliss. True to these earlier narratives of masculinity, the quality and the continuity of *everyone's* life finally depends on these white men.

And what a redemption for Reaganism. The Reagan policies of hard-edged anticommunism and "trickle down" economics may have seemed overwrought and misguided in a post–cold war, recession era, but these films offer a way to understand these acts: they were not committed by "bad" men who made the wrong decisions, only good-hearted men who didn't know any better and were simply following the social patterns that "no one" had told them not to pursue. Did Ronald Reagan intentionally break the law when he endorsed the arms sales to Iran? Or was he merely "misunderstanding" his role as president and "forgetting" exactly how those policies had been determined? While some pundits condemned Reagan for breaking the law and others condemned him for being "forgetful," Hollywood suggested that the unintentional crime should be understood and forgiven rather than punished, because if the Beast is to be punished for his callousness, all in the castle will suffer with him. If, by this logic, Reagan is to be impeached for his actions, the country as a whole will suffer, and no one will be released from the curse of past actions.

This more overt form of "forgetting" was mimicked during the 1980s by a pattern of internal amnesia typical of male action film sequences of this period—the *Rambo*, *Lethal Weapon*, and *Die Hard* films come most readily to mind. Where the first film in a given sequence is likely to reveal some emotional depth to its hero— Rambo's post-traumatic stress, Riggs's depression about his wife's death, or John McClane's distress over his wife's career—the second abandons even the momentary internal character developments in favor of the externalized spectacle itself. Eighties action sequels offer more explosions, more killings, and more outright violence. In the most extravagant shift, Rambo expertly kills no one in *First Blood*, forty-four people in *Rambo*, and countless numbers in *Rambo III*.[14] Even the most developed of the emotional subplots, Riggs's suicidal guilt over his wife's death in *Lethal Weapon*, is not only explained but externalized in *Lethal Weapon 2* when he has sex with another woman *and* kills his wife's murderer. *Lethal Weapon 3* (1992, Richard Donner) evaporates this memory altogether by linking Riggs romantically to a woman who is even tougher than he is.

The popularity and financial success of these films suggests that sequentiality itself was one of the mechanisms Hollywood employed to respond to crises in the representation and marketing of cinematic masculinity in this period. The challenge was to reproduce masculinity and the U.S. national identity with which it was linked in a post-Vietnam, post–civil rights, and post–women's movement era. These films attempted to meet that challenge through spectacular repetition, or, to be more specific, through the repetition of the spectacles of the masculine body, a body that, in this case, included the male hero, his weapons, and his environment. This strategy of sequentiality was motivated by more than economics. Indeed, it came to resemble the series of foreign policy decisions that placed the United States in military confrontations in Grenada, the Persian Gulf, Panama, and Iraq, for each of these successive policy decisions depended as much as any film sequel on audience amnesia.[15]

A good way to get at how this repetition works is to examine two of the best-selling serial films of this period, James Cameron's *The Terminator* (1984) and *Terminator 2: Judgment Day* (1991), films whose narratives center on masculinity and repetition, or, to be more concise, on the reproduction of masculinity. These films elaborate the shift from hard body to family man. At the same time, their ostensible themes take on the issue of nuclear armaments that was central to the Reagan era: the first film opens after a nuclear holocaust in which machines have taken over the planet and are methodically eliminating the human race, and the second challenges the inevitability of that future by proposing that nuclear war can be averted.

As with so many male action films of the 1980s, and reflecting Hollywood's altered marketing and production strategy of the same period, repetition is at the heart of both Cameron films. Fundamentally, as discussed in Chapter 3, with an aging president and a term-limited presidency, this was another way to get at a key question of the Reagan era, How to keep the revolution going? Tied as it was to the linked portrayals of masculinity and nationalism, Reaganism depended on the successful reproduction of certain images and definitions of masculinity. It is no accident then that these two films take as their focus how the future can be born and the extent to which men can control it.

In writing about *The Terminator,* Karen Mann and Constance Penley argue for the importance of repetition in the film. Mann suggests that at both a structural and a thematic level, the story of the film depends on repetition as self-reproduction, as the future steps back to rewrite the past. Of the future John Connor, leader of the humans fighting for their very existence in the year 2029, she argues: "He satisfies the fantasy of reaching back in time to control those who control him—his parents— by choosing who they are to be. . . . His choice [of his own father] provides the illusion of self-generation."[16] Penley takes on this same theme of rewriting the past, except that she reads it in psychoanalytic terms: "The fantasy of time travel is no more nor less than the compulsion to repeat that manifests itself in the primal scene fantasy."[17] Again, the rewriting of reproduction by the male child fulfills the primal-scene fantasy by being present at the moment of one's conception. In either case, both Mann and Penley recognize the importance of repetition as reproduction in these films, where the future son reaches back to the past, in effect, by choosing his own father (it is John Connor who decides that Kyle Reese—his father—should return to the past to "protect" his mother, and, coincidentally, to father himself, thereby alleviating the problem that Marty McFly faced in *Back to the Future* of having to retrain and improve a father that he wouldn't originally have chosen).

Much of the plot of *The Terminator* revolves around this form of repetition as self-reproduction. *Terminator 2* takes this repetition self-consciously, by reworking the plot, themes, and spectacles of its predecessor. Clearly, there is a certain logic in making a sequel as much like a successful predecessor as possible, if only to replicate its audience appeal and box office receipts. But in *Terminator 2* Cameron does more than merely repeat *The Terminator;* he self-consciously reworks elements of the first plot into the second, not simply to answer the questions raised by the earlier film (by finally showing us John Connor's face, for example, or how Sarah Connor (Linda Hamilton) learned the military skills that her son was later to put to such good use against the machines), but inverting them, so that nothing is repeated *exactly*. Everything is altered, if only slightly (even Schwarzenegger's chest is smaller), in a way that hints at how repetition, reproduction, and self-production are working in the shift from the masculinity of the 1980s to the early 1990s, how, in other words, masculinity is reproducing itself in this period through inversion rather than duplication.

Terminator 2's early trailers and commercials clued audiences in to the most obvious alteration, the shift in the character of the Terminator: "Once he was programmed to destroy the future. Now his mission is to save it." The very act for which this machine got its name in the first film—the relentless hunting and killing of human targets—is the key to its changed personality in the second. In *Terminator 2*, the killing task is left to the newer and sleeker Terminator, the liquid-metal T1000. The original Terminator, now reprogrammed by the future adult John Connor to protect his eleven-year-old self, is instructed not to kill humans any more. (Though the plot suggests that

From hard body to family man. (Terminator 2, *Tri-Star Pictures*)

it is young Connor (Edward Furlong) who gives the Terminator this instruction, from the time of its return to the present, the Terminator has already distinguished itself from its earlier counterpart by only injuring and not killing the people it meets; it's as if not hurting people was somehow now its "nature.") No longer the source of human annihilation, the Terminator is now the *single* guarantor of human

continuation. If, in the first film, the Terminator had killed Sarah Connor, John Connor would not have been born, there would have been no human rebellion against the machines, and the machines would have been able to exterminate all human life without opposition. In the second film, the Terminator is the only one capable of protecting the young Connor from the more efficient and sophisticated T1000. And here is the biggest reworking that comes from this shift: freed from its mission of destroying humanity, the Terminator can now become not simply the protector of human life but its generator. By "giving" John Connor his life, the Terminator takes, in effect, Sarah Connor's place as his mother. In one of the film's most astounding inversions, the Terminator can now be said to have given birth to the future of the human race.

But if the Terminator is now responsible for the future, what has happened to Sarah Connor, the woman who terminated the Terminator in the first film, and whose future included bearing the son who would save the human race? Like the Terminator, Sarah Connor's character is repeated and inverted in the second film. In the first she was uncertain, frightened, and weak; in her rebirth she is tough-minded, fearless, and strong (the first shot is of Sarah Connor doing chin-ups in her room at the mental hospital). This "new" Sarah Connor looks like the mercenary she has trained to be through all the intervening years. She wears fatigues, totes heavy weapons, and has a mission to perform. As final proof of her new hard character, she even forgets to love her son, chewing him out for rescuing her from the hospital: "You can't risk yourself, even for me! You're too important. . . . I didn't need your help. I can take care of myself." It is as if she is not a mother at all but only a soldier for the future.

Sarah Connor does remember that she is a mother, once. When she tries to kill Miles Dyson (Joe Morton)—the man responsible for developing Skynet, the computer system that will take on the task of eliminating humans—thinking thereby to change the future, she fails. Cracking off the first few rounds of her high-powered rifle, it seems that she has taken the Terminator's place and is doing what it can no longer do—kill human beings. But when she comes face to face with Dyson lying on the floor with his wife and son crying over him, she begins to cry. Then, when John Connor arrives, she finally tells him that she loves him, as if her admission of failure at being a tough combatant releases her to have the feelings of a mother.

In *The Terminator*, Sarah Connor was told that she would be, in effect, the mother of the future. That would seem, in the logic of this

*Sarah Connor's "tough love." (*Terminator 2, *Tri-Star Pictures)*

film, to be a pretty important job, since it's Sarah Connor who teaches her son all of the skills he will use to save humanity. Yet in the second film Sarah is effectively locked out of having any real role in the future. First, John tells the Terminator that he learned about weapons, machines, and fighting from the mercenaries his mother took him to meet, not directly from her. And second, for some years, she was not present for him as a mother at all but locked away in a mental ward where she was not allowed to see him. He was left with foster parents who taught him that everything his mother said about the future was a product of her deranged and obsessed mind. Third, as an audience, we are witness to how Sarah ignores her son for most of the film. The excuse, that she is concentrating on keeping him alive, puts her in direct competition for the Terminator's role, a job—and a body—that she just cannot fit. And while she is focusing on being a super-soldier, the Terminator is working on being a better mom, listening to and playing with the son that Sarah hardly notices for all the weapons she is carrying. Sarah Connor even acknowledges that the Terminator is doing a better job than she could and consciously decides to leave her son in its care when she goes on what promises to be a suicide mission to kill Dyson. While John is teaching the Terminator how to give high-fives, the camera pulls back to Sarah's point-of-view shot, and her voiceover reasons:

> Watching John with a machine. It was suddenly so clear. The Terminator would never stop. It would never hurt him. It would never leave him or get impatient with him. . . . It would die to protect him. Of all the would-be fathers who came and went over the years, this machine, this thing, was the only one who measured up. And in an insane world, it was the sanest choice.

Though Sarah refers to the Terminator as John's father here, it is apparent that, with her disappearance, it would be his sole parent, since, in the odd logic of this film, John's father was both killed in the past and has not been born yet. And though Sarah calls it a father, the Terminator clearly does not do things that the mercenary father-figures did. This father does not teach John about weaponry or survival skills, and does not freak out, like the others did, about John's role in the future. And unlike Sarah, it will always stay with him. The Terminator is thus not only a father but a mother as well to John Connor—to the hope of a human future. What had been its most frightening feature in the first film—Reese tells Sarah, "It will *never*

The Terminator as a better mom. (Terminator 2, *Tri-Star Pictures*)

stop!"—is now in Sarah's words its most admirable feature: it will never stop caring for John.

From the second film's outset then, Sarah Connor has been gently replaced as the mother and protector of the human future. Though she, better than any human, understands the consequences that await unchanged human actions, and would seem as a result to be an important source of knowledge, and her survival skills and patience are admirable, she is not presented as cool and clear-thinking. Instead, as Linda Hamilton chooses to play the part, Sarah Connor is more an animal than a human, or, better yet, a human whose animal instincts have been brought out in the face of death. As one film reviewer puts it: "She is an animal. She bares her teeth. She snarls. . . . She has an animal voice. Like an animal, she does anything to protect her young. That is her strongest emotion."[18] So not only does Sarah not have the machine body or efficiency to compete with the Terminator as a protector for her son, her emotions as a mother are primitive, stemming more from her animal instincts than from any loving relationship between two people. When she is shown as a mother, it is of the most brutish and unreflective kind.

Her final delegitimization is accomplished by none other than John Connor himself, showing how he has been able to surpass his mother's animal tendencies to remain human, even in the face of the future he knows he will confront. Most important, the scene in which he does this follows all of the other deteriorations of Sarah's role as mother— her brusque treatment of her son, her mental instability, her emotional breakdowns, her abandoning of her son to the care of a machine—and marks the final separation of Sarah and John, or, more precisely, the termination of his dependance on her and the beginning of the new alliance with the Terminator. After she has failed to kill Dyson, the Terminator sits down to tell Dyson the history of the future and the role he will play in it. When Dyson responds, "How were we supposed to know?" animal Sarah attacks: "Fucking men like you built the hydrogen bomb! Men like you thought it up. You think you're so creative. You don't know what it is to create a life, to feel something growing inside you." But just when her feminist critique of masculine birth compensation gets rolling, John Connor calmly interrupts: "Mom. We need to be a little more constructive here." Seated beside the Terminator, already taking command, John's retort relegates Sarah to the background. He and the Terminator programmed by his future self are in control.

To "flesh out," as it were, the Terminator's transformation from killer to protector, from stranger to parent, the audience is shown how it has changed. It shoots for the legs, à la Rambo of *First Blood*. It asks questions. It uses slang. It plays with children.[19] Perhaps most important, it learns. As it tells John Connor, "The more contact I have with humans, the more I learn." This learning is, in fact, one of the key thematic foundations of the film, since it is the Terminator's ability to learn that leads it to sacrifice itself for the survival of humanity: since humans once learned from its predecessor's computer chips how to produce the machines that would destroy the world, it must self-destruct, even though it is now a good Terminator, to prevent people from repeating that past mistake.

The Terminator offers the ostensible explanation for why men of the 1980s are changing their behavior: they learned that the old ways of violence, rationality, single-mindedness, and goal-orientation (there is no one more goal-oriented than the first Terminator; as Reese says to Sarah Connor, "He'll never stop. Not until he kills you!") were destructive, not only for individual men but for humanity as a whole. And the solution to this dilemma? According to this film, for the hard-bodied man to learn from his past (future?) mistakes to produce a change in character, a "new," more internalized man, who thinks with his heart rather than with his head—or computer chips.

But to show that "learning" is a universal characteristic of the "new" masculinity, the Terminator is not the only male in *Terminator 2* to change his behavior. Miles Dyson is the African-American scientist who constructs Skynet, the computerized military defense network that ultimately sets off the nuclear devastation that almost ends human existence. When Sarah Connor, the Terminator, and John Connor tell Dyson about how his current research will lead to a nuclear apocalypse, he volunteers to help them destroy all of his files, finally sacrificing his own life to set off the bomb that will explode the research institute he heads. (True to the new masculine ideal of non-killing, Dyson warns the police officers who have come to stop the break-in that they should leave before he sets off the bomb.) And like the Terminator, Dyson leaves behind him not only a woman and her son but the future of the entire human race. The message here is clear: in this narrative, masculinity transcends racial difference, suggesting that the forces of change—from killing to non-killing, from silence to speech, from indifference to love, from external display to internal exploration, from absent to active fatherhood—not only cross racial boundaries but draw men together. What more unlikely alliance than a white-skinned killing machine from the future and a dark-skinned benevolent scientist from the present? And yet, these "men" work together to preserve human futures; together, they give human life to the world. Yet, in keeping with the racial imbalances that mark Hollywood films of this period, the Terminator leads the way in this crusade, with the black scientist learning from it and following its lead.

The single feature that solidifies the alliance of Dyson and the Terminator is not simply that they both believe in the Terminator's future, or that they both understand the potential destructive power of Skynet, but that they are both "fathers" to young male children and, by narrative implication, to the future. The scenes immediately prior to Sarah Connor's attack on Dyson is the one in which she effectively turns her son over to the Terminator father. Dyson also has a son; in fact, he is the first member of the family we see besides Dyson, as the son's robot-controlled car drives into his father's computerized study. It is also the son who saves his father's life. While the wife cowers in terror at Sarah Connor's rifled commands ("Stay on the floor, bitch!"), the son cries over his father's body. It is this act which stops Sarah short and prevents her from terminating Dyson, as if Sarah knows that killing *any* son imperils the future. The alignment of Dyson and the Terminator is effected through the close proximity in which both men are shown as fathers. Their comparison is not, as it was between the African-American police chief and the Terminator in the first film, one of human vs. machine, or protector vs. killer, or even black vs. white, but instead one of self-sacrificing fathers who want to preserve a human future for their sons against the inhuman systems (mechanized or flesh) that are bent on carrying out a plan that will destroy all human life. Where humanity was the common denominator that erased racial difference in the first film, now fatherhood erases the difference between all "new" men, whether machine or human.

The introduction of Dyson serves to show not only that the new masculinity transcends racial and class difference but also that the vehicle for that transformation is fathering, the link for men to "discover" their "new" internalized selves. Throughout the late 1980s, fathering was a key characterization and narrative device for displaying the "new" Hollywood masculinities. In films such as *Three Men and a Baby* (1987, Leonard Nimoy), *Look Who's Talking* (1989, Amy Heckerling), *One Good Cop, Regarding Henry, Boyz n the Hood,* and others, fathering became the vehicle for portraying masculine emotions, ethics, and commitments, and for redirecting masculine characterizations from spectacular achievement to domestic triumph. But *Terminator 2* shows that this characterization is more than a simple warming of the individual male heart and an improvement of father-child relations, that it is instead a wholescale social patterning, in which these men not only replace the women whose work has interfered with their ability to mother their children (an indictment that links otherwise diverse films like *Terminator 2* and *Boyz n the Hood*) but father an entire human future. Mothers lay claim to giving biological birth to children, but these fathers ensure that there will be a world for these children to live in. And they accomplish this not with bombs and bombast but with love and protection.

In looking at discourse about nuclear warfare, Gillian Brown focuses on the emphasis on sequentiality in discussions of nuclear warfare and nuclear disarmament, suggesting that this interest in sequence is an indication of the preoccupation of both factions with continuity, futures, and reproduction, or what she phrases "the ideology of sequential self-extension": "When the antinuclear chain letter enjoins us to take a stake in futurity, or when the nursery rhyme reconstructs our self-extension in the world, they epitomize our familiarity with and reliance on a notion of projection in which we ourselves *are* our (possible) futures."[20] As she astutely goes on to say, this ideology of self-extension depends on a certain notion of individualism in which the individual not only owns the narrative and therefore the sequence that it articulates, but through that narrative, owns the self as well:

> Antinuclear thematics of affiliation and associationism share with pronuclear survivalism this desire for sequence and the narrative of possessive individualism it reprises. Thinking about the nuclear, then, is itself a sequence in the history of liberal humanism, a sequence that foregrounds the dynamic of disappearance and reappearance in the logic of self-proprietorship.[21]

The particular thinking about the nuclear that is narrated in *The Terminator* and *Terminator 2: Judgment Day* is equally based on a narrative of individualism that explains the apparent contradictions between the films' seemingly left-wing antinuclear conclusions and its star's right-wing Republican endorsements. What finally resolves this narrative spectacle of violence, technology, and mechanical genocide is the even greater spectacle of male individualism in the act of self-sacrificing fathers. For what greater and more powerful act of *individual* self-determination can there be than the *rational*, willing, and determined decision to end one's own life, not in the despair of defeat, but in the triumph of birth? of being the generator of the human future?

And this is what makes *Terminator 2* so disarmingly dangerous a narrative. The first film, like most Hollywood films before it, had to separate its male egos into good (Kyle Reese [Michael Biehn] and John Connor) and evil (the Terminator, automated vehicle for the destruction of human life) largely as a result of a pattern of masculinity that defines men by opposition to one another. *Terminator 2* works by a similar pattern, with the old Terminator validating itself by protecting John Connor against the T1000 and showing itself by contrast to be more "human." But this second film plays with so many oppositional reversals that this familiar pattern contains a few interesting realignments.

The most obvious reversal is that of goodness and authority, represented in *Terminator 2* primarily by the police. Whereas the first film showed police officers as well-intentioned but ineffectual—they tried to protect Sarah Connor from the Terminator, but did not believe her or Reese about its power, a failure that cost them their lives—in the second, the police are the greatest threat to both Connors and the Terminator. The T1000 disguises itself as a police officer, thereby not

The Terminator as a self-sacrificing father. (Terminator 2, *Tri-Star Pictures*)

only gaining access to automated police information but also winning the confidence of unwitting citizens such as John Connor's foster parents. But it is also the police who try to stop Sarah, John, Dyson, and the Terminator from destroying the Cyberdyne research lab where the computer chips and records about the first Terminator are being studied. Whereas in the first film the police are shown protecting people, in the second, they are shown protecting only property, principally the property of the very corporation that will send the human race down a path to destruction. And where the Terminator does not kill in the second film, the police do; they are responsible for the death of Dyson and are clearly trying to kill both Connors.

It is important to look not only at what reversals take place in the depictions of the police but also at what shifts these reversals imply about the oppositional definitions of masculinity in each film. In *The Terminator*, Kyle Reese was clearly defined against the Terminator: he was human, it was a machine; he wanted to protect Sarah, it wanted to kill her; he wanted to save the human future, it wanted to prevent it; he made love to her, it hurt her; he gave her a son, it gave her a nightmare. But Reese was also opposed to the police. They too wanted to protect Sarah, but they could not. And against everything Sarah Connor and, by then, the audience, knew, the police did not believe Reese's story about the future. In that film, the police functioned to show that it was not enough to be human; people had to be resourceful, have access to important information (what the future held; how to make pipe bombs; how to detect Terminators), and, most important, be able to act (the thematic anchor of masculinity in the 1980s). While the police stood around firing handguns at the Terminator (even the audience knew by this time that this was a laughable excuse for action), Reese helped Sarah escape. What *The Terminator* told its audiences was that if you wanted to be able to *father the future*—for this is literally what Reese did—you had to be more than good-hearted and human; you had to be strong, decisive, and powerful (through knowledge)—to not only *want* to protect the mother of the future but also be able to do it.

In the second film, the police serve again to show that being human is not enough. But here, they are opposed, not to an even more protective human (the cameras keep panning across the mottos written on the L.A. police cars: "To Serve and Protect"), but to a more human protector. The Terminator is opposed to the T1000 for purposes of the thematic battle of good and evil—the survival or destruction of humanity—but it is more effectively opposed to the police officers in terms of its character: the police despise John Connor (he is a delinquent), it cares for him; they kill Dyson, it treats his wounds after Sarah first shot him; they hide behind faceless machines, it is a machine with a face. But most important, in this second film, the Terminator protects humans (John Connor, and, through him, all humanity), but the police protect machines. They assemble their greatest force to protect a building housing the most sophisticated computer technology in the world. In contrast, the Terminator's most forceful act was to save Sarah and John Connor from the T1000.

These reversals of authority and oppositional presentations of police power are less a critique of institutional oppressions (the police mean well but are misinformed) and more an effort to distinguish individual actions from institutional action. By presenting the police as inefficient but well-meaning in *The Terminator* and ineffective and misguided in *Terminator 2*, individual men—Reese and the Terminator—are made to seem not only effective but *necessary*, both to the protection of women and children and to the survival of humanity. In the face of a society that is perceived as increasingly technologized, mechanized, routinized, and anonymous, the power of individual decisiveness and individual action is drawn as paramount in these films. Male viewers— particularly white male viewers—who may feel increasingly distanced from what they understand to be traditional male forms of power and privilege can be empowered through the assertions of the role male individualism must play in the future of humanity. *Terminator 2* can offer to these viewers not only a panacea for their feelings of disempowerment, but it can reinforce the culturally designated culprits of that scenario in the guise of technology, machines, active women, and men of color in managerial positions.

The film accomplishes this through one of the simplest and most reassuring frameworks available to many male viewers: individualism as fathering. In a slick rewriting of the traditionally gender-marked division between public and private, the *Terminator* films offer male viewers an alternative to the declining workplace and national structure as sources of masculine authority and power—the world of the family. It is here, this logic suggests, that men can regain a sense of masculine power without having to confront or suggest alterations in the economic and social system that has led to their feelings of deprivation. Throughout the 1980s, the Yankelovich Monitor of U.S. social attitudes recorded that men's primary definitions of masculinity rested in their sense of a man being "a good provider for his family."[22] The *Terminator* films capitalize on this sensibility—one that is becoming economically and socially obsolete—by implying a relationship not between men and their partners but between masculinity and future generations, an abstract and inverted repetition of both the public and private realms within which many American males are sensing a deterioration of their ability to define their identities or their privileges. And *Terminator 2* accomplishes this goal by portraying a father's relationship with his son.

In the previous chapter I argued that an alliance with the law was key to regenerating masculine power in the social justice films of the late 1980s; these fathering films return to the kinds of critiques of authority and police power that were more typical of films of the early 1980s. This is largely because the weight of the Reagan ideology, despite its support of corporate development, was on releasing the individual from federal control. Consequently, although invoking the law may have temporarily satisfied a desire for a more stable social order, the Reagan philosophy could ground that social order not on increased authority or institutional power but on the enhanced power of the individual to determine his own future, in other words, by being able to "father" that future with individual authority and determination.

In *Cassandra*, another narrative of nuclear apocalypse, (then East) German novelist Christa Wolf speaks about the same kind of "male rationalism" that Sarah Connor seemed to be criticizing in her attack on Dyson, saying,

> This in turn raises the question of what today could possibly still represent "progress" . . . , now that the masculine way has almost run its course—that is, the way of carrying all inventions, circumstances, and conflicts to extremes until they have reached their maximum negative point: the point at which no alternatives are left.[23]

It is as if Cameron had read *Cassandra*. The characters of *Terminator 2* seem to have "learned" the lesson Wolf was trying to impart about the inevitability of warfare within the framework of a "rational" way of thinking. Both the Terminator and Dyson seem to have understood that their forms of "progress"—computerized technologies, advanced weaponries, enhanced defense strategies, and increasingly efficient assessments of "life"—will lead nowhere, at least, to a human nowhere, in which the destruction of all life is the logical end product of their thinking. Wolf even anticipates the characters of these "new" men when her protagonist, Cassandra, tells a Greek chariot driver that "in the future there may be people who know how to turn their victory into life."[24]

This of course seems to be the most astonishing lesson that men of the Terminator's future have learned by looking at their own futures: that the continuation of their success and the accomplishment of their goals will lead only and inevitably to destruction. *Terminator 2* seems to have rightly earned its label as an "antinuclear" film,[25] one that short-circuits the nuclear nightmare by "learning" about the limitations of male mechanization. In this way, *Terminator 2* seems more than a direct response to characters like Rambo or Robocop, whose hard bodies imitated or integrated indestructible machines that led to the downfall of evil. Those 1980s machine-men get tossed into the steel melting pot at the end of *Terminator 2,* along with the T1000 and the self-sacrificing Terminator, leaving behind the young John Connor, bearer of a new and more human future.

But what Wolf didn't anticipate was the agility of U.S. culture to find venues for "alternative" masculinities. Rather than acknowledge a point at which masculinity must recognize its own negation—what seems on the surface to be the conclusion of *Terminator 2*—the film's complex reasonings supply a "new" direction for masculinity, not, as in the 1980s, outward into increasingly extravagant spectacles of violence and power (as Rambo and Ronald Reagan showed, these displays had become self-parody), but inward, into increasingly emotional displays of masculine sensitivities, traumas, and burdens. Rather than be impressed at the size of these men's muscles and the ingenuity of their violence, audiences are to admire their emotional commitment and the ingenuity of their sacrifices, sacrifices that are being made, *Terminator 2* reminds its viewers, for the sake of the future.

Terminator 2 also shows why this link between masculinity and the future is so problematic. Donald Greiner, in his discussion of the traditions of masculine representation in the American novel, identifies the two main "enemies" of men in these novels—space and time: "Time is always the enemy of spaciousness for the bonded male in the American novel because, if possible immortality is associated with space, certain mortality is equated with time. . . . If men are to fulfill the destiny of America . . . then they must avoid the reality of time for the illusion of space."[26] What *Terminator 2* offers is another way to resolve these anxieties about the ends of masculinity/territory through the manipulation of space and time via the male body. As John Connor not only chooses his own biological father in Kyle Reese (fathers himself, as it were) but also programs his mechanical father into the "kinder and gentler" Terminator, he seems to have conquered the restrictions of time, not by expanding into external territories (the solutions of Natty Bumppo, Huck Finn, or Theodore Roosevelt), but by territorializing the interior of the male body.

It is thus John Connor and not Sarah Connor or the Terminator who holds the real power of these films and marks himself as the hero of Hollywood sequels, for it is he who survives the destruction of the "old" masculinity, witnessing teary-eyed the Terminator's destruction. As he stands above the melting Terminators, audiences are to recognize in John Connor not only the father of his own and the human future but the new masculinity as well.

But in a remarkable inversion, the film manages not only to reveal the "new" masculinity/father but to excuse the "old" one as well. For though the Terminator must sacrifice itself in order to prevent a destructive future, the film's plot makes it clear that, like the Prince/ Beast, *it is not his fault.* Because the mechanized body from the movie's past has been shown, largely through the oppositional framework of the script, to be a "good Terminator," its elimination is tragic. The Terminator had to sacrifice itself not because it was "bad" or harmful or even useless but because others around it misused its components. Comparably, audiences can conclude that the aggressive and destructive 1980s male body that became the target for both ridicule and hatred may not have been *inherently* "bad" but only, in some sociologically pitiful way, misunderstood, just like the Reagan policy of SDI and increased military armaments. And who *does* understand this obsolete but lovable creature? None other than John Connor, the "new" man himself.

So, *Terminator 2* may present John Connor as the savior of the human race, but John Connor is finally saving something else, something far more immediate than a mechanized future and something far more dangerous than a mechanized killing machine. He is saving masculinity for itself, not only embodying the "new" future of masculinity but rescuing its past for revival.

Why did Arnold Schwarzenegger—gallant Republican, Bush-booster, head of the President's Council on Fitness and Sports, celebrator of the American way—take part in a film that seems to criticize the very militarist and rationalist policies that typify the administration he supports? Does his joke that he is playing a "kinder, gentler Terminator"[27]

The hard-bodied Schwarzenegger. / *The kinder, gentler Arnold. (*Terminator 2, *Tri-Star Pictures, and* Kindergarten Cop, *Universal Studios)*

explain enough? Certainly, the changes in Schwarzenegger's own image would demand some changes in the Terminator's character. As film critic Caryn James puts it:

> In the intervening years [between the two movies], Mr. Schwarzenegger transformed himself from a Hollywood joke to a likable superstar. . . . The bad old Terminator reflected the heady Reagan 80's; the good new one is a perfect Bush-era Terminator, a machine as sensitive war hero. . . . Could the chairman of the President's Council on Physical Fitness and Sports go around killing innocent people on screen? The softer Schwarzenegger image seemed to demand a softer Terminator.[28]

But while the pressures not to mar Schwarzenegger's new image with a return to the unflinching violence of the first Terminator might explain some of the alterations in the Terminator's role (though we still need to explain the alterations in Schwarzenegger's), they do not adequately explain how Schwarzenegger's politics—and Schwarzenegger's participation in the creation of this second film is clear—fit with those of the film. What shifts have occurred that make it possible for a Reagan-now-Bush Republican to take on the character of a gentle, protecting, humorous, emotional, antinuclear human machine?

First and most obvious, this *is* the political line the Bush administration was trying to take, and *Terminator 2* sold it across the country: that, against the rough-rider image of its predecessor (Reagan and *The Terminator*), the Bush government was a "kinder, gentler" place, where men were pledged to their families, were reluctant to kill, and were confident, firm, and decisive; where, the line goes, they were dedicated to the preservation of the future and not the destruction of the present. In the Bush era, the termination of the T1000 seems a perfect emblem for signaling a rejection of the Reagan image. What better symbol, after all, for the man to whom the only thing that seems to have stuck is his label as the "teflon president" than a liquid metal machine that changes shape at will, reconstructs its body after any attack, and looks like the clean-cut boy next door? And audiences are to reject this model for the "clunker," the older model Terminator that's been around the block and knows the battle scene (among the least of his credentials, Bush was director of the CIA and vice-president of the United States), but has been "reprogrammed" to be more "human" than its opponent, and to learn from its mistakes.

But the Terminator does sacrifice itself for the good of humanity, and I have not heard any reports that George Bush has done the same. How then can this film and Schwarzenegger's Republican boosterism be reconciled?

Let me try to pull all of this together: repetition, mothering, politics, masculinity, individualism, police forces, technology, and control of the future. Let me start by going back to Christa Wolf's conclusion about masculinity: "The masculine way has almost run its course . . . the point at which no alternatives are left." Both the films and the politics of the 1980s suggest that masculinity had done just this, had "almost run its course," primarily in that it was running out of repetitions. More and more spectacular film productions, larger and larger national deficits, increasingly demanding claims about U.S. military power, greater pressures for masculine success and appearance: the irony is of course that, while nothing seemed more easily successful than Rambo or Ronald Reagan, both characters had very little room left to move, having established their spectacular characters in such a way that even they had difficulty improving their performances. People began making fun not only of Rambo and his impervious skin but of Reagan as well and his impenetrable memory. These characters had made themselves so spectacular that they began to verge on comic representations of themselves.

But contrary to Wolf's conclusion that "no alternatives are left," the first years of the 1990s have offered both masculinity and the Bush administration an alternative: not to exceed their predecessors but to invert them, to show that the qualities of spectacle and violence are no longer sufficient for determining character, and that action takes more than ability—it takes heart. The "new" men of the 1990s have pulled the rug out from under Wolf's logic by shifting ground away from the externalities through which that logic had been defined in the 1980s to the "new" internal qualities of the more "human" man.

But, as these two films show, this is not a simple negation but rather a rewriting, a repetition, a retelling of the story of masculinity. Though the Terminator may have a different character in *Terminator 2*, it's still built on the same machine chassis. And though that rewriting seems on its surface to be a rejection of so many of the spectacular identifications of masculinity of the 1980s—technology, violence, power, command, strength—its mainframe is still very similar: the reproduction of masculine authority (now freed from civil authority) through the affirmation of individualism. For what finally saves humanity is not the power of the Terminator or the mothering of Sarah Connor but the individual will of the Terminator, and Miles Dyson before him, to sacrifice themselves to ensure that human life go on. What *The Terminator* showed was that, for masculinity to survive Reese's death and the Terminator's destruction, *humans* had to survive. Machines were not enough; there had to be flesh as well. In such terms, the act of masculine self-sacrifice turns out then to be, not so much a recognition of the flaws in masculine thinking (this analysis was rejected with John's putdown of Sarah's feminism) but an assurance that individualism would survive as a way of thinking. In the future–John Connor's message to Sarah—"No Fate"—audiences can read the messages of these films: that the future of masculinity has not yet been determined. But, at the same time, these films of 1991 argue, if there is to be a future for humanity at all, it lies in the hearts of white men.

Masculinity and the Reagan Legacy

R obert Bly opens *Iron John* with this observation:

> We are living at an important and fruitful moment now, for it is clear to
> men that the images of adult manhood given by popular culture are
> worn out; a man can no longer depend upon them. By the time a man
> is thirty-five he knows that the images of the right man, the tough
> man, the true man which he received in high school do not work in
> life. Such a man is open to new visions of what a man is or could be.[1]

Richard Nixon views the same period, 1990 and beyond, after the fall
of the Soviet Union, as a crucial test for the United States. With much
of the world having discarded communism, Nixon argues, the United
States remains the only "complete superpower," the only one that still
possesses "global economic, military, and political power."[2] Such a
position, he believes, offers the United States the unique role of
determining the future of the free world:

> Just as the free world turned to America for leadership to confront
> the post–World War II Soviet threat, the world as a whole will look
> to America for leadership to grapple with the post-cold-war prob-
> lems. . . . For the first time in history, there is a real chance to make
> the next century a century of peace, freedom, and progress. Today,
> only one nation can provide the leadership to achieve those goals.

The United States is privileged to be that nation. Our moment of truth has arrived. We must seize the moment.[3]

Arguing on the one hand for the personal fulfillment of men and on the other for the political fulfillment of a nation, Bly and Nixon together mark the 1990s as a period of challenge, a challenge that both see stemming from the deterioration of older models of behavior—whether fifties discipline or cold war anticommunism. Bly and Nixon even use similar rhetoric; Bly exhorts men, Nixon exhorts the nation, to become "complete." Bly charts a mythological and often mystical path that requires getting in touch with the "Wild Man" buried in all men, the part of their personalities that women have shamed them into repressing and that corporate structures have sterilized. Without this resource, according to Bly, men can be kind and nurturing, but they cannot act: "Wild Man energy . . . leads to forceful action undertaken, not with cruelty, but with resolve."[4] It is knowledge of this part of themselves that men, until this time, have lacked: "Making contact with this Wild Man is the step the Eighties male or the Nineties male has yet to take."[5]

Similarly, Nixon believes that the United States faces the challenge of recognizing its leadership role in the world, a role that isolationists and "idealistic internationalists"[6] would shun. Just as fearful men avoid seeing the Wild Man within them, Nixon holds that such idealists would fail to recognize that the United States needs to promote democracies around the world, would fail, in other words, to understand the need for "forceful action" undertaken with "resolve."

What kind of a masculine role will come out of Hollywood to respond to these calls for change and action? As Bly remarked, the "images of adult manhood given by the popular culture are worn out." The films of 1991, in which the male hard body has not only been critiqued but seen as the source of men's personal, emotional, and social problems, would seem to endorse Bly's conclusion that images of Rambo, "lethal weapons," and one-lining, hard-shooting cops are "worn out." Bly certainly is critical of these images and heralds the exploration by men of their "feminine," perhaps more domestic sides, as parents and lovers. And Nixon himself states that attention needs to be paid now to domestic as well as foreign policy issues: "When Moscow's cold war expansionism threatened the survival of the West, foreign policy necessarily became our top priority. But today foreign and domestic problems should receive equal priority."[7] But both agree that an exclusive focus on the domestic or "feminine" sides of the nation/man would be destructive. Both, while openly repudiating the hard body as a single model, are equally disenchanted with the "soft body" that could replace it. Somehow then, these recent images of Arnold Schwarzenegger being hugged by small children or Billy Crystal aiding in the birth of a calf are not quite what either would call for. If Nixon and Bly are in any way identifying sentiments available to the mainstream, then the warm-hearted fathers of 1991 will not be the models of masculinity for the 1990s.

In the concluding chapter of *Seize the Moment,* "The Renewal of America," Richard Nixon cautions that "those who have hailed the beginning of a new order in which peace and freedom are secure speak prematurely."[8] Consequently, in his terms, those who might have hailed the reformed and loving fathers of some of 1991's biggest Hollywood hits have also spoken prematurely. Nixon suggests that the peaceful environments in which such self-examination and familial intimacy can take place may not be as available as audiences are led to believe. Instead, Nixon warns, "The world remains a dangerous and unpredictable place."[9] Are the kind-hearted men of *The Doctor* (1991, Randa Haines), *One Good Cop, Regarding Henry,* and *City Slickers* prepared for such a world?

No. But William Munny is. The protagonist of the Academy Award winner for the best film of 1992,[10] Clint Eastwood's *Unforgiven,* William Munny is both father and gunfighter, able to live in a peaceful world but also able to survive in a "dangerous and unpredictable place." *Unforgiven* may offer the best clues to the kinds of masculine models being set forth for the United States in 1992, both as Hollywood heroes and as models of national identification and foreign policy action.

Like other films of the early 1990s, *Unforgiven* refers to the history of hard bodies that came before it. When a prostitute working in Big Whiskey, Wyoming, in 1881 has her face slashed by a client, her coworkers offer a reward to the assassin who will kill the two men responsible for her scars. The men who respond to the call are not hotheaded youths but former hard bodies, men about whom dime novels were being written, men whose exploits had formed the legends of the West. The only young man among them, the "Schofield Kid" (Jaimz Woolvett), is so nearsighted that he needs these older men to show him whom to shoot, which implies that he is old enough to pull a trigger but too young to determine who should live or die. Whether on the side of the law, like "Little Bill" Daggett (Gene Hackman), sheriff of Big Whiskey, or outside the law, like "English Bob" (Richard

Harris), William Munny, or Ned Logan (Morgan Freeman), the protagonists of this film are the men whose deeds earned them the titles
of the "hard bodies" of their era.

But these men are older now. As Ned tells Will when he first
explains about the reward, "We ain't bad men no more. Shit. We're
farmers." Ned Logan is married, he farms, and his Spencer rifle hangs
on display on his wall. Bill Daggett, now a small-town sheriff, is
building his own house, with a wide porch out front so that he can
watch the sun go down at night. Even English Bob, who still makes a
living by his gun, now works for the railroad, "shooting Chinamen."
But best of all is William Munny, the man whose reputation for being
"as cold as the snow" makes him the most ruthless of all the killers in
the film. After marrying Claudia Feathers, Munny settled down to
tend children and hogs. As the film opens, Claudia has been dead for
three years, and Munny has been left to raise two children and a pen
full of hogs on his own. In one of the least glamorous openings for any
Hollywood star, and one that certainly contrasts markedly with the
muscled close-ups of Rambo, Munny is seen flailing about in a hog
pen, trying to separate sick hogs from well ones. Audiences do not see
Eastwood full face for some time, as the camera tracks his falls in the
mud and his futile attempts to capture filthy hogs; when his face is
finally shown, it is full of mud, and there is nothing heroic about it.
When the Schofield Kid remarks, "You don't look like no rootin'
tootin' son-of-a-bitchin' cold-blooded assassin," the audience knows
he is right. If there were once any hard bodies here, they have long
disappeared.

They seem to have become the "soft men" that Bly identifies, men
who, like William Munny, became what women wanted them to be:
"The strong or life-giving women who graduated from the sixties, so to
speak, . . . played an important part in producing this life-preserving,
but not life-giving, man."[11] As Munny keeps explaining to everyone,
his wife reformed him. In what will become a refrain of the movie,
Munny tells the Schofield Kid, "I ain't like that no more. . . . My
wife—she cured me of that, of my drinkin' and wickedness." Claudia's
importance is underscored when Ned later comments to Munny, "If
Claudia was alive, you wouldn't be doing this," confirming how it was
she and not Munny himself who formed his "soft," nonviolent character and who turned him from his hard-bodied life.

But after the opening panoramic shots of William Munny's peaceful
cabin and Claudia's grave backlit by a spectacular sunset, audiences
are reminded, as Robocop put it, that "somewhere out there a crime is

being committed" no matter how peaceful and remote one's own homestead may appear. In other words, no matter how secure one's own nation may seem in a post–cold war period, the world outside the home, beyond the walls of domestic self-discovery and familial bliss of 1991, remains a "dangerous and unpredictable place." And who, in such a place, will protect the innocent?

Gene Hackman's character, like Special Agent Anderson in *Mississippi Burning*, again aligns himself with the law, now as Sheriff Bill Daggett. But where alliance with the law was the hallmark of a champion of justice in 1988, in *Unforgiven*, Daggett has gone too far and *become* the law in a role that reviewers have not hesitated to describe as "fascist."[12] A former hard body himself, Daggett runs his town with complete authority, being sheriff, judge, and enforcer of punishments. He is what Nixon fears would arise out of the former Soviet Union. In spite of the movements toward democracy in the former Soviet republic and in Russia, Nixon cautions that because of the "Russian imperial tradition" it is possible that "a demagogue will revive Russian imperialism," a conclusion grounded in Nixon's belief that "the Soviet people harbor a traditional desire for order imposed from above."[13] So while these hard-bodied men have retreated to their homes and farms or taken comfortable jobs with large corporations (like the railroad), authoritarian regimes have been allowed to flourish. And now, under those regimes, injustices have begun to occur.

When Delilah is first cut by Quick Mike and Davey, two cowboys from the Bar T ranch, Little Bill decides to whip them as punishment. But when Skinny, owner not only of the brothel where the women work but of the contract that brought Delilah from Boston in the first place, complains that a bullwhipping will not compensate him for the loss of Delilah's income, Little Bill forgoes the whipping and orders the men to bring seven ponies to Skinny as payment for his loss of Delilah's services. It is in the face of such an injustice that Strawberry Alice (Frances Fisher) and the other prostitutes decide to offer their own reward of $1,000 to anyone who will kill the two cowboys. The law, circumvented by individual power and capital, has been shown to be unable to uphold principles and values in the face of totalitarian rule. How can these women receive justice?

The answer offered by this film and by Richard Nixon is clear: Get those hard-bodied men back into circulation. As Nixon explains, "The peaceful revolution in Eastern Europe did not prevent the violent conquest of Kuwait by Iraq." And, perhaps more to the point,

*The autocratic Little Bill Daggett. (*Unforgiven, *Warner Brothers)*

"Those who two years ago touted the conventional wisdom that economic power had replaced military power as the major instrument of foreign policy were exposed as false prophets when Japan and Germany proved impotent in responding to Saddam Hussein's aggression."[14] Some may have argued that the end of the cold war meant an end to a need for military resolutions to world problems, but Nixon steps forward to remind Americans that "somewhere out there a crime is being committed," and that other nations are incapable of stopping those crimes. As he concludes, "America has an indispensable role to play in the world. *No other nation can take our place.*"[15] Similarly, the appearance that Big Whiskey is a "peaceful town" could not prevent atrocities occurring there. Even more pointed, not only did economic power prove incapable of stopping crimes, economic interests ensured that justice would not be implemented. In such a situation, if I might paraphrase Nixon, hard bodies have an indispensable role to play in the world. *No one can take their place.*

But in order to establish a national identity, Little Bill's actions must be distinguished from William Munny's and Ned Logan's. As in *Rambo*, where Rambo's hard body had to be distinguished from Sergeant Yushin's, *Unforgiven* must be able to show what kinds of hard bodies will be needed in the future. Whereas Little Bill's priorities seem to be to have a quiet town he can rule without dispute, Munny and Logan are motivated by a desire for justice. Though Munny declares initially that he is interested only in the money, his response to the Schofield Kid's description of the crime reveals the basis for his interest. When the Kid tells him that the job is to kill two men who should die "for cutting up a lady," Munny's response, as he tries to imagine the atrocity, is, simply, "Jesus." When Munny later approaches Ned about killing the two men, Ned replies, "If they done some wrong, I could see shootin' them," and then asks casually if they cheated at cards, stole some horses, or spit on a rich man, implying in his off-handed manner that these crimes were not worth killing for. But when Munny tells him about the cutting, Ned's face sobers up and he whispers, "I'll be damned. Well. Guess they got it coming." This is the American idealism that Nixon describes as follows:

American idealism—sometimes naive, sometimes misguided, sometimes overzealous—has always been at the center of our foreign policy. . . . This idealism has served as an indispensable foundation to sustain our commitment to the great moral causes of the twentieth century. It has enabled us to lead not on the basis of narrow and selfish interests but through the appeal of high ideals and common values.[16]

It is such idealism and not the desire for power that marks the difference between Little Bill's and William Munny's actions in *Unforgiven*. Whereas Little Bill was willing to overlook the atrocity committed against Delilah because she was someone who "was given over to wickedness in a regular way," Munny accepts the job of punishing the two cowboys, killing one himself and identifying the other for the Schofield Kid, without questioning Delilah's own behavior or status.

And, as he admits, he wants the money, but not to spend it on gambling or self-indulgent extravagences. William Munny wants to use his share of the reward "so the kids can get a new start." He may still have that hard-bodied character that America needs, but he remains a family man, thinking primarily of his children and their welfare. It is through such plot elements that *Unforgiven* manages to figure the task for the U.S. government in the 1990s—combining domestic and foreign policy interests in a way that best serves the nation. While Munny is responding to the foreign-policy challenges of the post–cold war era by reviving American idealism and force of action, he is invoking as well as the basis for such actions the U.S. family and the country's domestic future. Unlike Rambo, whom Colonel Trautman characterized as a "full-blooded combat soldier," and unlike the fathers of 1991 films who rediscovered their families as the centers of their lives, William Munny is both warrior and father, both defender and provider, both killer and nurturer. In Nixon's words, "We do not face a choice between dealing with domestic problems and playing an international role. Our challenge is to do both."[17] It is a challenge that men like William Munny seem to be best-suited to meet. Not only does he bring justice to Big Whiskey by killing the two cowboys and freeing the town from its autocratic ruler, he succeeds domestically by using the reward money to take his children to San Francisco "where it is rumored he prospered in dry goods."

As part of the foreign policy debate taken up in *Unforgiven*, a key feature of the film's plot is the presence of "Ordnance 14." Posted on a sign at the town's entrance, Ordnance 14 declared that there would be "no firearms in Big Whiskey," mandating that everyone turn over their guns to Little Bill when they entered town. After forcing both English Bob and William Munny to hand over their guns, Little Bill beats them mercilessly for violating his law and challenging his authority in Big Whiskey. But it is only when Munny returns to town with a rifle and pistol that justice is achieved, as he kills Little Bill and all of his deputies and then threatens to kill anyone else who dares harm women again or fails to give his friend, Ned Logan, also a victim of Little Bill's beatings, a decent burial. In a post–cold war era, when the need for armaments would seem to be diminished, *Unforgiven* argues that a weaponless world is not necessarily a just one. As Nixon argues, "We cannot count on the chimera of arms control alone. We need defenses."[18] Those who believe, as Nixon and *Unforgiven* characterize them, that peace can be achieved through domestic isolation or arms control are not only naive but also likely to be killed or abused by those who do not. Ned Logan, also a former hard body, decides that he is no longer capable of killing and that he will return to his farming. But although he did not kill either of the cowboys, he is captured and tortured to death by Little Bill. Such a man, according to the logic presented here, is naive in thinking that he can avoid the responsibilities and consequences of taking action, for it is precisely by opting out of the killing that Ned Logan brings about his own death. The message is clear: allowing someone else to hold all the guns in the name of peace will lead not to the freedom but to the oppression of everyone.

One of the most interesting aspects of *Unforgiven* is that it simultaneously presents and critiques a version of hard-bodied masculinity that verges on machismo, while debunking the myth of Hollywood westerns. In addition to showing Eastwood as a mud-covered hog farmer in the film's opening scenes, *Unforgiven* constantly reminds viewers of his body's failings, principally because he is unable to mount his horse, usually a casual act for every western hero. Later, when Munny contracts a fever that almost kills him, he admits to vivid and horrific images of death that haunt and terrify him, confessing to a fear that also seems uncharacteristic of western heroes. As one reviewer puts it, the film is "an all-out assault on the whole western cult of macho."[19]

In addition, in a subplot the film deflates the popular images of western heroism. W. W. Beauchamp, a dime-novel writer, enters the film as English Bob's biographer, recording for posterity the courageous deeds of Bob's hard-bodied gunfighting days. Beauchamp defends the authenticity of his tales until Little Bill, present at the events narrated in Beauchamp's books, tells him what really happened, including English Bob's cold-blooded murder of an unarmed man. At this point, Beauchamp switches sides to become Little Bill's biographer, now believing that he has found a more authentic source of heroic lore. The humor in these scenes clues the audience into the critique *Unforgiven* is offering, a critique that must extend to the very plots that make up the genre in which this film participates, a genre replete with the kind of hard-bodied heroics that fill the pages of Beauchamp's novels.

But although the film openly questions the validity of such tales and such heroes, it nonetheless holds out a space for a true western hero who is not like these men and whose exploits do not appear in popular fictions. No one has written a biography of William Munny, but everyone has heard some astounding story about him. The Schofield Kid first tells what he learned from his uncle about Munny, that he killed Charlie Pepper and William Harvey, but Munny claims not to remember. Later, when the Kid asks him if the story was true about his having killed two deputies when they had their guns pointed at him, Munny says, "I don't recollect." When Little Bill learns who killed Davey, he repeats what he has heard of Munny, that he killed women and children aboard a train, shot a U.S. Marshall, and killed numerous other men. Although each of these stories could easily be dismissed as the sort of exaggerated yarns that English Bob spun for Beauchamp, the film validates them as true. Unlike English Bob and Little Bill, Munny never tells any stories about himself, and consistently refuses to answer questions about stories that people have heard, underscoring that, for him, these are not tales but real events that cannot be recounted in simple ways. But more convincing, after hearing the Kid ask Munny about the two deputies, Ned, who was there, recalls the event as even more dangerous than the popular myth suggests, with Munny having killed not two but three deputies who all had their guns on him. Because Ned's character is only a sympathetic one throughout the film, his version of the story cannot be disputed, and it becomes apparent that Munny, unlike English Bob, is even more of an authentic hard body than the myths convey.

The combination of the debunking of English Bob and Little Bill with the validation of William Munny suggests that there is another line that must be drawn, not just between power-hungry and idealistic heroes, but between illusory and authentic ones. But what is most important is that *Unforgiven* insists that there are still authentic heroes, ones such as Richard Nixon invokes when he talks about the role the United States must play in the world's future. It is a heroic role that requires authentic not illusory leadership. When Nixon describes his view of the role the United States should play in world politics, it sounds remarkably like the characterization of William Munny:

As I have traveled around the world during the past forty-five years, I have found that some hate us, some envy us, and some like us. But I have found that almost all respect us. All know that without the United States peace and freedom would not have survived in the world in the past and will not survive in the future. But the question that has arisen again and again has been whether the United States had the will to play a world role over the long haul.[20]

In case anyone is worrying about the answer to this question, perhaps a screening of *Unforgiven* will ease their minds.

As part of the film's critique of self-promoting machismo, it offers a similar take on nationalism. Big Whiskey, Little Bill's town, is decorated throughout the bulk of the film with bunting and American flags, all for the purpose of celebrating Independence Day. Early in the film then, red, white, and blue are associated with the peaceful town that Bill authoritatively runs, suggesting that there is something hollow about the kind of patriotism and national identification Bill allows in his town. But in the closing scenes of the film after Munny has killed Bill and his deputies, he leaves the saloon, mounts his horse, and rides through the center of town, shouting to its inhabitants that they must bury Ned properly and not harm any more prostitutes. A low-angle shot of Munny astride his horse (which he is now able to mount without difficulty) captures as well the flag now draped behind him, as he concludes his warning that the town straighten up "or I'll come back and kill every one of you sons of bitches." Munny's promise, one that reminds everyone that authentic hard-bodied men are not going to disappear, is given in full view of the American flag that rests behind him, as if to say that this is not only a personal but also a national promise, one that, as William Munny has shown, Americans are more than capable of fulfilling.

If the presentation of nationalism is congruent with that of the masculine body that figures it, then it must be concluded that there is, as with the dime-novel and authentic heroes, an illusory and an authentic national identity. Whereas Little Bill's formulation of Big Whiskey's identity hinged entirely upon his control of the townspeople and their submission to his laws, Munny's offers a definition in which the residents of the town must be responsible for themselves and must be held accountable for the behavior of the entire town. When he threatens "every one of you sons of bitches," he invokes a democratic ideal that the town must uphold. Consequently, the film suggests not only that these authentic hard-bodied heroes are necessary to resolving injustices, but also that they are essential in structuring the futures of societies, setting out the democratic structures whereby people must live. Also important, in such terms, Munny does not stay in Big Whiskey to rule the town himself but departs for San Francisco with his children, leaving the town to move forward on its own to establish a democratic system. This is, of course, the very role that Nixon envisions for the United States: establishing the standard of freedom and democracy by which others may live, but not taking over other countries to dictate their social policies: "Only the United States has the military, economic, and political power to lead the way in defending and extending freedom and in deterring and resisting aggression. More important, our influence stems not only from our military and economic power but also from the enormous appeal of our ideals and our example."[21] Munny does what Nixon suggests: after righting the injustices done to women and to men of color, he returns to his own family and attends to his own domestic future, for it is from this commitment that the strength to be a hard body derives.

As audiences view the peaceful Munny farm at the film's opening, a prologue recalls how Claudia Feathers came to marry William Munny. No one, the script narrates, could understand why a woman such as the respectable and well-to-do Miss Feathers would attach herself to "a man notoriously vicious and of intemperate disposition." At the film's close, the camera still focused on the quiet, now deserted, cabin, the script recounts how Claudia's mother came west to find her, only to discover her daughter's grave and an absent son-in-law and grandchildren. This respectable lady, with no further information about her daughter, still could not understand why Claudia had married a man whose description has not altered from the film's opening lines, "a man notoriously vicious and of intemperate disposition." But although Claudia's mother may remain in the dark about her daughter's attraction to this notorious man, the audience has been invited to alter its understanding of that characterization of William Munny. For the man who was initially seen as a criminal and drunk who had been reformed by a good woman is now to be recognized as a hero.

Earlier in the film, English Bob tries to explain to a barber that it is more difficult to shoot royalty than a president (the assassination of President Garfield is one of the early pieces of historical information the film provides) because kings and queens inspire "awe" in their citizens, an emotion that would so overwhelm any would-be assassin that s/he would be unable to pull the trigger. Although *Unforgiven* shows that there is little hesitation on anyone's part to pull triggers in Big Whiskey, something different happens in the closing scene of the film, when William Munny makes his promise to the citizens of Big Whiskey and then rides out of town. The only surviving deputy, Charlie (William von Hamburg), watches Munny leaving the saloon, raises his rifle, and aims. But he is unable to fire. He hands the rifle to the man next to him, but he will not fire either. At this point, those remaining on the streets of town, including Beauchamp and Delilah, watch as Munny rides out of town. Their faces do not show fear, intimidation, anger, or revenge, but instead admiration, gratitude, respect. There is no better term to describe their gazes than the one offered by English Bob earlier in the film—"awe." "I have found that some hate us, some envy us, and some like us. But I have found that almost all respect us."

Unforgiven is not the only film to narrate these foreign and domestic policies. *Diggstown*, another popular 1992 release, shows Honey Roy Palmer (Lou Gossett, Jr.) participating in a con with Gabriel Cain (James Woods) in which Palmer must knock out ten men in twenty-four hours. Palmer holds a grudge against Cain because, in an earlier and similar con, Cain called the fight when he thought Palmer was too badly hurt. Palmer criticizes Cain for losing faith in him and not backing him the full ten fights. And in the current plot, when Palmer is several times knocked down by Hammerhead Hagan (Willie Green), his boxing nemesis, Cain is again about to call the fight. As he throws the towel into the ring, Palmer rises from the mat, catches the towel in the air, and hurls it back to Cain. He goes on from there to win.

As in *Unforgiven*, the successful resolution of the plot—including the just punishment of the town's oppressive owner, Gillon (Bruce Dern), and the restitution of the town's land to its original owners, as well as the vindication of Gillon's several murders—depends upon the strength of an aging hard body (Palmer is forty-eight), one who, like Munny, has turned to other, more peaceful pursuits in the intervening years (Palmer coaches boys' boxing at a gym), and who, like Munny, takes up this venture to gain money for his family. The plot is basically the same, with a similar "awesome" gaze delivered by the diegetic audience at the film's close. What *Diggstown* adds to the scenario provided by *Unforgiven* and Nixon's *Seize the Moment* is both the overt appeal—"Don't lose faith in me"—and the inclusion of a man of color as the heroic hard body. Though the plot's resolution finally depends upon the control a white man has over a man of color, as Cain orders Minoso Torres to throw the last fight, the emotional climax of the film rests more in Palmer's ability to overcome Hammerhead Hagan to win the most important bout of the series. But it is also more than likely because Palmer is black that he can make the more overt plea for support and faith that Munny could not do, voicing the essential cry of the 1980s hard bodies: that they are authentic, that they have not disappeared, and that they can still win the important fights and defeat the important villains, if only the country as a whole will support and believe in them, if only the nation will allow them to finish the fight for freedom they began without throwing in the towels of defeat and disarmament.

This is a Hollywood narration of the conservative national model for 1992, policies that seem once again to be returning to masculine hard bodies as emblems of national identities, resources, and heroics. In 1988, Martin Anderson confidently declared that, although "the end of the Reagan presidency is near, . . . the end of the ideas that swept him to power is nowhere in sight,"[22] and Haynes Johnson concluded in 1991 that the "underlying attitudes of the eighties are still exerting a powerful influence on Americans in the nineties."[23] Consequently, while critiquing the more spectacular hard bodies of the 1980s, these films of 1992 have not rejected that body so much as refigured it to incorporate a domestic component, one that acknowledges the family as the final justification for any foreign interventions. In an era when militarism is being openly questioned, either for its continued necessity or for its budgetary burden, it is important to identify this shift toward the family. Although the rhetoric of "family values" continues to dominate Republican party platforms, anti-abortion demonstrations, and local campaigns against gay and lesbians, spectacular media presentation should not lead us to perceive this rhetoric as an isolated legacy of Ronald Reagan's conservative rally, but instead as the linchpin of a redefined conservative movement in the post–cold war era. From enabling propositions of American "moral superiority" over foreign economic competitors, to reconstituting internal structures of racism, to rationalizing class divisions, "family values" have been one of the key political and social themes to effect the programs of the Reagan ideology. But these films of 1992 reveal that the illusions of family values are being reconstructed now to reinforce a continued militarism, in which external interventions are being justified to the

*The old . . . / . . . and the new hard bodies. (*Magnum Force, *Warner Brothers / Unforgiven, *Warner Brothers*)*

extent that they can revive the American family, both ideologically and economically.

At the center of this family and the nation it represents is the hard body, a body that has shifted its constitution throughout the 1980s. From its appearance in the early 1980s as a resuscitated body of the Vietnam War era, to its articulation in the mid-1980s as a re-masculinized foreign policy heroic, to its exteriorization and critique of the hard body in the late 1980s in order to "reveal" a more sensitive and emotional interior, to its reconfiguration in the early 1990s as a "family" value, to its resurfacing in 1992 as an aging but still powerful foreign and domestic masculine and national model, the hard body has remained a theme that epitomizes the national imaginary that made the Reagan Revolution possible. No longer the youthful and defiant Rambo, but now the aging and determined William Munny, the hard body continues, in the post-Reagan, post–cold war era, to find the national models of masculinity conveyed by some of Holly-wood's most successful films. They have shown their resiliency as models because they appear to critique, at times even to reject, their earlier versions, only to renarrate them in ways more complex and more intimately woven into the fabric of American culture. But they are dangerous models, not only because they depend on the kind of nationalism and militarism that brought the country to military actions in Panama, Grenada, and the Persian Gulf but also because they seem now to represent the desperation of an aging superpower that is reluctant, under a conservative framework, to relinquish its international status and influence and may, like William Munny, be willing to punish harshly those who insist it do so. They are the bodies that speak from Hollywood's screens the words that Richard Nixon uses to describe the United States, the words that he and those who share his views hope will continue to be the cry of American hard bodies everywhere: "Some hate us, some envy us, and some like us. But I have found that almost all respect us." But, without radical change, they may also be the bodies that would offer to those who do not accept Nixon's edict the warning William Munny gives to the citizens of Big Whiskey:

"I'll come back and kill every one of you sons of bitches."

NOTES

CHAPTER ONE. LIFE AS A MAN IN THE REAGAN REVOLUTION

1. Haynes Johnson, " 'High-Risk' President Reassessed," *Washington Post*, 8 November 1981, Op-Ed page.
2. Roger Rosenblatt, "Out of the Past, Fresh Choices for the Future," *Time*, 5 January 1981, p. 12.
3. Quoted in Martin Anderson, *Revolution: The Reagan Legacy* (Stanford: Hoover Institution Press, 1990), p. xxvii.
4. Ibid.
5. Rosenblatt, "Out of the Past," p. 12.
6. Rupert Wilkinson, *American Tough: The Tough-Guy Tradition and American Character* (Westport, Conn.: Greenwood Press, 1984), p. 6.
7. Richard Nixon, *Seize the Moment: America's Challenge in a One-Superpower World* (New York: Simon & Schuster, 1992), p. 277.
8. *Weekly Compilation of Presidential Documents*, 11 January 1989, pp. 53–54.
9. Lou Cannon, *President Reagan: The Role of a Lifetime* (New York: Simon & Schuster, 1991), p. 338.
10. Ibid., p. 337.
11. Anderson, *Revolution*, p. xxiv.
12. Bob Schieffer and Gary Paul Gates, *The Acting President* (New York: E. P. Dutton, 1989), p. 167.
13. *Weekly Compilation of Presidential Documents*, 7 February 1986, p. 184.
14. Cannon, *President Reagan*, p. 64.
15. Ibid., p. 286.
16. Rosenblatt, "Out of the Past," pp. 11, 14.
17. Anderson, *Revolution*, pp. xviii–xix.

18. Quoted in Maureen Dowd, "Of Knights and Presidents: Race of Mythic Proportions," *New York Times*, 10 October 1992, p. 1.
19. Ibid.
20. Quoted in Cannon, *President Reagan*, p. 141.
21. I am indebted to Michael Rogin's excellent book, *Ronald Reagan, The Movie* (Berkeley and Los Angeles: University of California Press, 1987), for his lucid and perceptive readings of Reagan's image in relation to the patterns of "demonization" in U.S. culture. I highly recommend Rogin's book to anyone interested in understanding the role "Ronald Reagan" played in this period.
22. Robert Bly, *Iron John: A Book About Men* (Reading, Mass.: Addison-Wesley, 1990), pp. 1 and 2.
23. Ibid., p. 2.
24. Ibid., pp. 2–3, 3, and 4.
25. Nixon, *Seize the Moment*, p. 276.
26. Richard Nixon, *The Real War* (New York: Simon & Schuster, 1980), p. x.
27. *Weekly Compilation of Presidential Documents*, 15 August 1988, p. 1065.
28. Nixon, *The Real War*, pp. 3, 169, 172, and 298.
29. Ibid., pp. 3, 309, 4, 243, 3–4, and 243.
30. Bly, *Iron John*, pp. 35, 102, 107, 109, and 99 (italics added).
31. Ibid., pp. 99 and 16.
32. Ibid., pp. 96 and 25.
33. John Orman, *Comparing Presidential Behavior: Carter, Reagan, and the Macho Presidential Style* (New York: Greenwood Press, 1987), p. 17.
34. Wilkinson, *American Tough*, p. 4.
35. Orman, *Comparing Presidential Behavior*, p. 39.
36. John Mihalic, "Hair on the President's Chest," *Wall Street Journal*, 11 May 1984, p. 30.
37. Bly, *Iron John*, p. 99.
38. Orman, *Comparing Presidential Behavior*, p. 18.
39. Lauren Berlant, *The Anatomy of National Fantasy: Hawthorne, Utopia, and Everyday Life* (Chicago: University of Chicago Press, 1991), p. 5.
40. Jochen Schulte-Sasse and Linda Schulte-Sasse, "War, Otherness, and Illusionary Identifications with the State," *Cultural Critique* 19 (Fall 1991): 68.
41. Lawrence Grossberg, "It's a Sin: Politics, Post-Modernity, and the Popular," in *It's a Sin: Essays on Postmodernism, Politics, and Culture*, ed. Lawrence Grossberg, Tony Fry, Ann Curthoys, and Paul Patton (Sydney: Power Publications, 1988), p. 7.
42. Ibid., p. 32.
43. Haynes Johnson notes this contradiction particularly in relation to Reaganism's position on religious issues: "Reagan and the members of the religious right, who wanted to get government off the people's back and God back into the classroom, proposed to achieve that goal by changing

the laws and putting government deeper into the thicket of church and state" (*Sleepwalking through History: America in the Reagan Years* [New York: W. W. Norton, 1991], p. 211).

44. David Stockman, *The Triumph of Politics* (New York: Harper & Row, 1986); Larry Speakes, *Speaking Out* (New York: Charles Scribner's Sons, 1988); Donald T. Regan, *For the Record* (San Diego: Harcourt Brace Jovanovich, 1988).

45. See, for example, books by Bob Schieffer and Gary Paul Gates, *The Acting President* (New York: E. P. Dutton, 1989); Mark Hertsgaard, *On Bended Knee* (New York: Farrar, Straus & Giroux, 1988); and Jane Mayer and Doyle McManus, *Landslide: The Unmaking of the President 1984–88* (Boston: Houghton Mifflin, 1988).

46. Anderson, *Revolution*, pp. xxvi–xxvii.

47. *Rambo* brought in $80 million in 1985; *Top Gun*, $82 million in 1986; *Lethal Weapon 2* $79.5 million in 1989; and *Batman*, $150.5 million in 1989. Moreover, Reagan's approval ratings were highest among the very audiences that Hollywood had learned to target—the young—87 percent of Americans between eighteen and twenty-nine approved of Ronald Reagan as a person.

48. Robin Wood, *Hollywood from Vietnam to Reagan* (New York: Columbia University Press, 1986), p. 28.

49. Ibid., p. 69.

50. Wilkinson, *American Tough*, p. 109.

51. Seth Cagin and Philip Dray, *Hollywood Films of the Seventies: Sex, Drugs, Violence, Rock 'n' Roll, and Politics* (New York: Harper & Row, 1984), p. xi.

52. Ibid., p. xii.

53. *Raiders of the Lost Ark* grossed $90.4 million in 1981; *Superman 2*, $64 million in 1981; *First Blood*, $24 million in 1982; *Terminator*, $17 million in 1984; *Top Gun*, $82 million in 1986; *Lethal Weapon*, $29.5 million in 1987; *Robocop*, $23.5 million in 1987; *Die Hard*, $35 million in 1988; *Batman*, $150.5 million in 1989.

54. Cagin and Dray, *Hollywood Films*, p. 216.

55. Ibid., p. 219.

56. Ronald Reagan, "Inaugural Address," *Weekly Compilation of Presidential Documents*, 26 January–1 March 1981, p. 2.

57. Ibid., p. 3.

58. Ibid.

59. Anderson, *Revolution*, p. xvii.

60. The top-grossing films of the decade in terms of box office receipts are as follows: *E.T.* $187 million, *The Return of the Jedi* $162.5 million, *Batman* $150.5 million, *Home Alone* $120 million, *Indiana Jones Crusade* $115.5 million, *Terminator 2* $112 million, *Back to the Future* $96 million, *Ghost* $95 million, *Tootsie* $94.6 million, and *Raiders of the Lost Ark* $90.4

million. Six of the top ten films of the decade fall under the categories of "hard bodies" that I am discussing here. Of the remaining four, one is a children's movie, one is a science fiction film geared toward children, and the remaining two are narratives that continue to indicate a fascination wth bodies and bodily changes in ways that support my thesis.

CHAPTER TWO. THE REAGAN HEROES

1. Robert Ajemian, "Where Skies Are Not Cloudy . . ." *Time*, 5 January 1981, p. 26.
2. Jurgen Link, "Fanatics, Fundamentalists, Lunatics, and Drug Traffickers—The New Southern Enemy Image," *Cultural Critique* 19 (Fall 1991): 35.
3. See John Mihalic's article "Hair on the President's Chest," in which he refers to Carter's "true feminine spirit," meaning that he didn't "twist arms," "threaten or rebuke," and "scrupulously avoided the trappings of power."
4. Roger Rosenblatt, "Out of the Past, Fresh Choices for the Future," p. 13.
5. Jochen Schulte-Sasse and Linda Schulte-Sasse, "War, Otherness, and Illusionary Identifications with the State," p. 78.
6. Ibid., p. 71.
7. Ibid., p. 70.
8. Antony Easthope, *What a Man's Gotta Do: The Masculine Myth in Popular Culture* (Boston: Unwin Hyman, 1990), pp. 39–40.
9. Lou Cannon, *President Reagan: The Role of a Lifetime*, pp. 148–149.
10. Schulte-Sasse and Schulte-Sasse, "War," p. 68.
11. See, for example, Bill Nichols's *Ideology and the Image: Social Representation in the Cinema* (Bloomington: Indiana University Press, 1981).
12. Quoted in Michael Rogin, *Ronald Reagan, The Movie*, p. 7.
13. John Orman, *Comparing Presidential Behavior: Carter, Reagan, and the Macho Presidential Style*, p. 110.
14. Haynes Johnson, *Sleepwalking through History: America in the Reagan Years*, p. 161.
15. Cannon, *President Reagan*, p. 115.
16. Johnson, *Sleepwalking through History*, p. 153.
17. Richard Nixon, *The Real War*, p. 3.
18. In David Morrell's original novel, Rambo does kill these men and more, requiring Rambo's own sacrifice at the end, as he is killed by Trautman himself (*First Blood* [New York: Ballantine, 1982]).
19. Orman, *Comparing Presidential Behavior*, pp. 7–8, 66, 7, and 18.
20. Jimmy Carter, *Keeping Faith* (New York: Bantam, 1982), p. 4.
21. Ronald Reagan, "The Trans World Airlines Hijacking Incident," *Weekly Compilation of Presidential Documents*, 2 July 1985, p. 869.
22. Rogin, *Ronald Reagan, The Movie*.

23. There are in fact several places where the *Rambo* films critique the government, particularly for its failure to retrieve U.S. POWs from Vietnam, to have properly received returning U.S. veterans and offered them training or jobs, or to have investigated Agent Orange contamination. Pointedly, Rambo refuses to return "home" at the end of *Rambo*, feeling that "[his] country does not love [him] as much as [he] loves it." But most of these critiques can be leveled at previous administrations and not at Reagan himself. Even where Rambo criticizes current government policies, the charges seem more to be laid at the door of an inactive Congress than an indifferent president.

24. Cannon, *President Reagan*, p. 321.

25. Quoted in Richard Crawford, *In the Era of Human Capital* (New York: HarperBusiness, 1991), p. 74.

26. Nixon, *The Real War*, pp. 11–12.

27. Orman, *Comparing Presidential Behavior*, pp. 13–14.

28. Clint Eastwood used this same gimmick in *A Mule for Sister Sarah*, but he needed assistance to perform the operation, and his shoulder gave him great pain afterwards.

29. Steve Neale, "Masculinity as Spectacle: Reflections on Men and Mainstream Cinema," *Screen* 24, no. 6 (1983): 2–17.

30. John Tower, Edmund Muskie, and Brent Scowcroft, *Report of the President's Special Review Board*, 26 February 1987, p. B-1.

31. Oliver North's interpretation of the law suggested that the National Security Council staff was not included in the congressional mandate. See North's account of Iran-contra in *Under Fire* (New York: HarperCollins, 1991).

32. Orman, *Comparing Presidential Behavior*, p. 25.

33. Ibid., pp. 112–113.

34. *Weekly Compilation of Presidential Documents*, 16 July 1986, p. 951.

CHAPTER THREE. FATHERS AND SONS

1. Robin Wood identifies what he calls the male duo film of the seventies, examples of which are *Butch Cassidy and the Sundance Kid, Easy Rider*, and *Thunderbolt and Lightfoot*, and explains their appearance as "a response to certain social developments centered on the emancipation of women and the resultant undermining of the home," in which the films' "implicit attitude is 'You see, we can get along pretty well without you' " (*Hollywood from Vietnam to Reagan*, p. 24). Such examples show the historical shift that has taken place from the seventies to the eighties in relation to alterations in gender positions. Whereas the characters in the male duo films are invariably "pals," with both sharing flaws and heroic qualities, the father/son films of the 1980s are much more oriented toward unequal relations between men. Whereas "buddy" films relate exchanges of power between these men and the society they oppose, inevitably in such a way

that the society retains its power by eliminating the duo, the father/son films show how that exchange has been internalized so that power is exactly a relation between men and not between marginalized men and society-at-large. Though power relations may be briefly destabilized in eighties films, it is always clear in what terms those relations are to be restabilized; that is, only in terms of masculine relations.

2. In "The New Vietnam Films: Is the Movie Over?" *Journal of Popular Film and Television* 13, no. 4 (1986), I describe how the U.S. government is depicted as feminine in recent films about the war in Vietnam. It is depicted not only as represented by women but also as weak, indecisive, and passive. In similar ways, bureaucracies seem almost maternal: Rambo cuts himself free from the equipment that threatens to kill him as he dangles from the plane that is to drop him in Vietnam. This is a clear reference to the need to sever an umbilical cord that threatens to strangle its fetus. That Rambo cuts his own cord is emblematic of the self-sufficiency of the masculine subject portrayed in this film.

3. George Bush, with Victor Gold, *Looking Forward* (New York: Doubleday, 1987), p. 225.

CHAPTER FOUR. THE BUSH STYLE

1. Haynes Johnson, *Sleepwalking through History: America in the Reagan Years*, p. 442.
2. George Bush, "Inaugural Address," 20 January 1989, *Weekly Compilation of Presidential Documents*, January–March 1989, p. 100.
3. Michael Duffy and Dan Goodgame, *Marching in Place: The Status Quo Presidency of George Bush* (New York: Simon & Schuster, 1992), p. 73.
4. Ibid., p. 70.
5. Ibid., pp. 21, 67, and 59.
6. Ibid., pp. 87 and 89.
7. Ibid., p. 53.
8. Bush's campaign announcement speech, Houston, Texas, 12 October 1987. Quoted in Duffy and Goodgame, *Marching in Place*, p. 22.

CHAPTER FIVE. A FEW GOOD WHITE MEN

1. Michael Ryan and Douglas Kellner, "Technophobia," in *Camera Politica: The Politics and Ideology of Contemporary Hollywood Film* (Bloomington: Indiana University Press, 1988), p. 58.
2. Ibid.
3. Richard Nixon, *The Real War*, p. 299.
4. Reagan used this phrase in a speech delivered to the National Association of Evangelists, 8 March 1983.
5. Wilbur Edel, *The Reagan Presidency: An Actor's Finest Performance* (New York: Hippocrene Books, 1992), p. 52.
6. Ryan and Kellner, "Technophobia," p. 65.

7. James S. Albus, "To Pay for the Future," *Omni*, October 1980, p. 54. In *The Computer Revolution and the U.S. Labor Force*, (Washington, D.C.: Government Printing Office, 1985), p. 10, a study produced for the House Subcommittee on Oversight and Investigations of the Committee on Energy and Commerce, the government's own figures indicate widespread layoffs due to automation, with as much as 11.4 percent of the total work force being displaced by automation.

8. The degree to which Reagan's advisers operated on the "not-Carter" principle is best exhibited by their support of the Weinberger plan for the deployment of MX missiles in "superhardened" Titan or Minuteman silos. Under the Weinberger plan, the Soviets would have been able to destroy the entire U.S. arsenal of MXs with only two hundred missiles. In contrast, under the Carter plan, which entailed continually shifting the missiles among silos, the Soviets would have needed nine thousand additional missiles to destroy the same arsenal. In spite of this obvious discrepancy, the Weinberger plan was approved by the Reagan administration primarily because it was not the Carter plan. For a discussion of this decision, see Lou Cannon, *President Reagan: The Role of a Lifetime*, pp. 163–171.

9. Needless to say, the system of equal justice was first and foremost a system for white men in which women and men of color make apparent the mechanisms of operation.

10. For a closer examination of the events surrounding the murders, see Seth Cagin and Philip Dray's definitive study, *We Are Not Afraid: The Story of Goodman, Schwerner, and Chaney and the Civil Rights Campaign for Mississippi* (New York: Macmillan, 1988).

11. "The Crime that Tarnished a Town," *Time*, 5 March 1984, p. 19.

12. "The Tavern Rape: Cheers and No Help," *Newsweek*, 21 March 1983, p. 25.

CHAPTER SIX. TERMINAL MASCULINITY

1. *Alien 3* is one notable exception to this trend, as Ripley's body becomes host to an alien queen. But like these nineties men, she finally regains control of her body, and, in a perverse way, fulfills the impetus toward family as well, as she sacrifices herself so that the aliens cannot be reproduced by the Company, clutching her newborn infant to her breast as she plummets into a fiery furnace.

2. Elayne Rapping, "Boys of the Summer," *The Progressive*, November 1991, p. 36.

3. As Donald Bogle states in his study of blacks in U.S. films, *Toms, Coons, Mulattoes, Mammies, and Bucks: An Interpretive History of Blacks in American Films*, rev. ed. (New York: Continuum, 1990), the heydey of black male action-adventure heroes was in the early 1970s, with the appearance of films such as *Shaft* (1971, Gordon Parks, Sr.) and *Superfly* (1972, Gordon

Parks, Jr.), films that were made largely for black audiences. *Passenger 57*, a 1992 film starring Wesley Snipes, seems to be challenging the black/white buddy films in its presentation of a black male as a single action hero.

4. *Beauty and the Beast*, adapted from the film by A. L. Singer (New York: Disney Press, 1992), pp. 2 and 3.

5. Ibid., p. 25.

6. Ibid., p. 1.

7. Ibid., p. 48.

8. *Beauty and the Beast*, retold by Deborah Apy (New York: Holt, Rinehart & Winston, 1980), p. 44.

9. Singer, *Beauty and the Beast*, p. 49.

10. Ibid., p. 6.

11. Ibid., p. 19.

12. Ibid., p. 7.

13. Ibid., p. 35.

14. David H. Van Biema, "With a $100 Million Gross(out), Sly Stallone Fends Off *Rambo*'s Army of Adversaries," *People*, 8 July 1985, p. 35.

15. Michael Rogin has written persuasively on the use of amnesia in the Reagan era. See his excellent article, " 'Make My Day': Spectacle as Amnesia in Imperial Politics," *Representations* 29 (Winter 1990): 99–124.

16. Karen B. Mann, "Narrative Entanglements: *The Terminator*," *Film Quarterly* 43 (Winter 1989–1990): 21.

17. Constance Penley, "Time Travel, Primal Scene, and the Critical Dystopia," in *The Cultural Politics of "Postmodernism*," ed. John Tagg (Binghamton: Department of Art History, SUNY Press, 1989), p. 47.

18. Julie Baumgold, "Killer Women," *New York*, 29 July 1991, p. 26.

19. This recharacterization is reinforced by one of Schwarzenegger's intervening Hollywood hits, *Kindergarten Cop*, in which viewers are treated to the spectacle of Arnold frollicking with five-year-olds.

20. Gillian Brown, "Nuclear Domesticity: Sequence and Survival," in *Arms and the Woman: War, Gender and Literary Representation*, ed. Helen M. Cooper, Adrienne Auslander Munich, and Susan Merrill Squier (Chapel Hill: University of North Carolina Press, 1989), p. 294.

21. Ibid., pp. 292–293.

22. Quoted in Susan Faludi, *Backlash: The Undeclared War Against American Women* (New York: Crown, 1991), p. 65.

23. Christa Wolf, *Cassandra*, trans. Jan Van Heurck (New York: Farrar, Straus & Giroux, 1984), p. 244.

24. Ibid., p. 116.

25. Caryn James, "A Warmer, Fuzzier Arnold," *New York Times*, 14 July 1991, p. H9.

26. Donald Greiner, *Women Enter the Wilderness: Male Bonding and the Ameri-*

can Novel of the 1980s (Columbia: University of South Carolina Press, 1991), p. 13.

27. Quoted in James, "A Warmer, Fuzzier Arnold," p. H9.
28. Ibid.

CHAPTER SEVEN. MASCULINITY AND THE REAGAN LEGACY

1. Robert Bly, *Iron John*, p. ix.
2. Richard Nixon, *Seize the Moment: America's Challenge in a One-Superpower World*, p. 26.
3. Ibid., p. 40.
4. Bly, *Iron John*, p. 8.
5. Ibid., p. 6.
6. Nixon, *Seize the Moment*, pp. 32–33.
7. Ibid., p. 39.
8. Ibid., p. 273.
9. Ibid.
10. *Unforgiven* also won Clint Eastwood honors as best director and Gene Hackman as best supporting actor. The film also won the Golden Globe Award for Best Film.
11. Bly, *Iron John*, p. 3.
12. Hillary De Vries, "The Squint-Essential Tough Guy," *Seattle Post-Intelligencer*, 6 August 1992, p. C1.
13. Nixon, *Seize the Moment*, pp. 43 and 71.
14. Ibid., p. 273.
15. Ibid.; italics added.
16. Ibid., pp. 274–275.
17. Ibid., pp. 277–278.
18. Ibid., p. 279.
19. Arnold, "Surprise," p. 5.
20. Nixon, *Seize the Moment*, p. 302.
21. Ibid., p. 274.
22. Martin Anderson, *Revolution: The Reagan Legacy*, p. xix.
23. Haynes Johnson, *Sleepwalking through History: America in the Reagan Years*, p. 462.

BIBLIOGRAPHY

Ajemian, Robert. "Where the Skies Are Not Cloudy. . . ." *Time*, 5 January 1981, pp. 26–30.

Albus, James S. "To Pay for the Future." *Omni*, October 1980.

Anderson, Martin. *Revolution: The Reagan Legacy*. Stanford: The Hoover Institution Press, 1990.

Apy, Deborah. *Beauty and the Beast*. New York: Holt, Rinehart & Winston, 1980.

Arnold, William. "Surprise: Eastwood's Latest Is Near Perfect." *Seattle Post-Intelligencer*, 7 August 1992, p. 5.

Baumgold, Julie. "Killer Women." *New York*, 29 July 1991, pp. 24–29.

Berlant, Lauren. *The Anatomy of National Fantasy: Hawthorne, Utopia, and Everyday Life*. Chicago: University of Chicago Press, 1991.

Bly, Robert. *Iron John: A Book About Men*. Reading, Mass.: Addison-Wesley, 1990.

Bogle, Donald. *Toms, Coons, Mulattoes, Mammies, and Bucks: An Interpretive History of Blacks in American Films*. Rev. ed. New York: Continuum, 1990.

Brown, Gillian. "Nuclear Domesticity: Sequence and Survival." In *Arms and the Woman: War, Gender and Literary Representation*, ed. Helen M. Cooper, Adrienne Auslander Munich, and Susan Merrill Squier, pp. 283–303. Chapel Hill: University of North Carolina Press, 1989.

Bush, George. "Inaugural Address," 20 January 1989. *Weekly Compilation of Presidential Documents*, January–March 1989, pp. 99–102.

Bush, George, with Victor Gold. *Looking Forward*. New York: Doubleday, 1987.

Cagin, Seth, and Philip Dray. *Hollywood Films of the Seventies: Sex, Drugs, Violence, Rock 'n' Roll, and Politics.* New York: Harper & Row, 1984.

————. *We Are Not Afraid: The Story of Goodman, Schwerner, and Chaney and the Civil Rights Campaign for Mississippi.* New York: Macmillan, 1988.

Cannon, Lou. *President Reagan: The Role of a Lifetime.* New York: Simon & Schuster, 1991.

Carter, Jimmy. *Keeping Faith.* New York: Bantam, 1982.

The Computer Revolution and the U.S. Labor Force Washington, D.C.: Government Printing Office, 1985.

Crawford, Richard. *In the Era of Human Capital.* New York: HarperBusiness, 1991.

"The Crime That Tarnished a Town." *Time,* 5 March 1984, p. 19.

De Vries, Hillary. "The Squint-Essential Tough Guy." *Seattle Post-Intelligencer,* 6 August 1992, p. C1.

Dowd, Maureen. "Of Knights and Presidents: Race of Mythic Proportions." *New York Times,* 10 October 1992, p. 1.

Duffy, Michael, and Dan Goodgame. *Marching in Place: The Status Quo Presidency of George Bush.* New York: Simon & Schuster, 1992.

Easthope, Antony. *What a Man's Gotta Do: The Masculine Myth in Popular Culture.* Boston: Unwin Hyman, 1990.

Faludi, Susan. *Backlash: The Undeclared War Against American Woman.* New York: Crown, 1991.

Greiner, Donald. *Women Enter the Wilderness: Male Bonding and the American Novel of the 1980s.* Columbia: University of South Carolina Press, 1991.

Grossberg, Lawrence. "It's a Sin: Politics, Post-Modernity, and the Popular." In *It's a Sin: Essays on Postmodernism, Politics, and Culture,* ed. Tony Fry, Ann Curthoys, and Paul Patton, pp. 6–72. Sydney: Power Publications, 1988.

Hertsgaard, Mark. *On Bended Knee.* New York: Farrar, Straus & Giroux, 1988.

James, Caryn. "A Warmer, Fuzzier Arnold." *The New York Times,* 14 July 1991, p. H9.

Jeffords, Susan. "The New Vietnam Films: Is the Movie Over?" *Journal of Popular Film and Television* 13, no. 4 (1986): 186–195.

Johnson, Haynes. " 'High-Risk' President Reassessed." *The Washington Post,* 8 November 1981, Op-Ed page.

————. *Sleepwalking Through History: America in the Reagan Years.* New York: W. W. Norton, 1991.

Link, Jurgen. "Fanatics, Fundamentalists, Lunatics, and Drug Traffickers— The New Southern Enemy Image." *Cultural Critique* 19 (Fall 1991): 33–55.

Mann, Karen. "Narrative Entanglements: *The Terminator.*" *Film Quarterly* 43 (Winter 1989–1990): 17–27.

Mayer, Jane, and Doyle McManus. *Landslide: The Unmaking of the President 1984–88.* New York: Houghton Mifflin, 1988.

Mihalic, John. "Hair on the President's Chest." *The Wall Street Journal*, 11 May 1984, p. 30.

Morrell, David. *First Blood*. New York: Ballantine, 1982.

Mosse, George. *Nationalism and Sexuality: Middle Class Morality and Sexual Norms in Modern Europe*. Madison: University of Wisconsin Press, 1985.

Neale, Steve. "Masculinity as Spectacle: Reflections on Men and Mainstream Cinema." *Screen* 24, no. 6 (1983): 2–17.

Nichols, Bill. *Ideology and the Image: Social Representation in the Cinema*. Bloomington: Indiana University Press, 1981.

Nixon, Richard. *The Real War*. New York: Simon & Schuster, 1980.

———. *Seize the Moment: America's Challenge in a One-Superpower World*. New York: Simon & Schuster, 1992.

North, Oliver. *Under Fire*. New York: HarperCollins, 1991.

Orman, John. *Comparing Presidential Behavior: Carter, Reagan, and the Macho Presidential Style*. New York: Greenwood Press, 1987.

Penley, Constance. "Time Travel, Primal Scene, and the Critical Dystopia." In *The Cultural Politics of "Postmodernism,"* ed. John Tagg, pp. 33–49. Binghamton: Department of Art History, SUNY Press, 1989.

Rapping, Elayne. "Boys of the Summer." *The Progressive*, November 1991, p. 36.

Reagan, Ronald. "Inaugural Address," 20 January 1981. *Weekly Compilation of Presidential Documents*, 26 January–1 March 1981, pp. 1–6.

———. "The Trans World Airlines Hijacking Incident." *Weekly Compilation of Presidential Documents*, 2 July 1985, p. 869.

Regan, Donald T. *For the Record*. San Diego: Harcourt Brace Jovanovich, 1988.

Rogin, Michael. *Ronald Reagan, The Movie*. Berkeley and Los Angeles: University of California Press, 1987.

———. " 'Make My Day' ": Spectacle as Amnesia in Imperial Politics." *Representations* 29 (Winter 1990): 99–124.

Rosenblatt, Roger, "Out of the Past, Fresh Choices for the Future." *Time* 5, January 1981, pp. 10–24.

Ryan, Michael, and Douglas Kellner. *Camera Politica: The Politics and Ideology of Contemporary Hollywood Film*. Bloomington: Indiana University Press, 1988.

Schieffer, Bob, and Gary Paul Gates. *The Acting President*. New York: E. P. Dutton, 1989.

Schulte-Sasse, Jochen, and Linda Schulte-Sasse. "War, Otherness, and Illusionary Identifications with the State." *Cultural Critique* 19 (Fall 1991): 67–97.

Singer, A. L. *Beauty and the Beast*. New York: Disney Press, 1992.

Speakes, Larry. *Speaking Out*. New York: Charles Scribner's Sons, 1988.

Stockman, David. *The Triumph of Politics*. New York: Harper & Row, 1986.

"The Tavern Rape: Cheers and No Help." *Newsweek*, 21 March 1983, p. 25.

Tower, John, Edmund Muskie, and Brent Scowcroft. *Report of the President's Special Review Board*, 26 February 1987, p. B-1.

"Two Outrages." *The Los Angeles Daily Journal*, 16 January 1984, p. 4.

Van Biema, David. "With a $100 Million Gross(out), Sly Stallone Fends Off *Rambo*'s Army of Adversaries." *People*, 8 July 1985, p. 35.

Wilkinson, Rupert. *American Tough: The Tough-Guy Tradition and American Character*. Westport, Conn.: Greenwood Press, 1984.

Wolf, Christa. *Cassandra*. Trans. Jan Van Huerck. New York: Farrar, Straus & Giroux, 1984.

Wood, Robin. *Hollywood from Vietnam to Reagan*. New York: Columbia University Press, 1986.

INDEX

(Page numbers for illustrations are in italics.)